D1203223

Italian Renaissance Ceramics

Italian Renaissance Ceramics

From the Howard I. and Janet H. Stein Collection
and the Philadelphia Museum of Art

Wendy M. Watson

PHILADELPHIA MUSEUM OF ART

Published on the occasion of the exhibition

Italian Renaissance Ceramics: The Howard I. and Janet H. Stein Collection

December 7, 2001, to April 28, 2002, at the Philadelphia Museum of Art

Exhibition organized by Dean Walker

The exhibition and publication are generously supported by The Pew Charitable Trusts, The Women's Committee of the Philadelphia Museum of Art, and the Robert Montgomery Scott Endowment for Exhibitions.

This book is also supported by Howard I. Stein and family and by an endowment for scholarly publications established by grants from CIGNA Foundation and the Andrew W. Mellon Foundation at the Philadelphia Museum of Art.

Produced by the Department of Publishing
Philadelphia Museum of Art
Benjamin Franklin Parkway at 26th Street
P.O. Box 7646
Philadelphia, Pennsylvania 19101-7646
www.philamuseum.org

Edited by Nicole Amoroso
Production managed by Richard Bonk
Designed by Katy Homans, New York
Map by David Noble, Berkeley, California
Color separations by Professional Graphics, Inc., Rockford, Illinois
Printed and bound in Great Britain by Butler & Tanner Ltd., Frome

Text and compilation © 2001 Philadelphia Museum of Art
All rights reserved. No part of this publication may be reproduced or transmitted in any form or by any electronic or mechanical means (including photocopying, recording, or any other information storage and retrieval system), without prior permission in writing from the publisher.

Cover: *front* Dish with Orsella (cat. 56) *back* reverse of dish with Orsella (appendix 8)

Frontispiece: Workshop of Guido Durantino, Plate with Apollo and Daphne (detail; cat. 18)

Page 16: Workshop of Guido Durantino or Orazio Fontana, Snake-handled vase with scenes from *Amadis de Gaula* (detail; cat. 19); Page 38: Giulio Romano, *Marriage Feast of Cupid and Psyche* (detail; fig. 1); Page 46: Footed jar with arms of the Pittigardi family (detail; cat. 2); Page 56: Francesco di Piero, Dish with destruction of Troy (detail; cat. 4); Page 92: Molded ewer basin with Judith holding the head of Holofernes (detail; cat. 37); Page 110: Plate with allegory relating to Vespasiano Gonzaga (detail; cat. 55); Page 130: Francesco Durantino, Footed bowl of a childbirth set (interior; cat. 60a); Page 150: Ewer basin with coat of arms (detail; cat. 69).

Library of Congress Cataloging-in-Publication Data
Watson, Wendy M., 1948–
    Italian Renaissance ceramics from the Howard I. and Janet H. Stein collection and the
    Philadelphia Museum of Art / Wendy M. Watson.
        p. cm.
    Published on the occasion of an exhibition held at the Philadelphia Museum of Art,
    Dec. 7, 2001–Apr. 28, 2002.
    Includes bibliographical references and index.
    ISBN 0-87633-154-1 (cloth : alk. paper) — ISBN 0-87633-155-X (pbk. : alk. paper)
        1. Majolica, Italian—Exhibitions. 2. Majolica, Renaissance—Italy—Exhibitions. 3. Stein, Howard I.—Art collections—Exhibitions. 4. Stein, Janet H.—Art collections—Exhibitions. 5. Majolica—Private collections—Pennsylvania—Philadelphia—Exhibitions. 6. Philadelphia Museum of Art—Exhibitions. 7. Majolica—Pennsylvania—Philadelphia—Exhibitions. I. Philadelphia Museum of Art.

NK4315.W348 2001
738.3'0945'07474811—dc21

                                    2001052379

CONTENTS

FOREWORD

Anne d'Harnoncourt

The George D. Widener
Director, Philadelphia Museum
of Art

An abiding passion for great ceramics—across many centuries, countries, and cultures—has characterized the Philadelphia Museum of Art and its succession of directors, curators, and collectors since our founding in 1876. From ancient tomb figures of Han dynasty China to the most daring contemporary example of the ceramicist's art, from the supreme refinement of eighteenth-century Sèvres porcelain to the earthy sentiments inscribed in Pennsylvania German redware, the Museum's galleries bear witness to the infinite potential of clay under a master's hand.

The extraordinary achievements of Italian Renaissance ceramicists are now represented in depth in the Museum's collection thanks to the generosity of another passionate collector, Howard I. Stein. Together with his late wife, Janet, Howard Stein assembled the distinguished holdings recorded in this catalogue over twenty-five years of informed and judicious acquisition, object by beloved object. The partial and promised gift to the Philadelphia Museum of Art of the Howard I. and Janet H. Stein Collection constitutes one of the high points of the Museum's 125th anniversary celebration—transforming our fine but small existing collections through the range and remarkable quality of the Stein objects and ensuring that this brilliant and imaginative aspect of Renaissance culture will fascinate our public for generations to come.

This handsome book is published on the occasion of the first exhibition of the Stein Collection at this Museum and in context with the Museum's own holdings; it reveals the wealth of information that these beautiful objects contain about the society in which they were created, used, and treasured. We are deeply grateful to Wendy M. Watson for her scholarship, so eloquently imparted, which unfolds the delights of maiolica to every reader. We are also indebted yet again to Howard Stein himself, whose generosity has ensured that these vivid works of art are illustrated in the splendid color they deserve.

Dean Walker, the Museum's inimitable Senior Curator of European Decorative Arts, has matched his boundless enthusiasm for this splendid gift with thoughtful attention to every detail of its presentation in the galleries and on the printed page. I join him in expressing the warmest thanks to Wendy Watson, and to the team of Museum staff who have carried out the exhibition installation and this publication with elegance, and the conservation of many objects with thorough research and skill.

We are also deeply grateful to The Pew Charitable Trusts and The Women's Committee of the Philadelphia Museum of Art for their support of this project, and to all the contributors to the Museum's endowment for exhibitions created in honor of Robert Montgomery Scott. It is a special joy to have that fund support a beautiful exhibition in which every work of art is destined to belong to the Museum. This book is also supported by an endowment for scholarly publications at the Museum established by grants from CIGNA Foundation and the Andrew W. Mellon Foundation. The late Barbara B. Rubenstein—dedicated chairman of the Museum's Committee on European Decorative Arts, longtime trustee, and former vice president of the Women's Committee—was enormously excited about this marvelous acquisition. I know she would share our delight upon the occasion of its first presentation to the public.

ACKNOWLEDGMENTS

Dean Walker

The Henry P. McIlhenny
Senior Curator of European
Decorative Arts and Sculpture,
Philadelphia Museum of Art

One brilliant February afternoon in 1997, I visited Howard Stein's house for the first time. Without interrupton, we proceeded to handle and discuss the collection piece by piece, passing each object back and forth. It was an encounter of complete absorption. So began an acquaintance that has ripened into a warm relationship, the logical but wondrous results of which are the publication and exhibition of the Howard I. and Janet H. Stein Collection, marking the gift of the collection to the Philadelphia Museum of Art. It is a pleasure here to thank Mr. Stein for his trust in this Museum as the proper home for a collection so carefully assembled over a quarter century and one so deserving of a sympathetic gallery setting.

For the choice of the author of the book, the obvious person was Wendy M. Watson, a friend of Mr. Stein's since the publication in 1986 of her well-known catalogue of the maiolica in the William A. Clark Collection at the Corcoran Gallery of Art in Washington, D.C., and someone already knowledgeable about the Stein Collection. Responding to Anne d'Harnoncourt's challenge to create a book useful for both neophites and specialists, Wendy has written an original text whose graceful accessibility belies its command of the field and perceptive observations about numerous individual objects.

Over the years, members of the Philadelphia Museum of Art's staff and volunteers have carried out research on maiolica in the Museum's collection, notably Donald J. LaRocca, former Assistant Curator of European Decorative Arts, and John Giura, a graduate student from New York University.

Former departmental assistants Erik Goldner, Scott A. Williams, and Robb Bunnell contributed to the establishment of an extensive catalogue database for all the maiolica in the Museum and in the Stein Collection, while volunteer Eunice Smith patiently entered and reentered much of the information. As the present book neared completion, Hillary Belzer, Departmental Assistant, helped with a multitude of tasks, and Jonathan P. Canning, Research Assistant, coped with scholarly investigations on many fronts.

Melissa S. Meighan, Conservator of Decorative Arts and Sculpture, analyzed and treated a number of the ceramics, beginning with the examination of the Museum's three Fontana vases, the subject of an exhibition we organized together in 1992. She has also supervised the examination and treatment of selected Museum pieces by Julie Solz, Samuel H. Kress Fellow;

Gwynne Barney, Andrew W. Mellon Fellow; Adam Jenkins, third year Winterthur Fellow; and Amanda Gadola, Conservation Technician.

Our colleague Timothy Wilson, Keeper of Western Art at the Ashmolean Museum, Oxford University, reviewed the Museum's collection of maiolica in 1997, when visiting Philadelphia to deliver a lecture on our dish by Nicola da Urbino. Tim's wide-ranging comments were crucial in our reevaluation of a number of objects acquired by the Museum over the years.

In the Museum's Department of Publishing, the planning of the book was initiated by George H. Marcus. The final form and the completion of the book were accomplished under the interested eye of Sherry Babbitt, his successor as Director of Publishing. Anne d'Harnoncourt made a strong plea for a publication with a fresh look. Designer Katy Homans has once again created for this Museum a striking volume that is innovative and unusually sympathetic to the material. The texts were scrupulously and thoughtfully edited by Nicole Amoroso, whose dedication has been truly exceptional. Photography, mostly taken expressly for this publication, was carried out by Graydon Wood. Richard Bonk supervised the production of the illustrations, comparing many of the proofs with the objects themselves, and oversaw the printing of the book.

The exhibition was designed by Jack Schlechter assisted by Andrew Slavinskas. Installation mounts were crafted by Randall Cleaver of the Department of Installations and Packing.

Jane Spencer, Senior Graphic Designer, designed gallery texts and the gallery guide that accompanied the exhibition. Texts were edited by Graphics Editor Maia Wind in helpful consultation with Marla K. Shoemaker, Senior Curator of Education.

As part of the Museum's exhibition, we were very pleased to be able to include "Methods of the Renaissance Potter," a video written by Catherine Hess, Associate Curator of Sculpture and Works of Art, and Stepheny Dirden, Assistant Manager, Event Production, at the J. Paul Getty Museum in Los Angeles, which elegantly demonstrates the basic techniques of the making of maiolica.

The financial support for this book and exhibition joins both the oldest and newest sources connected with the Museum. The Women's Committee of the Philadelphia Museum of Art—founded before the Museum itself—has contributed generously to this project, continuing a long tradition of commitment to the decorative arts, which embraces objects from the distant past and the newest creations of today. We are also grateful to the Robert Montgomery Scott Endowment Fund, established in 1996 to honor the achievements and dedication of our former president and honorary chairman, and for the purpose of helping make the exhibition dreams of curators into realities to be enjoyed by the Museum's public.

NOTE TO THE READER

Translations are by Wendy M. Watson unless otherwise noted.

The Bible is cited according to *The New Oxford Annotated Bible*, edited by Michael D. Coogan, 3rd ed. (Oxford and New York: Oxford University Press, 2001).

FOR THE CHECKLIST:

DIMENSIONS: Although every effort has been made to report the dimensions accurately, the objects have been measured by different people at different times and under varying circumstances.

INSCRIPTIONS: All inscriptions original to the manufacture of an object have been provided. An [n] indicates that the previous letter is surmounted by a curved line that acts as an abbreviation for the letter *n*. In some instances labels or inscriptions that postdate manufacture have been included because of the important information they supply. All inscriptions and labels are recorded in the object files in the Philadelphia Museum of Art's Department of European Decorative Arts and Sculpture.

PROVENANCE: Brackets indicate art dealers; parentheses indicate sales.

REFERENCES: The bibliographic citations provided for each object are a selection of the most important references; they are not comprehensive.

The condition and repair of objects is mentioned only when it provides information about notable alterations. Basic condition reports exist for all objects in the Stein Collection and for many pieces in the Philadelphia Museum of Art. These reports are kept in the Museum's Department of European Decorative Arts and Sculpture and in the Department of Conservation.

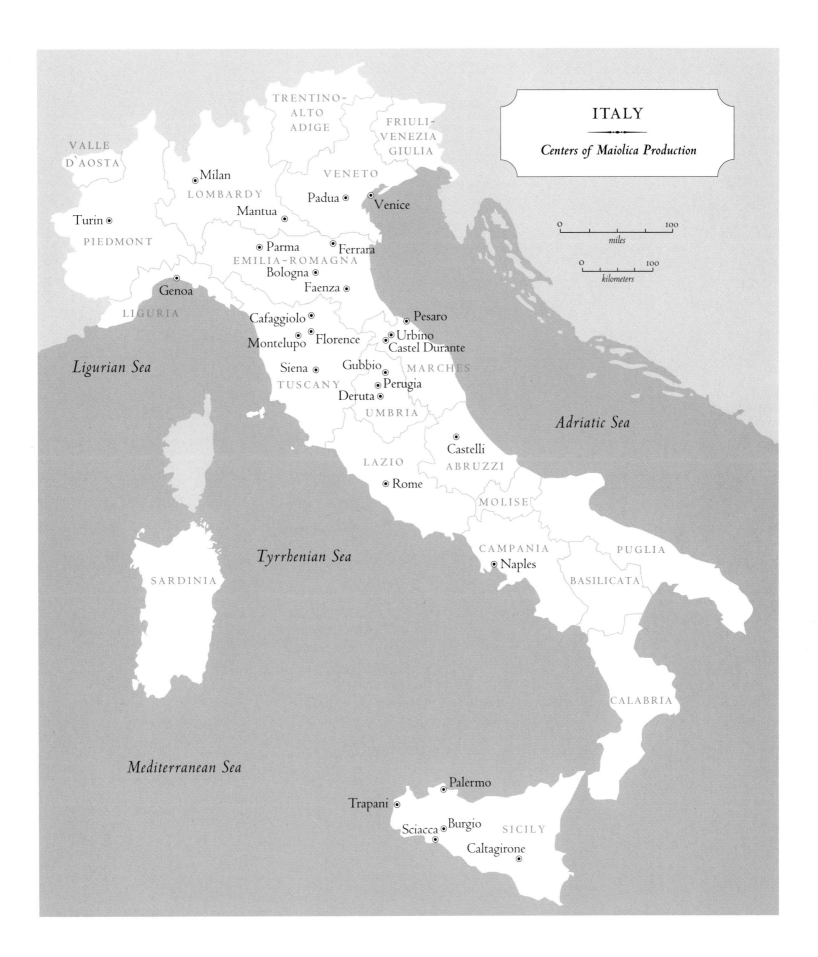

ITALY

Centers of Maiolica Production

VALLE D'AOSTA

TRENTINO-ALTO ADIGE

FRIULI-VENEZIA GIULIA

VENETO

LOMBARDY

Milan

Turin

PIEDMONT

Mantua

Padua

Venice

Parma

Ferrara

EMILIA-ROMAGNA

Bologna

Faenza

Genoa

LIGURIA

Cafaggiolo

Pesaro

Montelupo

Florence

Urbino
Castel Durante

Ligurian Sea

Siena

Gubbio

MARCHES

TUSCANY

Perugia

Deruta

UMBRIA

Adriatic Sea

Castelli

LAZIO

ABRUZZI

Rome

MOLISE

CAMPANIA

PUGLIA

Tyrrhenian Sea

Naples

BASILICATA

SARDINIA

CALABRIA

Mediterranean Sea

Palermo

Trapani

Sciacca

Burgio

SICILY

Caltagirone

0 ——— 100
miles

0 ——— 100
kilometers

Maiolica Comes to the United States, the Philadelphia Museum of Art, and the Howard I. and Janet H. Stein Collection

DEAN WALKER

The acquisition and exhibition of the Howard I. and Janet H. Stein Collection are fitting 125th anniversary events for the Philadelphia Museum of Art, for it was at the Centennial Exhibition of 1876, from which the Museum arose, that Renaissance maiolica was given its first grand presentation in the United States. As with many aspects of art collecting in this country, that of maiolica has been little explored to date. The richness of this story can only be suggested here, but a brief survey is worth attempting, both for its own sake and because it provides a context for highlighting aspects of the maiolica in the Stein Collection and at the Museum.[1]

During the Centennial in Philadelphia, a gallery at Memorial Hall was given over to the maiolica from the collection of Alessandro Castellani, well-known then as a jeweler, collector, and connoisseur. Consisting of 350 pieces arranged by date, the comprehensive collection was a small version of the one in London belonging to the South Kensington Museum (renamed the Victoria & Albert Museum in 1899).[2] In 1876, it was generally known that the Castellani collection was for sale, and in 1877, it was lent to the Metropolitan Museum of Art in New York, then still on West Fourteenth Street. The catalogue prepared for that exhibition states that the museum desired to acquire the collection.[3] Sadly, Castellani's high price and the financial crisis of 1877 defeated this aim. The collection was sent to Paris, where it was auctioned the following year.[4] Castellani did manage to secure at least one American institutional client for his Renaissance ceramics. In 1876–77, the Boston Athenaeum purchased from him a dozen pieces of maiolica, along with textiles and other decorative arts, for the Lawrence Room in the new Museum of Fine Arts in Boston.

The Metropolitan Museum of Art, the institution with the longest and most interesting

1. The love of tin-glazed sculpture in the United States, notably by the della Robbia workshop, is beyond the scope of this essay, as is the related appreciation of Hispano-Moresque pottery. For the former, see Marquand 1912.

2. See Italian Maiolica 1876. For a description of the exhibition of maiolica, see Frank H. Norton, *Illustrated Historical Register of the Centennial Exhibition, Philadelphia, 1876, and of the Exposition Universelle, Paris, 1878* (New York: The American News Company, 1879), pp. 178–79.

3. See Castellani Collection 1877.

4. Winifred E. Howe, *A History of the Metropolitan Museum of Art with a Chapter on the Early Institutions of Art in New York* (New York: The Gilliss Press, 1913), p. 167. For the Castellani sale in Paris at the Hôtel Drouot, see Charles Pillet, *Catalogue des faïences italiennes . . . composant l'importante collection de M. Alessandro Castellani*, May 27–29, 1878.

Figure 1
Detail of the Gothic Room, Marble House, Newport,
Rhode Island. Residence of Mr. and Mrs. William
Kissam Vanderbilt. Photograph taken by Mattie Edwards
Hewitt (1868–1954) in 1926

history of collecting maiolica in the United States, responded to its earlier loss by acquiring

pieces in 1884 from the sale of the Fountaine family's collection at Narford Hall in Norfolk,

England—famous for its China Room filled with elaborate ceramics from Urbino—and from

the auction of the estate of Castellani, then recently deceased.[5] At the time, the rising pur-

chasing power of the United States was feared in London. J. C. Robinson, the brilliant former

keeper of the Museum of Ornamental Art at Marlborough House (transferred to the South

Kensington Museum in 1857), used the threat of the Rothschilds and the Vanderbilts as the

reason for forming a syndicate to buy Fountaine maiolica for the benefit of English institu-

tions and collectors.[6] Nevertheless, in the United States, private collectors do not appear to

have become interested in maiolica until a few years later.

❧ ❧ ❧ ❧

In the last decades of the nineteenth century, the creation of colossal wealth among the newly

rich gave a small number of Americans the means to act as patrons on a prodigious scale.

5. For the sale of the Fountaine collection, see Moore 1988, pp. 435–47. For
the sale, which was held at the Palazzo
Castellani in Rome after Castellani's
death, see *Catalogue des objets d'art antiques*
du Moyen-Age et de la Renaissance dépendant de
la succession Alessandro Castellani, March
17–April 10, 1884.

6. Reitlinger 1963, p. 118.

Their aspirations required the acquisition of European tastes and included the creation of grand residences as settings for recently purchased European treasures. It is not yet easy to draw generalizations about early purchasers of maiolica in the United States. In Baltimore, the future museum founders William and Henry Walters, father and son, wrote about the ceramics in the 1880s, but bought nothing at the time.[7] The distinguished New York collector Henry G. Marquand gave some maiolica to the Metropolitan in 1891 and 1894.[8] However, Isabella Stewart Gardner, whom one might have expected to be interested in Renaissance ceramics, acquired no maiolica for Fenway Court, her Venetian-style palazzo in Boston, completed in 1903. Nor does maiolica appear prominently in the contemporary interiors of the important architects McKim, Meade and White.

When American collectors eventually purchased maiolica, the role of the Paris art world was crucial. Around 1890 Alva (Mrs. William Kissam) Vanderbilt, later Mrs. O.H.P. Belmont, acquired maiolica from the collection of Emile Gavet for Marble House in Newport, Rhode Island, where the pieces were installed anachronistically in the Gothic Room (fig. 1).[9] The designer of the interior and likely guide to the purchase was her adviser, the Parisian decorator Jules Allard, who had bought from the Gavet collection, probably in 1889.[10] The appearance of maiolica in Marble House could have inspired E. J. Berwind's purchases of maiolica, also through Allard and from the Gavet collection, that filled two vitrines at The Elms, his Newport house completed in 1901 (fig. 2). However, since Berwind's wife, Sarah, had lived in Italy and owned some Italian bronzes, the ceramics may have had a personal appeal.[11] At the "sale of the century" of collector-dealer Frédéric Spitzer's possessions in Paris in 1893, Mr. and Mrs. Martin Ryerson from Chicago included maiolica among their purchases of fine decorative arts.[12]

After 1900, the pace of American acquisitions quickened so much that it is difficult to determine influences with any certainty. The opening of the Wallace Collection in London that year could have been an important event, since maiolica had a prominent place there, and we know that Americans were impressed with other aspects of the collection. As in the Gavet collection earlier and other collections sold later, maiolica in the Wallace Collection was a component of a sumptuous interior densely installed with precious art objects. These rooms had little in common with the orderly, scientific presentation of the maiolica displayed in cases

7. W. T. Walters assisted by Henry Walters, *Oriental Collection of W. T. Walters, 65 Mount Vernon Place, Baltimore* (Baltimore: I. Friedenwald, 1884), pp. 111–14.

8. For maiolica given by Marquand to the Metropolitan Museum of Art, see Pier 1911.

9. See Miller 1994, pp. 176–85.

10. Molinier 1889.

11. Miller 1994, p. 185 n. 9. Maiolica from The Elms was given to the Metropolitan Museum of Art by Berwind's sister Julia in 1953. Recently, some of the pieces have been returned to The Elms on loan.

12. Objects files, Department of European Decorative Arts and Sculpture, Art Institute of Chicago. A photograph in the Ryerson Papers at the Art Institute of Chicago Archives shows maiolica in a vitrine at the foot of the staircase in the open-plan entrance hall of the Ryerson's house in Chicago. For a brief biography of Frédéric Spitzer, see Charles Turner, "Spitzer, Frédéric," in Jane Turner, ed., *The Dictionary of Art* (London: Macmillan, 1996), vol. 29, pp. 415–16.

Figure 2
Detail of the South Alcove, The Elms, Newport, Rhode Island. Residence of Mr. and Mrs. E. J. Berwind Photograph taken by Childs in 1901

at the Victoria & Albert Museum. Maiolica was also an interest of the dynamic and powerful director general of the Berlin Museum, Wilhelm Bode (von Bode after 1914), who had featured the ceramics in his important exhibition of medieval and Renaissance art from Berlin private collections in 1898.[13] There, the maiolica appeared in cases adjacent to a space divided into alcoves devoted to individual collectors. As a scholar and collector, Bode was increasingly interested in the earliest Italian ceramics and exerted an important influence in the international change of taste toward wares not included in the collections of the second half of the 1800s.[14]

In the new century, the role of the decorator-dealer continued to be important for private collectors in the United States. Duveen Brothers, working from their Paris gallery, were instrumental in the sale of maiolica eventually given to two museums in Washington, D.C. In 1906, the firm bought the Oscar Hainauer collection in Berlin, a loss to German museums that enraged Emperor Wilhelm II. With the collection came one of the finest groups of maiolica in Germany, previously exhibited by Bode. Much of the Hainauer maiolica, roughly one hundred pieces, was sold to Senator William A. Clark from Montana.[15] According to gallery staff member Edward Fowles, Joseph Duveen supervised the creation of the interiors

13. The exhibition was held from May 20 to July 3, 1898. The commemorative catalogue appeared the next year; see Bode 1899.

14. See Bode 1911, which includes a number of pieces owned by Bode himself.

15. There are no surviving bills for Clark's purchases of maiolica. The Clark Collection was bequeathed to the Corcoran Gallery of Art in Washington, D.C. in 1925, and opened to the public in 1928. On Clark as a collector, see *The William A. Clark Collection* (Washington, D.C.: The Corcoran Gallery of Art, 1978); Dare Myers Hartwell et al., *The Salon Doré* (Washington, D.C.: The Corcoran Gallery of Art, 1998); and Watson 1986.

Figure 3
View of the Faience Gallery. Residence of Senator William A. Clark, Fifth Avenue and East Seventy-seventh Street, New York

for Clark's Fifth Avenue mansion, drawing on the skills of specialized French craftsmen.[16]
One gallery in the house featured an arrangement of vitrines of maiolica along with French ceramics from the Gavet collection and early terracottas (fig. 3). Again, it was from Duveen Brothers in Paris, in 1910, that P.A.B. Widener and his son Joseph purchased most of the maiolica for Lynnewood Hall, their estate outside Philadelphia.[17] About thirty pieces came from the fabulous collection of Maurice Kann, whose Paris house and the adjoining one of his brother had been filled with treasures intended to form a house-museum.

By 1909, to judge from the dated photograph of the interior court of the Walters Art Museum in Baltimore, Henry Walters had a sufficient number of pieces of maiolica to fill a vitrine to compare with his exceptional French Renaissance enamels (fig. 4). His interest in maiolica must have been recent because, although records are incomplete, Walters's first few pieces were acquired as part of the Don Marcello Masseranti collection from Rome in 1902.[18] He obtained more maiolica in 1905, and another group in 1908.

For these American collectors the role of J. Pierpont Morgan may have set a determining example. The careful charting of Morgan's collecting of maiolica has yet to be done, nevertheless existing evidence suggests that the ceramics began to interest him around 1900,

16. Fowles 1976, p. 10.

17. For the Widener maiolica, see Alison Luchs and Timothy Wilson, introduction to Distelberger 1993, p. xiii; and Wilson 1993. Of the Widener maiolica only plates and dishes were given to the National Gallery of Art. For other pieces sold at auction, see the sale catalogue for Samuel T. Freeman & Co., Philadelphia, *The Valuable Furnishings and Objects of Art at "Lynnewood Hall", the Residence of the Late Joseph E. Widener*, June 20, 1944. Two of the drug jars are now at the J. Paul Getty Museum, Los Angeles; see Hess 1988, pp. 75–81, nos. 24–25.

18. Henry Walters destroyed most of the bills for his purchases. For Walters as a collector, see Johnston 1999. For the Walters maiolica, see Prentice von Erdberg and Ross 1952.

Figure 4
View of the Lower Court. The Walters Art Museum, Baltimore, 1909

perhaps because of the precedent of the Wallace Collection.[19] In 1901 Morgan acquired the maiolica collection of the Parisian art expert Charles Mannheim. It was lent immediately to the Victoria & Albert for display, with other pieces added subsequently. Morgan's collection was essentially formed by 1911, when a catalogue was in preparation.[20]

Interest in maiolica arose again at the Metropolitan in 1904, the year Morgan was first elected vice president and then president of the museum. In that year, the Metropolitan purchased thirty pieces of maiolica from J. & S. Goldschmidt in Frankfurt and the large glazed earthenware Lamentation group from Duveen Brothers.[21] Henry Walters could well have known about the Metropolitan's activity as one of the new trustees selected by Morgan in the year he became president.

The astonishing comprehensiveness of the Morgan collections was visible only after his death, when they were assembled and lent to the Metropolitan Museum of Art from 1914 to 1916. Among the treasures arranged by period was a large gallery devoted to twelve cases of maiolica, which constituted the most important collection formed by an American (fig. 5).[22] Accompanying the maiolica were other Renaissance treasures—Raphael's Colonna Altarpiece;[23] three sculptures; tapestries; and cases with metalwork, rock crystal, and glass. In its

19. For Pierpont Morgan's maiolica, see Linda Horvitz Roth, "J. Pierpont Morgan, Collector," in Horvitz Roth 1987, pp. 34–35; and Jörg Rasmussen and Wendy M. Watson, "Majolica," in Horvitz Roth 1987, pp. 58–81.

20. Alessandro Imbert to Belle da Costa Greene, July 30, 1911, Early Acquisition Files, Pierpont Morgan Library, New York.

21. Ballardini 1930, vol. 1, p. 41, no. 7, fig. 7.

22. Joseph Breck in Robinson 1914, pp. 53–60.

23. Federico Zeri with the assistance of Elizabeth E. Gardener, *Italian Paintings, A Catalogue of the Collection of the Metropolitan Museum of Art: Sienese and Central Italian Schools* (New York: The Metropolitan Museum of Art; Vicenza: Neri Pozza, 1980), pp. 72–75, pl. 110.

Figure 5
Detail of the Large Renaissance Room (Gallery 14)
Loan Exhibition of the J. Pierpont Morgan
Collection, *The Metropolitan Museum of Art, New
York, 1914–16*

entirety, Morgan's maiolica collection is notable for its range, which surveyed Italian ceramics

from the 1400s through the better-known sixteenth-century productions, although few of his

earliest Italian pieces were included in the 1914–16 exhibition. A prized Medici porcelain ewer

and several ceramics were given by the Morgan estate to the Metropolitan. Maiolica was not,

otherwise, among the Morgan collections donated to the museum.[24] However, a group of

about fifty pieces were among the many objects presented to the Wadsworth Atheneum in

Hartford, Connecticut, the native city of the Morgan family, in accordance with Pierpont

Morgan's wishes.[25] This selection was officially accessioned in 1917. The dispersal of Morgan's

maiolica benefited other important collections, including those of V. Everit Macy, William

Randolph Hearst, Mortimer L. Schiff (who bought many of the best early pieces), and the

stock of Duveen Brothers in New York.

Although during his lifetime Morgan lent most of his maiolica to the Victoria & Albert

Museum, a few pieces were displayed in the West Room, his study at the Pierpont Morgan

Library in New York. In this grand room, maiolica can still be seen, along with sculptures

and other decorative objects, arranged on top of low bookcases.[26] It is worth considering

whether this room set a precedent in New York. The Renaissance Room in the Fifth Avenue

24. For the Pierpont Morgan decorative arts given to the Metropolitan Museum of Art, see Breck and Rogers 1925; and Strouse 2000. For the Medici porcelain ewer, see ibid., p. 56, no. 67. The recent biography on Morgan (Jean Strouse, *Morgan: American Financier* [New York: Random House, 1999]) provides the best account of the man and his life. The book includes valuable information about Morgan's collecting, although the creation of the collections is not treated in great detail.

25. For Pierpont Morgan and the Wadsworth Atheneum, see Horvitz Roth 1987.

26. For a photograph of the West Room at the Pierpont Morgan Library, see ibid., p. 36, fig. 12.

mansion of Thomas Fortune Ryan, around which a small number of fine pieces of maiolica were distributed as decoration, is one example that could be used to support this suggestion.[27]

Before and after World War I, with the shift of many European art dealers to New York, a number of galleries in the city began to offer maiolica. Many of their names will be found among the provenances of the objects in this book: Duveen Brothers, Arnold Seligmann & Rey, M. and R. Stora, P. W. French & Co., Dikran G. Kelekian, Durlacher Brothers, and C. and E. Canessa. Also, a succession of auctions of large Italian collections of furniture and decorative objects, including maiolica, were held in New York—Elia Volpi in 1916, Stefano Bardini in 1918, Raoul Tolentino in 1920 and 1925, C. and E. Canessa in 1924. In terms of numbers and quality the finest maiolica appeared in the sale of Achille de Clemente's collection from Florence in 1931. In general, these collections included earlier maiolica, drug jars, and vessels rather than the *istoriato* (narrative) pieces to be found in English, French, and German collections. Did the apparently plentiful supply of maiolica allow dealers to create a sharply rising market, as they had achieved for Chinese porcelain? Little information has been published yet about the economics of the trade in maiolica.[28] Competition must have been keen for objects perceived as trophies, since the assembled garniture of three large vases by members of the Fontana family of Urbino in the William Salomon sale achieved the astounding record price of $101,000 at auction in 1923.[29]

Maiolica appeared in a new light in 1923 in the Metropolitan's exhibition *The Arts of the Italian Renaissance*, in which ceramics were included within a survey of paintings, sculpture, furniture, textiles, prints, and illustrated books. All of the objects (except those on paper) were chosen from private collections, mostly in New York (fig. 6).[30] In time a number of the works from the exhibition were acquired by the Metropolitan. One prominent lender, V. Everit Macy, gave his maiolica collection of about forty pieces to the Museum in memory of his wife in 1927.

The Metropolitan also augmented its display of maiolica with loans from William Randolph Hearst (1923–38) and the collection of Mortimer L. Schiff (1937–41). New York auction sales catalogues from the twenties through the forties indicate that maiolica was not a rarity. Some people with large collections had only a small number of pieces of maiolica,

27. Sale, American Art Association, Anderson Galleries, New York, *Gothic and Renaissance Art, Collection of the Late Thomas Fortune Ryan*, November 23–25, 1933, pp. 78–80, lots 370–76. The frontispiece depicts the Renaissance Room.

28. For the market for maiolica at auction, see Reitlinger 1963. Most collectors in the United States, however, bought maiolica from dealers. An interesting reflection of the market could be found in a comparison of Morgan's bills and the valuations given for pieces after his death. Another important source is the Duveen Brothers archive, now at the J. Paul Getty Research Center. For additional comments about the price of maiolica in the twentieth century, see Wilson 1994, pp. 79–99. I only saw this essay when my own was already edited.

29. Reitlinger 1963, pp. 252, 505.

30. See New York 1923.

Figure 6
Detail of Gallery II. The Arts of the Italian Renaissance, The Metropolitan Museum of Art, New York, 1923

31. See Leslie A. Hyam's foreword in the sale catalogue for Parke-Bernet Galleries, New York, *Italian Majolica of the XV–XVII Century . . . Collected by the Late Whitney Warren, Property of Mrs. Whitney Warren,* October 7–9, 1943.

32. Hearst began collecting again when his fortunes improved. Some of his maiolica was given later to the Los Angeles County Museum of Art.

33. Earlier, maiolica was shown in San Francisco at the California Midwinter International Exposition in 1895 and at the International Panama-Pacific Exhibition in 1915.

34. The Great Hall of Treetops is illustrated in the sale catalogue for Christie's, Sewickley Heights, *The George R. Hann Collection,* part 2, May 19, 1980. The maiolica was acquired from Duveen Brothers, the likely source for many of the other works in the collection. Previously, the maiolica had belonged to Carl W. Hamilton of New York, another important Duveen client.

35. Mrs. Joanne Flannery and Father Donald Roe, conversations with the author, January 2001.

36. See especially, Conforti 1995, pp. 323–26; and McNab 1995, pp. 517–41.

while others with sizable collections of the ceramics had particular interests, like the architect Whitney Warren, who preferred boldly designed pieces and included interesting fragments.[31] The natural passing of a generation as well as continued economic difficulties eventually brought much of this material onto the market. The Hearst, Schiff, and Warren collections were all sold at auction.[32]

A taste for maiolica extended across the country in the course of the twenties.[33] Provenances of ceramics in the Stein Collection include owners from Philadelphia, Pittsburgh, Detroit, Minneapolis, and San Francisco. For George R. Hann at Treetrops in Sewickley Heights, outside Pittsburgh, maiolica contributed to the overall display of a mixture of Gothic and Renaissance objects.[34] The legendary precedents of Spitzer and Morgan continued to inspire later collectors including Thomas Flannery in Chicago.[35] One such collection with a number of fine objects remains intact. At the Taft Museum, in Cincinnati, maiolica figures among the choice selection of decorative objects.[36] For Charles Phelps and Anna Sinton Taft, the founders of the museum, maiolica was a late interest added perhaps to balance their enamels, as Henry Walters had done earlier. The Tafts acquired their fourteen pieces of maiolica at Duveen Brothers in New York on March 6, 1924.

When maiolica was recognized by Americans as desirable after 1900, Morgan, Clark, the Walters, and the Tafts imagined their collections on view for the public. It is interesting to see that pieces of maiolica now belonging to the Stein Collection and at the Philadelphia Museum of Art were also acquired by other people with institutional interests or ambitions. William Salomon intended his Fifth Avenue house to be a museum. George Booth bought maiolica for the young Cranbrook Academy of Art in Bloomfield Hills, Michigan. T. B. Walker displayed various collections, including an impressive survey of ceramics, in his house and after 1927 in his own museum, the Walker Galleries in Minneapolis. Later, Sydney N. Blumberg's drug jars were a component within a large pharmacological collection suitable for a science museum or a corporation.[37] In the 1980s Dr. Arthur M. Sackler's maiolica provided the material for temporary museum exhibitions at the National Gallery of Art in Washington, D.C. and the Fine Arts Museums of San Francisco.[38] That these pieces came onto the market for one reason or another indicates the inevitably fluctuating, and even the vagarious, nature of collecting in the United States. The example of Norton Simon is especially telling about changes in taste after World War II. In 1964 he acquired the remaining stock of Duveen Brothers, a collection that still contained many of the kinds of luxurious items preferred by collectors in the twenties. By 1971, as the specific areas of his collecting interests had become defined, these objects of types so sought after by an earlier age were returned to the market through auction.[39]

❧ ❧ ❧ ❧

To this broad survey in which New York is the center, the history of collecting maiolica in Philadelphia is peripherally related. At this museum, as with other institutions without large donations, the collecting pattern has been one of random accumulation of pieces by gift and purchase. This history runs parallel to that of other museums in the United States, including Boston, Chicago, and San Francisco.[40]

The first notable examples of maiolica acquired by the young Pennsylvania Museum of Art (as the Museum was named originally) came as gifts from the collection of Dr. Francis W. Lewis in 1893 and 1903 (cats. 92, 29). The few pieces of maiolica may have been intended

37. Sale, Sotheby Parke-Bernet, New York, *Pharmacy Wares of the Late Sydney N. Blumberg,* April 26, 1973. This sale contained, in addition to maiolica, pharmacy wares from Holland, Spain, and England. Blumberg also owned other apothecary objects. After his death, some of these pieces were purchased for the National Museum of American History, Smithsonian Institution, Washington, D.C.

38. See Washington, D.C. 1982–83; and San Francisco 1986–88. On Sackler as a collector of maiolica, see Cyril Humphris in the sale catalogue for Christie's, New York, *Important Maiolica from the Arthur M. Sackler Collections,* part 1, October 6, 1993, p. 11.

39. Sale, Parke-Bernet Galleries, New York, *Chinese Porcelain, Italian Majolica, European Porcelain, Gothic & Renaissance Sculpture Works of Art . . . Property of the Norton Simon Foundation . . . ,* May 7–8, 1971.

40. At another museum, the Detroit Institute of Arts, the acquisition of maiolica was different than elsewhere. It began with a purchase of fifteenth-century pieces from A. Satori in Florence in 1923. Bode's protégé, W. R. Valentiner, came to work at the museum soon after. In 1927, Valentiner gave a group of early Italian ceramic fragments to the museum.

Figure 7
View of Gallery D (East Gallery). Pennsylvania Museum of Art, Memorial Hall, Philadelphia, 1916

41. For a description of the Pennsylvania Museum of Art at Memorial Hall, see Helen W. Henderson, *The Pennsylvania Academy of the Fine Arts and Other Collections of Philadelphia* (Boston: L. C. Page, 1911), pp. 218–312.

42. William P. Blake, *International Exhibition, Vienna, 1873: Ceramic Art, a Report on Pottery, Porcelain, Tiles, Terra-cotta and Brick* (New York: D. Van Nostrand, 1875).

43. For Fiske Kimball and the Philadelphia Museum of Art, the best source is Roberts and Roberts 1959.

to provide needed specimens of these wares. A photograph from 1916 shows the gallery devoted to a survey of ceramics, glass, enamels, and silver at Memorial Hall, an installation reminiscent of the presentation of ceramics at the Victoria & Albert Museum, the original model for the Pennsylvania Museum (fig. 7).[41] The early approach to collecting ceramics answered the need defined by William P. Blake, United States commissioner and delegate to the 1873 International Exhibition in Vienna, in his report on the ceramics shown there.[42] He challenged American museums to assemble comprehensive collections of the pottery of all countries and all periods to help improve artistic education and stimulate the creativity of U.S. manufacturers. These issues were central to the foundation of the Pennsylvania Museum and its related school in 1876. Although the Museum's collections grew subsequently, notably under the distinguished ceramics curator and later director Edwin AtLee Barber, his interests did not include Renaissance maiolica.

In 1928 the Museum moved from Memorial Hall into its monumental, empty temple on Fairmount. In conceiving the Museum's future galleries and collections the brilliant director Fiske Kimball proceeded to acquire architectural ensembles and to shape the visitors' experience of related works of art contextually, a program that came to be known as a "walk through time."[43] With the brave purchase of the collection formed by the Frenchman Edmond Foulc acquired with funds contributed by many donors in 1930, after the stock

44. For Foulc, see ibid.; Leman 1927; and Hiesinger 1987. After the opening of the new museum, the city of Philadelphia transferred to it the collection of Sallie Crozer Hilprecht, which included a group of maiolica pieces, a number of them problematic. The collection was bequeathed to the city by her husband Herman V. Hilprecht, the former curator and archaeologist at the University Museum of the University of Pennsylvania.

45. The then recently opened study galleries of ceramics are briefly described in the 66th Annual Report of the Philadelphia Museum of Art (May 31, 1942), p. 15.

46. Widener Archives, National Gallery of Art, Washington, D.C.

47. For the Wideners and the Philadelphia Museum of Art and the National Gallery of Art, see Roberts and Roberts, passim; and Walker 1974.

48. Fiske Kimball to Paul M. Byk, Arnold Seligmann & Rey, New York, February 2, 1943, Philadelphia Museum of Art Archives, Fiske Kimball Records, Series 1. During these years, Joan Prentice, [later von Erdberg], was a young member of the Museum's curatorial staff. After leaving the Museum, she went to France to study maiolica, especially the collection at the Musée de Cluny, Paris. Upon returning to the United States, she conducted research on the Clark Collection at the Corcoran Gallery of Art. For the Walters Art Gallery, she was coauthor of the maiolica catalogue with Marvin Ross; see Prentice von Erdberg and Ross 1952.

49. The Metropolitan Museum of Art, Department of Arms and Armor, Mackay Collection Archive.

market crash, the Museum acquired a European collection of importance.[44] Among the masterpieces was a large circular relief by Luca della Robbia (cat. 6), who raised tin-glazed earthenware sculpture to the status of high art; fine lustered pieces from Deruta (cats. 35, 36); and two drug bottles from Faenza that bear the arms of a member of the Gonzaga family, the rulers of Mantua and important patrons of maiolica (cats. 75a,b). This grouping contained just enough pieces for a modest display in the imposing interior Foulc created for his Paris residence. Kimball intended that these objects would eventually take their place either on the Museum's second floor within evocative period interiors that combined the fine and applied arts—for which Wilhelm Bode's aesthetic and recent installations at the Metropolitan were influential—or in bright, modern study galleries on the first floor that opened in 1942.[45]

A great uncertainty facing Kimball was the eventual disposition of the collection formed by P.A.B. Widener and his son Joseph. Known best for its superb old-master paintings, the Widener collection also contained about fifty fine pieces of maiolica. At Lynnewood Hall, outside Philadelphia, the maiolica was displayed primarily on shelves in a vitrine placed in a vestibule off the large entrance hall.[46] The visitor could have glimpsed the case before ascending the stair to the main floor dominated by the famous picture galleries. Other pieces adorned the mantelpiece in one gallery, and a few lustered ceramics were placed in the dining room. By late 1942, the Wideners' collection had been given to the National Gallery of Art.[47]

The timing of the Widener donation to Washington influenced the growth of the Museum's maiolica collection. In 1943, reacting to the loss of maiolica that might have stayed in Philadelphia, Kimball used endowed purchase funds from the Museum to buy four important pieces then available from the collection of William Randolph Hearst, perhaps the finest private collection of maiolica in the United States at the time (cat. 16). Kimball boasted that his choices were the pick of the collection.[48] In the following year, Kimball achieved another coup by acquiring the three vases from the Fontana family of artisans as part of a purchase that included important Renaissance furniture, all of which was the property of the ruined magnate Clarence H. Mackay (cat. 53). The maiolica had previously graced the Main Hall in Harbor Hill, the Mackay house in Roslyn, New York, designed by McKim, Meade and White (fig. 8).[49]

Figure 8
Detail of the Main Hall, Harbor Hill, Roslyn, New York. Residence of Mr. and Mrs. Clarence H. Mackay

50. Kimball to Byk, February 2, 1943; see note 48. Other institutions and individuals were also buying maiolica during these years. Notable among them were Dr. Robert Bak and especially Robert Lehman in New York. The Metropolitan made important acquisitions at the Baroness Lambert sale in 1941, the Mortimer L. Schiff sale in 1946, and from Rosenberg & Stiebel (by exchange) in 1965.

51. Correspondence between Charles D. Kelekian and Fiske Kimball, September–November, 1951, Philadelphia Museum of Art Archives, Fiske Kimball Records, Series 1.

52. For John D. McIlhenny as a collector, see Roberts and Roberts 1959; "John D. McIlhenny Memorial Exhibition," *Pennsylvania Museum Bulletin*, vol. 21 (February 1926); and "The McIlhenny Collection Inaugural Exhibition," *Philadelphia Museum of Art Bulletin*, vol. 39 (January 1944).

In a letter, Kimball explained that the Museum's trustees had instructed him to buy only fine pieces, taking advantage of Depression prices.[50] For the three Fontana family vases, this was certainly the case. Kimball paid a tenth of the sum they had fetched at the Salomon sale in 1923. In 1951, again profiting from an unforeseen opportunity, Kimball responded to the impending closing of the gallery of Dikran G. Kelekian in New York by selecting three pieces of maiolica, including two beautifully lustered Deruta dishes, then still available at rock-bottom prices (cat. 39).[51]

As far as we know at present, maiolica was an interest of only a few of Philadelphia's private collectors in the twentieth century, aside from the Wideners. In the early 1910s, John D. McIlhenny bought a few pieces of maiolica for Parkgate, his house in the Germantown section of the city. There some maiolica and tin-glazed sculptural reliefs decorated interiors notable for McIlhenny's important Oriental carpet collection and fine early European furniture.[52] (Much of these collections was bequeathed to the Museum.) Years later some of the maiolica came to the Museum as gifts from his son, Henry, and his daughter, Mrs. John Wintersteen. These include the large vase signed and dated by Andrea Pantaleo (cat. 13) and the fine seated Virgin and Child (cat. 86), the latter purchased by John D. McIlhenny from the Palazzo Davanzati auction held in New York in 1916.

A local house with a distinctly Italianate decor was Timberline, the suburban Bryn Mawr mansion of W. Hinckle Smith, which was designed by Charles A. Platt.[53] This residence contained Renaissance and later Italian furniture and maiolica purchased in the 1910s and 1920s from the New York auctions of the Palazzo Davanzati, Stefano Bardini, Luigi Grassi, and Rita Lydig collections.[54]

The only other significant group of maiolica in Philadelphia in the mid-1920s was acquired by the brothers Philip and Dr. A.S.W. Rosenbach.[55] By 1926, most of these pieces, small in number but of notably fine quality, were placed in Dr. Rosenbach's private Spanish-style library in the Rosenbach townhouse at 2006 Delancey Place (fig. 9). The chosen decor was probably a reflection of interiors in New York, such as J. Pierpont Morgan's or Thomas Fortune Ryan's, rather than a local taste. The Smith collection was sold at auction in 1971 and the Rosenbach maiolica in 1974.[56]

At the Museum, which now had pieces sufficient to decorate several galleries—reinstalled in 1946 by the decorative arts curator Henry P. McIlhenny, after his return from service in the Navy during World War II—there were few additional purchases. Later on, curator David DuBon added French plates (cat. 25) and Spanish lusterware, including a classic drug jar (cat. 1). In the 1995 reinstallation of the European galleries, a wall case was devoted to maiolica, and the Fontana family vases were featured as prominently as they had been at Harbor Hill.

ↄ ↄ ↄ ↄ

History demonstrates over and over that the formation of a collection is an activity of passion. It can begin innocently enough. The Steins' first purchase, a Sicilian jar dated 1701, occurred in November 1970, during a trip to New Orleans (cat. 14).[57] The Steins had recently bought a new house, and Howard Stein selected the piece without knowing anything about it. Back at home they saw maiolica at the house of Marie Barcus, a local antique dealer. Like so many admirers of the ceramics, the Steins were struck by the ageless colors and rich decora-

53. For Timberline, see Keith N. Morgan, *Charles A. Platt: The Artist as Architect* (New York: Architectural History Foundation; Cambridge and London: The MIT Press, 1986), pp. 108–9.

54. Sale, Samuel T. Freeman & Co., Philadelphia, *The W. Hinckle Smith Collection*, April 26–29, 1971.

55. Edwin Wolfe 2nd with John F. Fleming, *Rosenbach: A Biography* (Cleveland and New York: World Publishing, 1960), pp. 244–48.

56. In 1954, the Rosenbach brothers turned their residence, then at 2010 Delancey Place, and its contents into a museum, which later sold the maiolica at auction.

57. Howard Stein kindly discussed his collecting with me and patiently answered my questions. Essential to the presentation of the development of the collection here are the Steins' records, which include sale catalogues and an inventory of art objects.

Figure 9
*Detail of the Spanish Library. Residence of Philip and
Dr. A.S.W. Rosenbach, Philadelphia, mid-1920s*

tion of these pieces from the distant Renaissance. In December, at a local auction Janet Stein

acquired a group of small drug jars, one of which depicts an engaging putto playing with a

pinwheel (cat. 61).

This was not an obviously propitious moment to begin collecting maiolica. In 1970,

the historian of art at auction Gerald Reitlinger bemoaned the lack of good collections in

the sale room and wrote that maiolica did not appeal to "the smart international taste of

today."[58] However, the market—first in London and later in New York—was already begin-

ning to rise as good, if not overly plentiful, material appeared. Dr. Arthur Sackler had begun

58. Gerald Reitlinger, *The Economics of Taste,*
vol. 3, *The Art Market in the 1960s* (London:
Barrie and Jenkins, 1970), p. 570.

to acquire maiolica in the 1960s, and a perspicacious London dealer was forming the collection later purchased by the J. Paul Getty Museum in Los Angeles.[59] In the course of the decade, museums and scholars turned their attention to maiolica, too. There were important events, such as the opening of the Robert Lehman Collection galleries at the Metropolitan Museum of Art in 1976. Research in the United States and abroad produced monumental studies as well as numerous carefully reasoned articles on many aspects of the subject.

In May 1971, the Steins made their first important purchases from the Norton Simon Foundation's sale of the former stock of Duveen Brothers, a time capsule of the luxurious objects from the heyday of American collecting after 1900. The Steins attended the exhibition preview prior to the sale because it contained early Italian furniture of a type they had selected for furnishing their house. But in the showroom it was the sight of the vitrine filled with maiolica that enthralled and excited Howard Stein. He threw himself into the study of the objects, following up all the references in the sale catalogue. The Steins chose four accouchement pieces (cats. 83a,b) from Urbino—then of little interest to collectors—and the unique Gonzaga allegorical dish dated 1555.

At a pace slowing only at the end of the 1970s, the Steins bought at public auction in New York almost every season, with Howard Stein doing the bidding. They sometimes acquired objects in groups, such as the ten drug jars from the pharmacy collection of Sydney Blumberg in April 1973, and the six pieces from the Rosenbach brothers' collection in March 1974. But more often they selected a few pieces of maiolica at a time.

In 1974, the Steins made their first acquisitions from a London art dealer, Kate Foster. However, they continued to buy mostly at auction, including the London sales beginning with the Robert Strauss collection in 1976, the source for the signed and dated plates by Francesco Xanto Avelli da Rovigo and the workshop of Guido Durantino. With these acquisitions the Steins had assembled, by careful selection, a choice collection of *istoriato* pieces within the short span of five years. Foster suggested that they consider expanding the collection by adding earlier pieces. Taking her advice, in 1977 the Steins bought from the Lehman family the Deruta dish with the arms of Pope Clement VII and the early Deruta Orsella plate (cats. 71, 56). Urbino wares drew the Steins' interest again in the early 1980s, with the plate

59. For the Sackler exhibition at the National Gallery of Art, see Shinn 1982. There was no catalogue for San Francisco 1986–88. For the maiolica at the Getty, see Hess 1988.

with the coats of arms of the Böckhli and Christell families of Augsburg, Germany, and one from the Lanciarini family service (cats. 74, 72).

Howard and Janet Stein collected maiolica together, although in time, Mr. Stein's interest in the ceramics grew to be more absorbing than his wife's. Their activity was private, aside from their discussions with experts at the auction houses and a few dealers. Mrs. Stein's illness and subsequent death in 1985 interrupted the growth of the collection. Mr. Stein met Wendy Watson through a mutual friend in 1986, at the time of the circulating exhibition of the Clark Collection of maiolica for which she wrote the catalogue. For fifteen years, on summer visits to Italy, Watson has studied aspects of the ceramics, as amply demonstrated in her text that follows, and she encouraged Mr. Stein in his collecting.

In 1990, after a hiatus of five years, Howard Stein looked again to London for several seasons, where the auctions provided pieces one by one, including the superb early Florentine globular jar with the arms of the Pittigardi family (cat. 2) and the Scipio plate. The sales held in New York of the important maiolica of Dr. Arthur Sackler and the well-known London dealer Cyril Humphris were the sources for the last pieces added to the collection. Among the latest acquisitions were the large plate from one of the Hannibal services, another work from the Fontana family (cat. 51). The impressive Deruta drug jar, dated 1501, for which Mr. Stein had been the underbidder to Dr. Sackler in 1978, was an especially satisfying prize thirteen years later (cat. 10).

ల ల ల ల

The Stein maiolica collection, as assembled over a quarter century, embraces an unusual number of interests. Early on, the Steins recognized the wide-ranging functions of Renaissance ceramics. Plates or dishes, preferred by many collectors, are only about a third of the collection. The appeal of objects with distinctive uses explains their choice in 1971 of four accouchement pieces, which the Steins understood to be rarities that might not appear on the market again. Later came maiolica for other purposes, like a writing box (cats. 85a,b), a puzzle jug (cat. 88), an apparently unique plaque (cat. 63), and small beads usually identified as spindle whorls (cats. 84a–e).

The ceramics associated with pharmacies constitute a virtual collection within the Stein Collection. Representing many of the centers of production, including Montelupo, Faenza, Castel Durante, and Venice, these objects display a range of forms and styles of decoration. Some of the pharmacy wares belong to the best-known and most admired apothecary series, such as the dragon-spouted jar from Castelli (cat. 12) and the pieces from Urbino decorated with a seated queen (cats. 78a,b, 79).

Almost a third of the ceramics in the collection display coats of arms or emblems. In their attraction to heraldry, even when the arms remain to be identified, the Steins evince an interest that is traditional among maiolica collectors. A few pieces are signed with names or maker's marks, including the major figures Xanto and Guido Durantino. More numerous are works that bear dates. Pieces decorated with metallic luster glaze, so loved by earlier American collectors of maiolica, are present in fine works from Deruta. The shimmering luster is notably successful on the plate with the Medici arms, the Xanto dish, and the plate with a putto playing a drum from the workshop of Maestro Giorgio Andreoli, who was active in Gubbio (cat. 33). Also present in the collection are works in unusual styles, like the large dish with the Deposition (cat. 64), and uncharacteristic pieces, such as an early Deruta basin and a drug bottle probably from Faenza (cats. 69, 28).

An important development of the Stein Collection in the mid-1970s was a movement toward the acquisition of earlier works. Pieces before 1530 comprise only a quarter of the collection, with but a few dating before 1500. Nevertheless, they constitute some of the most memorable works and the rarest masterpieces—the globular footed jar, the large Deruta drug jar dated 1501, and the plate inscribed *Orsella*. The reemergence of these and other previously published pieces will be especially noted by scholars. Additional early maiolica are a rare small bowl and a drug jar in exceptionally fine condition (cats. 32, 30).

The most distinctive part of the Stein maiolica is their collection of *istoriato* ceramics decorated with narrative subjects. In recent decades, scholars have renewed their interest in these pieces through the study of the identity of the painters and their activities, the graphic sources for their designs, and the patronage that gave rise to this most characteristic form of Renaissance ceramics.

The initial phase of *istoriato*, from the 1520s to the late 1530s, has received particular attention, and pieces from this period have become especially prized. Of greatest interest recently have been the gradually reidentified works by the artists Nicola da Urbino and the prolific Xanto. The Museum's collection has long contained pieces by each of these figures, including a dish by Nicola from the service for Isabella d'Este, probably the most famous of all Renaissance maiolica. The Stein Collection contains complementary works: the large plate representing Pluto abducting Persephone in which the impact of Nicola's style is unmistakable (cat. 47); a fine Xanto plate depicting a favorite subject Eriphyle and Amphiaraus (cat. 50); and the dishes from the workshop of Guido Durantino. Two of the latter pieces are dated 1535, the same year as Guido Durantino's well-known service for Anne de Montmorency, the powerful French military leader (cats. 18, 73).

In the succeeding phase of *istoriato*, from 1540 to 1580, one important innovation was the adaptation to maiolica of the grotesque style, a system of ornamental design devised by Raphael for his decorations in the Vatican Loggie, a scheme inspired by rediscovered ancient Roman wall paintings. The most prominent artisans from this period are members of the Fontana family—Guido Durantino, his son Orazio Fontana, and other relations in Urbino. In the mid-nineteenth century, these wares were the most admired of all maiolica. The scholar J. C. Robinson even characterized Orazio as "a really great industrial artist," whose wares were not to be surpassed until the perfection of porcelain at Sèvres in the eighteenth century.[60]

The Stein Collection possesses notable strength with plates securely associated with the Fontana family as well as accouchement pieces and drug jars also related to their workshops. These wares complement the Museum's holdings of two rare vases with inscribed bases referring to Orazio's workshop, another exceptional vase from a set with scenes from the epic Spanish romance *Amadis de Gaula* (cat. 19), and a plate depicting the sacrifice of Marcus Curtius. The joining of the Stein and Museum collections will form the most instructive group of these ceramics in the United States and an important resource for scholars for whom understanding the Fontana workshops remains a challenge.

The *istoriato* plates issued from other Urbino workshops can also be studied in a group of Stein pieces. They include a plate from the service created for the Lanciarini family of Rome,

60. J. C. Robinson, ed., *Catalogue of the Special Exhibition of Works of Art of the Mediaeval, Renaissance, and More Recent Periods. . . .*, part 4 (London: G. E. Eyre and W. Spottiswoode, 1862), p. 429.

and works associated with the Patanazzi family of artisans, as well as pieces by currently anonymous hands (cat. 20). Fine *istoriato* wares from other centers can be seen in plates painted by various masters, such as the peripatetic Francesco Durantino (cat. 21), Sforza di Marcantonio of Pesaro (cat. 22), and the Venetian Francesco di Piero to whom the important, large dish dated 1546 in the Museum's collection is attributed (cat. 4). A very great rarity is the design concerning a specific contemporary figure to be found on a plate dated 1555 (cat. 55). In the pages that follow Wendy Watson identifies the subject as an allegorical scene relating to a moment in the life of Vespasiano Gonzaga, a member of the cadet branch of the famous Mantuan family.

The strength of the Stein maiolica made after 1540 extends to non-narrative pieces. The collection contains characteristic ceramics from Faenza with compartmentalized designs from the 1550s (cat. 66), pieces from important workshops, such as the prolific Venetian potter Maestro Domenego da Venezia (cat. 5), and two large baluster jars, one dated 1562, from the workshop of Maestro Simone da Colonello in Castel Durante (cats. 23, 24). Later wares include pharmacy jars with a figure of Fortune from around 1580 (cats. 80a,b). To these works can be added the Museum's jar by Andrea Pantaleo, who was active in Palermo in the early seventeenth century.

The number of later Stein works from 1540 to 1580 and beyond is unusual for an American collection. The Steins' fondness for the brilliant palette in these ceramics and the painters' skill at rendering complicated compositions, even those depending on graphic sources by other artists, is reminiscent of the assessment of Giovanni Battista Passeri, the eighteenth-century historian, who characterized designs on Renaissance maiolica as "full of thought and feeling."[61]

The considerable amount of maiolica that has survived over four centuries and come down to us is proof that these ceramics were admired and preserved by later generations. While much about the ownership of maiolica until the 1850s is currently unknown, it is not surprising that pieces as fine as those in the Stein Collection formerly belonged to significant collectors.[62] As one might expect, the previous owners of pieces now in the Stein Collection include well-known Italian names like Alessandro Castellani, Stefano Bardini, and Achille

61. Quoted in Arthur Beckwith, *Majolica and Fayence: Italian, Sicilian, Majorcan, Hispano-Moresque and Persian* (New York: D. Appleton, 1877), p. 9. For Passeri's full text, see Passeri (1752) 1980.

62. For a revealing presentation of the history of maiolica collecting in England, see Norman 1976.

de Clemente. Other works also come from such famous German collectors as James Simon, Dr. Alfred Pringsheim, Hermann Emden, and Adalbert Freiherr von Lanna in Prague. Nevertheless, the number of Stein ceramics that can be traced to English and French collectors of the second half of the nineteenth century is striking. They include the English Robert Stayner Holford, Alexander Barker, and Sir Francis W. Cook and the French Eugène Piot, Baron Adolphe de Rothschild, and the Chabrières-Arlès family, originally from Lyon. These pieces represent a certain European taste that came naturally to the Steins, but is distinctive within American collections. By happy coincidence, these objects reinforce the strengths of the Museum's collection as well.

During the last thirty years, among the changes in American taste has occurred a rediscovery of the brilliant creations of master craftsmanship associated with late-Renaissance or mannerist styles. Demand among collectors has increased for such characteristic wares as tapestries, enamels, and metalwork. Currently, the drawings of almost any sixteenth-century Italian artist are avidly sought after. Although the supply of good pieces of maiolica on the art market has diminished dramatically, the ceramics in general have attracted a new audience and engage a new generation of scholars. The distinguished and personal collection formed privately by Howard and Janet Stein during this interval now emerges to join and transform the holdings of the Philadelphia Museum of Art. The publication and exhibition of the Stein Collection should provide ample stimulation for museum visitors, connoisseurs, and historians alike. Within its riches are objects to offer viewers and readers many varieties of enjoyment—the strength of early pieces, the brilliance of lusterwares, and the meditated control of earlier *istoriato*—as well as a host of objects that display the deft elegance of later ceramic artists.

This essay depends to an unusual degree on the generous cooperation of curatorial colleagues, museum archivists, and others. It is a pleasure to acknowledge them here: The staff of the Philadelphia Museum of Art Library, Tracey Albainy, Susan Anderson, Betsy Baldwin, Graham Berwind III, Martin Chapman, Dr. Alan P. Darr, Mrs. Joanne Flannery, Brian Gallagher, Ann Halpern, Catherine Hess, Linda Horvitz Roth, William R. Johnston, Marisa Keller, Donald J. LaRocca, Douglas Lewis, Dr. Reino Liefkes, Lee Miller, Paul F. Miller, Jeffrey Munger, Christine Nelson, Father Donald Roe, Bart Ryckbosch, Ian Wardropper, Michael Wentworth.

As far as we know, the Romans were not aware of this type of painting on pottery. The vessels from those days that have been found filled with the ashes of their dead are covered with figures incised and washed in with one colour in any given area, sometimes in black, red, or white, but never with the brilliance of glaze nor the charm and variety of painting which has been seen in our day. —Giorgio Vasari, 1550[1]

CHAPTER I

The Pottery of Humanism

The golden age of Italian Renaissance maiolica occurred between the late-fifteenth and late-sixteenth centuries. Half a millennium later, in an era deluged with commodities and images, we may not fully appreciate the impact that these brilliantly painted wares had upon their contemporary culture. Humbler than the gold and silver vessels that Giulio Romano (1499?–1546) depicted in a mythological banquet scene at the Palazzo del Te in Mantua (fig. 1), maiolica, or tin-glazed earthenware, was nonetheless a valued product in a luxury economy that was unprecedented since antiquity. It is the good fortune of the Philadelphia Museum of Art to have a collection that represents many of the highest points of this art form, thanks in good part to the recent gift of the Howard I. and Janet H. Stein Collection.

Ceramics have been created, owned, and used by people in every era, culture, and class, beginning thousands of years ago with the first humans who crudely molded clay into functional containers. By their very nature, ceramics have become touchstones of civilizations that archaeologists and historians use to reconstruct the past. Pervasive throughout societies, they are produced in quantity and are remarkably durable. Most importantly, ceramics offer considerable insight into the cultures that produced them. Their shapes, decoration, and function

1. Vasari-Milanesi 1878–85, vol. 6, pp. 581–82. Vasari's interest in ceramics developed honestly, since his name itself was derived from the word *vasaio* (potter), and his own grandfather had plied the trade in Arezzo; see Patricia Lee Rubin, *Giorgio Vasari: Art and History* (New Haven: Yale University Press, 1995), p. 61.

provide eloquent testimony about a particular time and place, and about their original makers and owners.

In the pages that follow, some of this history will unfold through an examination of the Museum's splendid maiolica collection. For example, how did upper-class Italians decorate their palaces; how did they dine, celebrate, worship, and treat illness; how did they see them-

Figure 1
Giulio Romano, Marriage Feast of Cupid and Psyche, *detail, fresco. Sala di Psiche, Palazzo del Te, Mantua, c. 1528*
Scala/Art Resource, New York

selves and convey their character, intellect, and social and economic status to others? This quintessentially Italian medium, which the English scholar Bernard Rackham referred to as the "pottery of humanism," reflects the basic themes and ideals of the Italian Renaissance in the same way that Greek vase painting embodied those of Periclean Athens in the fifth century B.C.E. Indeed, E. P. Richardson has noted that the minor arts give us a "picture of the artistic genius of those centuries in their smaller expressions, in forms which are equally wonderful but much less familiar. . . . The decorative arts enable us to discover with greater intimacy something of the powerful and decisive personalities for whom the artist worked," like Isabella d'Este or the Gonzaga family.[2]

In recent years, scholars and museums have modified their approach to the broad spectrum of the arts, reversing a long-held trend in which the fine arts—painting, sculpture, and architecture—were treated as distinct and separate from the decorative arts. The reintegration of art objects from both sides of that vanishing boundary—evident now in the literature of art as well as in museum galleries in Boston, Los Angeles, and Philadelphia, to name a few—presents a more coherent picture of the aesthetic experience of a particular moment in history. Seen alongside paintings and sculpture of the period, Italian Renaissance textiles, metalwork, furniture, and maiolica can be appreciated as integral elements of the same artistic culture, social fabric, and intellectual milieu.[3] Far from being disconnected, the decorative objects

2. E. P. Richardson, foreword to *Decorative Arts of the Italian Renaissance, 1400–1600* (Detroit: The Detroit Institute of Arts, 1958), p. 13.

3. For a useful discussion of the value of the decorative arts and an exploration of the relationship between art objects and their originating culture, taking tapestries as an example, see Jardine and Brotton 2000, pp. 61–131.

created by Italian artists and artisans in the fifteenth and sixteenth centuries were part of a veritable flood of commodities that were produced for patrons with an overriding enthusiasm for artistic beauty. As John Shearman has written of these Renaissance epicureans: "Beauty they desired and cultivated in every imaginable context: in deportment, in hunting or in the theatre, in their tables and in the objects they placed upon them, in the music they performed, the books they read and all the works of art around them."[4]

Artists in the Italian Renaissance, particularly court artists, were expected to respond to the desires of their patrons for every decorative commodity imaginable, from altarpieces and frescoes to festival banners, playing cards, textiles and tapestries, liturgical vestments, tablewares, wedding chests, and theater costumes.[5] And since artists were regarded with rare exceptions as craftsmen, it was not considered inappropriate to make such demands upon them. They were expected to be flexible, imaginative, and as Leonardo da Vinci (1452–1519) asserted, "universal."[6] While examples of artistic crossover are far less common today—although David Hockney's theater sets or Michael Graves's teapots come to mind—it was the norm in Renaissance courts. The role of the modern artist, anticipated by Leonardo himself, is individualistic, entrepreneurial, and generally free from the requirements of patrons. In the sixteenth century, by comparison, it was not unusual for major artists to turn their talents toward the *arti minori,* or minor arts, as Giorgio Vasari (1511–1574) noted.[7] Duke Guidobaldo II of Urbino (1514–1574), for example, commissioned Michelangelo (c. 1475–1564) to design a silver inkwell for him, ordered a painted harpsichord cover from Agnolo Bronzino (1503–1572), and was an important patron of the thriving ceramic workshops nearby. The mannerist painter Rosso Fiorentino (1494–1540), best known for his painted altarpieces, designed every sort of decorative item, including whimsical festival masks that were recorded in engravings. In what may be one of the more bizarre examples of this kind, Giulio Romano's responsibilities at the Palazzo del Te went well beyond fresco painting, and included the fashioning of a chamber pot with fish in relief on the bottom and bullrushes around the sides.[8]

The desire for material luxury and the unrestrained pursuit of consumer goods in the Renaissance have been the subject of vigorous scrutiny in recent years. This is fortunate, for to understand the significance of maiolica, we must be familiar with the new consumption

4. Shearman 1979, p. 187.

5. See Holman 1997, pp. 6–8, for examples.

6. Leonardo da Vinci, *The Notebooks of Leonardo da Vinci,* comp. and ed. Jean Paul Richter (New York: Dover Publications, 1970), vol. 1, pp. 250–51.

7. Vasari mentions this idea several times in the *Lives.*

8. Shearman 1979, p. 156.

phenomenon and the ways in which it affected Italian artists and artisans of the period. The fifteenth-century humanist, philosopher, and courtier Giovanni Pontano summarized the newly emerging values in a pair of treatises written for his patron, Alfonso II of Naples.[9] In *De principe* (1468) and *I trattati delle virtù sociali*,[10] Pontano outlines the appropriate manner in which a prince, his courtiers, and even members of the upper-middle class should conduct their lives—that is, with dignity, decorum, urbanity, and refinement. For Pontano, the concept of "magnificence" was manifested in the virtuous spending of money on public projects, such as architecture, while the notion of "splendor" was the logical extension of that idea into the private sphere. He describes in detail how private houses—both city residences and country villas—should be characterized by elegance and impeccable taste, decorated with the most luxurious and splendid things possible, while remaining within the bounds of propriety.[11]

The value of objects, according to Pontano and others, was based not only upon their intrinsic worth, but on the artisanry with which they were made, whether of gold, silver, or "porcelain."[12] Antiquities, although not always the most valuable items in terms of materials, were among the most highly regarded possessions, as Lorenzo de' Medici's 1492 inventory attests.[13] But it was not enough merely to *possess* wealth in order to garner admiration. One needed also to *demonstrate* one's social and intellectual worth through the ambience in which one lived. In his chapter on the artistic furnishings of a household, the mid-sixteenth-century writer Sabba da Castiglione noted that it was both the selection and the combination of objects—works of art, medals, musical instruments, and all manner of decorations—that conveyed the taste, refinement, and erudition of the owner.[14] The moral and humanistic quality of consumption that surfaces in his writings as well as those of Pontano, Niccolò Machiavelli, Baldassare Castiglione, and others is an essential element of the phenomenon, and something quite new in the Renaissance.

Clearly, the Renaissance desire for worldly goods was a momentous break from the medieval emphasis on the spiritual, the metaphysical, and the afterlife. The earlier condemnation by church and state alike of any conspicuous display of wealth was gradually replaced in the fourteenth century by the approval, and even the active encouragement, of public and private splendor. Indeed, the eminent humanist Leonardo Bruni (1370–1444) inveighed against

9. See Pontano 1965; and Kidwell 1991.

10. Pontano's treatise on magnificence was written c. 1486; the one on splendor was first published in 1498. Both were included in *I trattati delle virtù sociali*.

11. In the 1540s, Marco Benavides constructed an elegant loggia in Padua and had this message carved into the stone: "It is praiseworthy to do what is appropriate, not what licence permits"; see John Onians, *Bearers of Meaning: The Classical Orders in Antiquity, the Middle Ages, and the Renaissance* (Princeton: Princeton University Press, 1988), p. 319.

12. Pontano 1965, pp. 272–73; see also Syson and Thornton 2001, chapter 5.

13. See Giovanna G. Bertelà and Marco Spallanzani, eds., *Libro d'inventario dei beni di Lorenzo il Magnifico* (Florence: Associazione Amici del Bargello, 1992); cited in Goldthwaite 1993, p. 248 n. 148.

14. Sabba da Castiglione, *Ricordi overo ammaestramenti* (Venice: Paolo Gherardo, 1555), chapter 109; cited in Goldthwaite 1993, p. 249.

unwarranted frugality, saying that it was ridiculous to save one's riches for an elaborate tomb, and much better to be known by one's virtuous spending. Moral strictures and social disapproval of consumption fell away as expenditures in the name of liberality and magnificence became the rule in Italian courts and city-states.[15] At the same time, the expansion of the economy, with its burgeoning merchant class and its increasingly wealthy aristocracy, gave rise to a situation in which there was more money to spend and more items on which to spend it. Social competition among peers was also a crucial factor in the development of the market for paintings, sculpture, decorative arts, and antiquities. Economic historian Richard Goldthwaite has noted: "As a consumption phenomenon, the patronage of art in Renaissance Italy represents something new in the history of art in a quantitative as well as a qualitative sense, for men not only redirected their spending habits according to new canons of taste but they demanded substantially more art and a greater variety of it."[16]

In the twenty-first century, we tend to take a commodity-driven economy for granted, but in the Renaissance the system operated in a different way, through a demand and supply mode rather than the reverse.[17] Buyers sought new and evermore elaborate decorations for their homes as those residences became imbued with deeper symbolism. This trend should resonate for us today, in an age characterized by a striking upsurge of interest in domestic architecture, interior decoration, household consumer products, and "shelter magazines" that tell us what to want, where to buy it, and how to display it once we have it. The modern expression "lifestyle" is one that could accurately be applied to the impulse that was so central to the Italian Renaissance.

The rise of the potter's art in Italy was the direct result of this drive to refine one's style of life, and the industry benefited enormously from the new market for luxury goods.[18] Artists and craftsmen rushed to fill the void and provided greater varieties and quantities of decorative objects, ranging from paintings and sculptures to furniture and elaborately painted tablewares. Domenico Ghirlandaio's (1449–1494) fresco of the *Birth of Saint John the Baptist* (fig. 2) illustrates the new impulse toward sumptuousness and splendor in patrician households of late-fifteenth-century Florence. This "empire of things," a phrase Goldthwaite borrowed from the novelist Henry James, brought with it fundamental transformations in

15. Holman 1997, p. 5; see also A. D. Fraser Jenkins, "Cosimo de'Medici's Patronage of Architecture and the Theory of Magnificence," *Journal of the Warburg and Courtauld Institutes,* vol. 33 (1970), pp. 162–70; and Cole 1995, pp. 17–35.

16. Goldthwaite 1987a, p. 154; see also Goldthwaite 1989.

17. Goldthwaite 1987a, p. 154.

18. Maiolica was relatively inexpensive compared to other luxury goods. The price of a service of seventy-five or eighty pieces, for example, would have been about one-tenth the cost of a painted and gilded *cassone* (chest). Perhaps surprising to us is the fact that textiles were among the costliest items of all in the Renaissance.

Figure 2
Domenico Ghirlandaio, Birth of Saint John the
Baptist, *fresco. Santa Maria Novella, Florence, 1485–90*
Scala/Art Resource, New York

patronage, manners, entertaining, cuisine, furnishings, and the use of domestic spaces.[19] In all
of these domains, maiolica played a part. Although the Italian pottery industry had a relatively modest share of the overall economy, in many ways it reflected the development of other
luxury markets, such as textiles, glass, and metalwares, throughout the peninsula. Tin-glazed
earthenware satisfied, at least for a time, the appetite for gleaming white porcelain tablewares,
whose manufacture remained a well-guarded secret in China.

The maiolica technique developed in the Middle East, and was introduced by foreign
artisans into Sicily and southern Italy. Influenced by imports from Spain, it spread rapidly
throughout the peninsula. Artisans quickly developed new shapes in response to the demand
from pharmacies and hospitals, changes in dining and display customs, the evolution of
devotional practices, and the desire for decorative architectural details, like tiles and facade
decorations. Maiolica designs were inspired by a wide variety of sources, ranging from Roman
sculpture and medieval manuscript illuminations to Spanish and Chinese floral schemes.
Perhaps the greatest innovation of the maiolica artisans was the introduction of *istoriato*
(literally, storied) wares, the first narrative ceramics since antiquity. Although a less-exalted
medium than painting or sculpture, maiolica also took an active part in the current of antique

19. Goldthwaite 1987a, p. 154.

revivalism that was at the heart of the Italian Renaissance. The design motifs and narrative subjects that appear on many of the pieces in the Museum's collection are frequently linked to ancient works of art as well as classical literature. This directly reflects the engagement of patrons with the ancient world and humanist thought.

The desire for maiolica diminished after true porcelain began to be produced in Germany in the eighteenth century. And although tin-glazed earthenware enjoyed a resurgence with collectors in the nineteenth century, that eventually subsided as well, relegating these precious ceramics to the storerooms and less-frequented galleries of museums. In recent decades, however, attention has been deservedly redirected to the decorative arts and to these beautiful ceramics in particular. This book is not intended as a comprehensive history of maiolica. Rather it is a narrative told through holdings of the Philadelphia Museum of Art, which has now been significantly enhanced by the addition of Howard and Janet Stein's exceptional collection.

The art of the potter has two sources as its principal basis. One comes from the art of design, the other from various alchemical secrets and elemental mixtures . . . the perfection of this art depends on the diligence of the master, on good clay, on good colors, and then on the fire. —Vannoccio Biringuccio, 1540[1]

CHAPTER 2

Making Maiolica

The Venetian traveler Marco Polo (1254–1324) recounted the many marvels he saw during his long stay at the Chinese court of Kublai Khan. Among these wonders were the delicate white ceramics the Italians called *porcellana*, after a type of smooth, white seashell. Chinese porcelain was made from a white refractory clay known as kaolin mixed with petuntse, a felspathic rock that fuses into a natural glass. Fired to a high temperature—around 1,450 degrees centigrade—the resulting wares were thin, hard, translucent, and white, qualities that made these Eastern wares eminently desirable. From the late-thirteenth century, when Polo spoke of it, through the Renaissance, porcelain was a highly sought rarity that was imported into Italy and Europe along with Islamic versions of the ware. The very idea of tin-glazed earthenware was born out of the desire to imitate Chinese porcelain, and it was the Middle Eastern potters who developed a white tin-glaze to cover the brown earthenware clay and provide a surface on which to apply colors. Introduced into Sicily and southern Italy by the twelfth century, the revolutionary glazing technique soon spread northward. Within a few decades it had reached the central part of the peninsula, where many active workshops were to flourish in the Quattrocento and Cinquecento (the Italian designations for the fifteenth and sixteenth centuries). The late-medieval ceramics of Italy were quite limited in shape and color.[2] The famous wares of Orvieto, for example, were painted primarily with copper green and manganese purple. In time, that palette expanded to include other pigments like yellow, orange, turquoise, and blue, as well as gold and ruby metallic lusters made using silver and copper.

1. Biringuccio 1959, pp. 392, 395.

2. Much of what we know about late-medieval wares comes from material excavated from wells or other disposal sites. Some bowls were set into building facades, where they can still be seen today (for example, Spanish fourteenth-century bowls in the campanile of Santa Maria Maggiore in Rome [see Ravanelli Guidotti 1992, p. 26]); see Hugo Blake, "The Bacini of North Italy," in *La Céramique Médiévale en méditerranée occidentale Xe–XVe siècles, Valbonne, 11–14 septembre 1978, Colloques Internationaux du Centre National de la Recherche Scientifique*, no. 584 (Paris: Centre National de la Recherche Scientifique, 1980), pp. 93–111.

Lusters, applied to the already glazed ceramic surface and fired a third time, added an iridescence that simulated metalwares.

The production of native wares in Italy was paralleled by the importation of tin-glazed, lustered earthenware from the workshops of Spain. Originally, the Italians applied the term *maiolica* only to those Spanish lusterwares, later to their own lustered pottery, and eventually to all types of tin-glazed earthenware.[3] A traditional explanation for the origin of the mysterious word comes to us from Dante himself, who referred in his *Divine Comedy* (c. 1310–14) to Majorca, a stopover for ceramics traders, as the *isola di majolica*.[4] It is more likely, however, that the word derives from the Spanish term *obra de Mallequa* (Malaga wares) for the lustered pottery of Valencia on the east coast of Spain. Indeed, it was the Moorish artisans of Malaga who introduced the style to that region, where it flourished and became one of the most desired imports for wealthy Tuscan families whose coats of arms appear on them.[5] A classic example of Valencian production is a graceful lustered albarello (cat. 1), or cylindrical drug jar, with bryony flowers and parsley leaves (the name *albarello* was most likely derived from *al barani*, the Arabic word for *container*). This particular jar probably originated in Manises, Spain, the source for most high-quality export wares. Intended to be used by pharmacists and spice-sellers, its shape was tailored for easy retrieval from a shelf. The bryony pattern was particularly popular with Italian customers, who referred to the motif as *fioralixi* (fleur-de-lys). It was often combined with parsley leaves, forming a tightly woven decorative pattern.[6] This long-lived Spanish design had a great influence on Italian artisans, who adopted it for its functional simplicity. A rare Tuscan vase made for the Pittigardi family of Florence bears its coat of arms in a wreath set against a more schematic bryony-pattern background (cat. 2). The special fondness of Florentine aristocratic families for Valencian imports may have influenced local potters to quote the popular Spanish styles. The Pittigardi vase exemplifies that new competitive spirit of fifteenth-century Italian potters, who effectively cut into the foreign market despite their lack of luster technology.

The glittering Spanish imports clearly had an impact on Italians, who were just embarking on their quest for luxury items in the new Renaissance "empire of things." As technological strides were made in the medium of maiolica, local artisans—who were more adventurous

3. As late as the 1550s, Cipriano Piccolpasso applies the term *maiolica* exclusively to lustered wares, although by that time such usage was somewhat antiquated.

4. Dante, *Inferno*, canto 28; cited in Mallet 1998, p. 13.

5. See Wilson 1987b, pp. 28–32. Thornton (1997, pp. 201–10) also refers to inventories of fine Italian households that list Spanish wares.

6. See Ray 2000, p. 73.

CAT. I
ALBARELLO WITH BRYONY FLOWERS, SPAIN, VALENCIA, PROBABLY MANISES,
C. 1430–70

CAT. 2
FOOTED JAR WITH ARMS OF THE PITTIGARDI FAMILY, TUSCANY, PROBABLY
FLORENCE, SECOND HALF OF THE FIFTEENTH CENTURY

than their Spanish brethren—moved quickly to create new forms and decorative styles. They were influenced by trends in the other arts—painting, sculpture, printmaking, and textiles—and by imported goods from the Middle East.[7] Remarkable advances occurred in Italian ceramics between the mid-fifteenth century and the 1530s, by which time artisans were creating *istoriato* wares with complex narrative scenes as well as purely decorative schemes.

The workings of the maiolica industry in Italy have been illuminated in recent years by archaeological excavations, archival discoveries, and various publications. However, the detailed documentation that often exists in contracts for paintings, sculpture, and architecture is less common for the decorative arts. There is the occasional, but all too rare, self-referential work, like a plate made in Cafaggiolo that shows a painter with two clients (fig. 3), or another plate that illustrates a potter's wheel and tools and bears the inscription *Qui se lavora de pigniate* (Here pottery is made).[8] More significant for our knowledge of the medium, however, is Cipriano Piccolpasso's extraordinary treatise, "Li tre libri dell'arte del vasaio" (The Three Books of the Potter's Art), written around 1557.[9] A native of the flourishing pottery center of Castel Durante, Piccolpasso (1523/24– 1579) was commissioned by Cardinal François de Tournon (1489–1562), an eminent humanist and patron of the arts, to write this work, perhaps as a guide for craftsmen in France. By the mid-sixteenth century, the manufacture of tin-glazed earthenware was already established in Lyon (de Tournon's own see), Nevers, and elsewhere, thanks to the northward migration of Italian artisans. Piccolpasso and his patron may have intended to publish the work in Venice, but that plan was never realized, perhaps due to the cardinal's death in 1562. Miraculously, the treatise survived in a single manuscript copy now in the National Art Library at the Victoria & Albert Museum in London.

Piccolpasso was a small-town patrician who led an eventful, if star-crossed life. He was an amateur artist who followed Castiglione's dictates that a good courtier must have a "knowledge of how to draw and an acquaintance with the art of painting itself."[10] The information that Piccolpasso reported in the "Arte del vasaio" was gained not from practical experience, but from the study and observation of workshops in operation. In the case of metallic luster

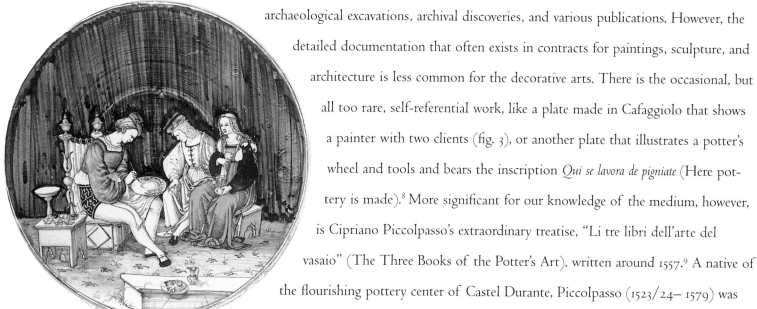

Figure 3
Plate showing a maiolica painter at work, Cafaggiolo, c. 1510
Victoria & Albert Picture Library, London

7. I think it is likely, as John Mallet has remarked, that textiles had a larger impact on the other decorative arts than may be realized. Their fragility and limited survival rate hampers study in this area; see Mallet 1998, pp. 15–16; and Thornton 1991, with many references in the index.

8. Rackham (1940) 1977, nos. 307, 746.

9. See Piccolpasso 1980 for a two-volume facsimile and translation of the treatise.

10. Baldesar [Baldassare] Castiglione, *The Book of the Courtier*, trans. Charles S. Singleton (New York: Anchor Books, Doubleday & Company, 1959), p. 77.

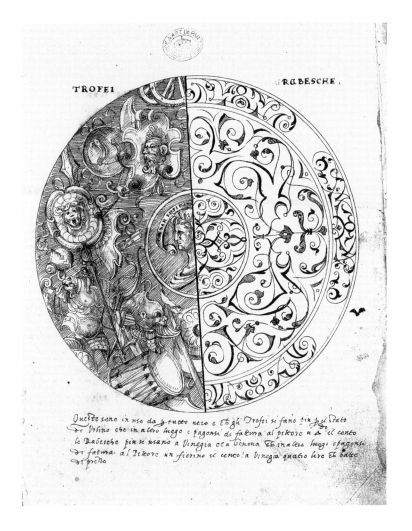

Figure 4
*Cipriano Piccolpasso, Sample design with trophies, from
"The Three Books of the Potter's Art," c. 1557
Victoria & Albert Picture Library, London*

Figure 5
*Cipriano Piccolpasso, Potters at work, from "The Three
Books of the Potter's Art," c. 1557
Victoria & Albert Picture Library, London*

11. Piccolpasso 1980, vol. 2, p. 86. Only certain ceramic shops, like some at Gubbio and Deruta, were privy to these secrets that they guarded jealously.

pigments—the highly prized secret of making what he calls "gold maiolica"—Piccolpasso noted that his report was based on "what I have heard of it from others, not that I have ever made it myself, or even seen it being done . . . [although] I do know that it is painted over finished wares."[11] He freely acknowledged that he relied in part on Vannoccio Biringuccio's *De la pirotechnia* (1540), a work concerned mainly with metallurgy. Unlike Biringuccio (1480– c. 1539), who treats the subject of pottery only fleetingly, Piccolpasso provides such minute details about the materials and procedures that his treatise could be used as a practical manual today. Accompanying the texts are drawings that cover every step of the process, from the digging of clay and forming of vessels to their painting and firing. At the conclusion, Piccolpasso illustrates a number of decorative schemes, along with some notes about their cost and popularity (fig. 4). Strangely, he does not illustrate any *istoriato* wares, which were among the most highly praised products of his home province at the time he was writing. In a subtle way, however, Piccolpasso invokes the popular themes that appeared on the wares in the historiated initials that introduce various sections of his treatise: Venus and Adonis, the Trojan War, Samson, Fortune, river gods, Hercules and the Hydra, Pluto and Persephone,[12] and the Judgment of Paris.

As Piccolpasso describes, the making of maiolica began with the digging of clay from river beds and its purification. The clay was then shaped either on a foot-powered wheel or in molds (fig. 5). Spouts, handles, or other decorative elements were applied to the still-damp clay using a slip (clay thinned with water). The pieces were fired in wood-fueled kilns, heated to about 1,000 degrees centigrade. After cooling, the semiporous wares were dipped into a white glaze mixture. The mixture, called *bianco*, was made with expensive tin imported from England or Flanders, since the metal was not common in Italy. The pigments applied atop the dried *bianco* were made from metallic oxides: copper green, manganese purple and brown, cobalt blue, antimony yellow, and antimony-iron orange. As with fresco or watercolor techniques, a sure hand was required because the colors were absorbed quickly into the white surface, and errors were difficult or impossible to correct. The best brushes, which needed to be soft and flexible, were made from goat hair or the manes of asses, or sometimes, as Piccolpasso noted, mouse whiskers. Painters either drew their designs freehand or worked out their compositions—especially in the case of *istoriato* subjects— by consulting prints after paintings by Raphael (1483–1520) and other masters.[13] Sometimes entire compositions would be copied wholesale, while in other cases, the artisans would invent their own arrangements by excerpting figures from different sources. The craftsman's drawing of the design would then be transferred to the white surface of the ceramic either by tracing the lines with a stylus or by pricking small holes in the paper, dusting it with charcoal, and using the dots left on the *bianco* to re-create the composition.

Finer works were normally coated with a second clear glaze called *coperta* (covering), which added a sparkling finish that enhanced the colors beneath. The second firing then took place at a slightly reduced temperature, around 950 degrees centigrade. If gold or red metallic lusters were desired, compounds of silver or copper mixed with ocher would be applied to the pottery, which was then fired at a lower temperature in a smoke-reducing atmosphere within

12. Derived from Marcantonio Raimondi's print of the *Martyrdom of Saint Lawrence* (Bartsch, vol. 26 [14], no. 104-1 [89]).

13. See Landau and Parshall 1994, especially pp. 294–97, for details about the cost of prints.

CAT. 3
LARGE DISH WITH LION, DERUTA, FIRST HALF OF THE SIXTEENTH CENTURY

the kiln. The completed works would have appeared much as they do today, since their brilliant colors locked permanently within the glaze (cat. 3). Unlike Renaissance paintings that are frequently transformed by the chemical reactions of the pigments or obscured under layers of dull yellow varnish, maiolica never fades. In fact, these ceramic wares echo the vivid tones and *colori cangianti* (iridescent colors) now seen in Michelangelo's newly cleaned ceiling frescoes in the Sistine Chapel, or in the perfectly preserved miniature paintings of Giulio Clovio's Farnese Hours.[14]

14. For illustrations of Michelangelo's ceiling frescoes (1508–12), see Michael Hirst et al., *The Sistine Chapel: A Glorious Restoration* (New York: Harry N. Abrams, 1994). For the Farnese Hours (c. 1535–46; now in the Pierpont Morgan Library, New York), see Thornton 1991, fig. 147; and for a full facsimile edition, see *Das Farnese-Stundenbuch aus dem Besitz der Pierpont Morgan Library in New York* (Graz: Akademische Druck-u, 2001).

I have been in Urbino and have seen really excellent ware painted with landscapes, fables, and histories, to my eyes of surpassing beauty . . .

—Ioanfrancesco to Gianjacopo Calandra, 1530[1]

CHAPTER 3

Workshops and Artisans

Maiolica workshops produced two general types of wares: simple domestic pottery used for cooking, food storage, and tablewares, and more elaborate painted ceramics that were prized for their decorative qualities as well as their functionality. It is difficult to know the proportion of plain to decorated wares, since everyday vessels were undoubtedly made, broken, and discarded far more often than their painted and much more valuable counterparts. Clearly, though, painted ceramics were less common and required more experienced artisans to turn them out. Piccolpasso tells us that a typical smaller maiolica workshop might comprise eight or nine individuals: an owner or manager (who may or may not have been a master craftsman himself), two potters, two or three painters, a kiln man, and two general workers.[2] The size of a shop could vary depending upon the quantity and type of business, and it might expand to include contract painters when special commissions were received. Larger workshops also used apprentices learning the trade and probably employed artisans specializing in certain types of painting, like the designs on the rims of Deruta's *piatti da pompa* (display plates).[3] In one of his most memorable illustrations (fig. 6), Piccolpasso shows four painters at work in a communal studio and writes: "Painting on pottery is different from painting on walls, since painters on walls for the most part stand on their feet, and painters on pottery sit all the time; nor could the painting be done otherwise . . . the ware that is being painted is held on the knees with one hand beneath it . . . the hollow ware is held with the hand inside it."[4]

The scholar's challenge in attributing maiolica to one center or another, or to one painter

1. Cited in J. V. G. Mallet, "Mantua and Urbino: Gonzaga Patronage of Maiolica," *Apollo,* vol. 114 (September 1981), p. 167. Gianjacopo Calandra was secretary to Duke Federico II Gonzaga of Mantua.

2. Piccolpasso 1980, vol. 2, p. xxii.

3. Mallet 1996, p. 45.

4. Piccolpasso 1980, vol. 2, p. 101.

Figure 6
Cipriano Piccolpasso, Painters at work, from "The Three Books of the Potter's Art," c. 1557
Victoria & Albert Picture Library, London

or another, can be complicated by the division of labor and by collaboration between artisans, a practice that was also common in ancient Greece. Although Piccolpasso draws four painters working side by side in a studio, an arrangement that could foster such artistic interchange, he refrains from commenting upon it. In addition, the mobility of craftsmen, a factor that is only now being fully taken into account by scholars, has made it increasingly difficult to assign a work of maiolica to a particular geographic location without knowing the identity of the painter.[5] Maiolica designs and styles were transmitted from place to place by artisans traveling between towns. Their mobility was undoubtedly the means by which the *istoriato* style, which developed around Urbino in the 1520s and 1530s, gained a foothold in Venice and became an important component of the market there by the 1550s. One peripatetic painter, Francesco di Piero, maintained studios in both his native Castel Durante and Venice, as did several other Urbino-area painters of the 1540s and 1550s. An important *istoriato* dish marked "1546 made in Venice in Castello," is most likely from Francesco's workshop in the Castello district (cat. 4).[6] The scene is identified as the destruction of Troy, and a roiling battle takes place in a hilly landscape. Themes from the Trojan War appear frequently in Renaissance art and literature, but here the artist downplays the story of the destructive conflagration and instead emphasizes the combat, which is based on Giulio Romano's *Battle of Constantine* in the Vatican.[7]

Ceramics were also routinely shipped from place to place, although certain cities like Venice maintained protectionist laws that banned the importation of maiolica made elsewhere.[8] On the other hand, Venetian wares were actively exported. At least three consignments from the city's workshops were ordered for the Medici court between 1544 and 1551,

5. As noted by Timothy Wilson (2001).

6. Francesco di Piero may be the artist to whom Piccolpasso refers in his treatise as having a kiln twice the size of those in Urbino; see Piccolpasso 1980, vol. 2, pp. 64–65. See also Wilson 1987a, pp. 186–89, where he notes that some of the figures on the right seem to echo an engraving by Giulio Bonasone (1510–c. 1576) after an early design of Raphael's for the same painting (Bartsch, vol. 28 [15], no. 84-1 [134]).

7. Stefania Massari, *Giulio Romano pinxit et delineavit* (Rome: Fratelli Palombi, 1993), cat. 176. Francesco di Piero undoubtedly used a reproductive print after that fresco, a common practice that will be discussed in chapter 5.

8. As a major focal point of trade with the rest of Europe and the East, Venice was experienced in protecting its interests; see Wilson 1987a, p. 185.

CAT. 4
LARGE DISH WITH DESTRUCTION OF TROY, VENICE,
FRANCESCO DI PIERO, 1546

requiring a long journey for the fragile objects from the Adriatic port to Florence.[9] In addition there was a significant ceramic trade between Venice and even more distant Sicily. This active exportation should not come as a surprise, however, given the Venetians' exceptional experience in the overseas trade of luxury goods.

Venice had a remarkably vigorous ceramics industry despite the fact that every manufacturing component had to be imported, in contrast to centers like Urbino and Castel Durante, which had ready access to fine clay from their local riverbanks. The most famous and prolific of all Venetian maiolica-makers and exporters was Maestro Domenego (or Domenico) da Venezia, who was listed as "painter or potter" in documents as early as 1547, and signed many pieces between 1562 and 1568.[10] A large pharmaceutical service from his shop was sent south to a hospital in Messina, and there is overwhelming evidence that he served a large German clientele as well.[11] The quality of the work from this shop varies widely, as might be expected from one with a large production; its output included both the characteristic "foliage and flowers" styles described by Piccolpasso and *istoriato* wares.[12] In a large storage jar in the Museum's collection, vigorous scrolls surround medallions with images of two men—one older and bearded, the other younger and sporting a feathered hat (cat. 5). Set within in a deep blue ground with sweeping fronds, daisies, and calligraphic strokes scratched through the blue pigment, the free brushwork of the anonymous heads echoes the painterliness of Titian and other Venetian artists.

Venice, of course, was the northernmost of the Italian ceramic centers, but the heartland of Italian Renaissance maiolica was to be found in cities farther to the south.[13] As was noted, Cinquecento Florence was a major destination for Spanish lustered wares that were avidly acquired by wealthy merchant families. As Italy's own ceramic industry gained momentum, local workshops sprang up around Florence, in nearby Montelupo and Cafaggiolo, and farther south in Siena. The industry was encouraged by growing consumerism and by consistently supportive patrons like the Medici.[14]

Between 1420 and 1450, pharmacy jars with stylized cobalt blue oak leaves and animals were produced in and near Florence. The thick pigment applied atop the white surface of the tin glaze gave rise to the term "relief-blue" wares. Although there are no examples of these jars

9. See Marco Spallanzani, "Maioliche veneziane per Cosimo I de' Medici ed Eleanora di Toledo," *Faenza*, vol. 67 (1981), pp. 71–77.

10. Maestro Domenego da Venezia is probably the person listed as "domenego depentor over bochaler" in a painter's will of 1547; see Concina 1975, p. 136.

11. For the Messina service, see M. P. Pavone, "Maestro Domenico da Venezia e la spezieria del grande ospedale di Messina," *Faenza*, vol. 71 (1985), pp. 49–67. Timothy Wilson cites the fact that there are numerous pieces from this workshop with German heraldry, and that German museums contain surprising quantities of the Venetian master's work; see Wilson 1987a, p. 188.

12. Piccolpasso 1980, vol. 2, pp. 114–15.

13. A number of important maiolica-producing areas—Naples, Liguria, and others—will not be dealt with here because they are not represented in the Museum's collection.

14. See Spallanzani 1994; and Timothy Wilson, "Some Medici Devices on Pottery," *Faenza*, vol. 70 (1984), pp. 433–40.

CAT. 5
GLOBULAR JAR WITH MALE HEADS, VENICE,
WORKSHOP OF MAESTRO DOMENEGO DA VENEZIA, C. 1560–70

in the Philadelphia Museum of Art at present, the collection does contain other ceramics typical of the region's production. One of the best-known Florentine ceramic workshops was that of the della Robbia, although its output consisted mainly of sculpture, rather than vessels. The atelier was founded by Luca della Robbia (c. 1399/1400–1482), who gained renown for his lyrical marble sculptures. He was also known for his work in clay and for his technical innovations, which included the creation of impervious polychrome glazes that allowed for the outdoor installation of terracotta sculptures.[15] Members of the della Robbia shop often chose the tondo format, a challenging shape familiar to ceramic artisans but also used by painters for religious works and *deschi da parto*, the painted wooden trays made for women at the time of childbirth.[16] A fine ceramic relief (cat. 6) shows a tender rendition of the Adoration, with a youthful Virgin and chorus of angels paying homage to the infant Jesus, a theme repeated in paintings and inexpensive prints.[17] Devotional objects of every sort—paintings, sculpture, prints, or ceramic reliefs like this one—were almost universal in the bedchambers of the elite as well as the less prosperous. For example, in the 1492 inventory of the Medici villa at Poggio a Caiano, which listed few works of art, records that each bedroom had a small painting of the Virgin or a saint. In addition to reliefs, busts, and sculpture groups, the della Robbia *bottega* (workshop) turned out smaller works such as inkstands and molded vases, and continued to do so well into the sixteenth century.

By the end of the fifteenth century, Florence's ceramic industry was in decline except for the della Robbia workshop, but those of other nearby towns like Montelupo prospered. A two-handled pharmacy vase probably made there around 1500–1520 is decorated with blue and white palmettes that originated in thirteenth-century Persian lusterwares and textiles (cat. 7).[18] These motifs begin to appear in Italian wares as early as the first quarter of the Cinquecento and in Florentine velvets and brocades somewhat later. Two spouted apothecary jars made a century later in Montelupo are decorated with curling foliage; one with a crescent under the handle (cat. 8), and the other with a monogram (cat. 9), both of which are probably marks of their still-unidentified makers. While many distinguished potters worked in Montelupo, others set up shops elsewhere. In 1498 two brothers, Stefano and Piero di Filippo, established a pottery that continued for a century at the Medici villa at Cafaggiolo, north of Florence.

15. The techniques developed by Luca della Robbia around 1441 for tin-glazed terracotta sculptures were somewhat different from those used by maiolica potters. His glazes contained a higher percentage of tin and no sand, resulting in a more opaque appearance. Instead of being painted onto the white ground, the pigments were mixed into the glaze and then applied to the surface. Since many of their works were made using molds, they could be easily replicated, ensuring a widespread market for the workshop's output.

16. Vasari describes these elaborately painted trays as "round panels which carry food to the women in birth"; cited in Musacchio 1999, pp. 70–71. For more on *deschi da parto*, see ibid., especially chapters 3 and 4.

17. See Landau and Parshall 1994, fig. 72.

18. Poole 1995, cat. 171, with numerous comparative pieces listed there. See also Biscontini Ugolini 1997, p. 68, for textile references.

CAT. 6
CIRCULAR RELIEF OF THE ADORATION, FLORENCE, ATTRIBUTED TO LUCA DELLA
ROBBIA AND ANDREA DELLA ROBBIA, C. 1460–70S

CAT. 7
TWO-HANDLED PHARMACY JAR WITH DECORATIVE PALMETTES,
MONTELUPO, C. 1500–1520

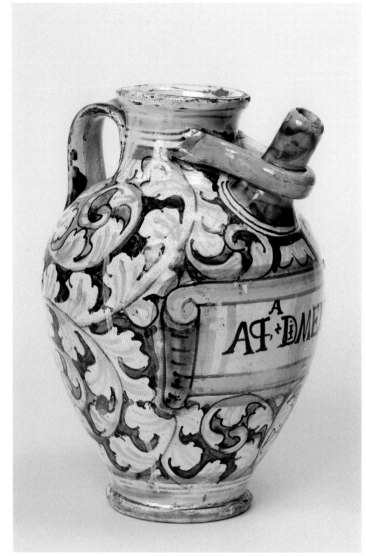

CAT. 8
SPOUTED PHARMACY JAR WITH FOLIATE DECORATION,
MONTELUPO, FIRST QUARTER OF THE SEVENTEENTH CENTURY

CAT. 9
SPOUTED PHARMACY JAR WITH FOLIATE DECORATION, MONTELUPO, FIRST
QUARTER OF THE SEVENTEENTH CENTURY

There they successfully experimented with lusterwares and were the only Tuscan shop to master the technology.[19]

In Florence, ceramics played only a small part in the city's overall economic picture. For towns like Montelupo, Castelli, and Deruta, however, maiolica was a major product. Set in the broad Umbrian plain, Deruta was an extremely prolific ceramic center as it remains today, with thirty or forty kilns operating in the early sixteenth century. Its potteries were busily supplying wares as early as the mid-1300s to the convent of Saint Francis in nearby Assisi, and two hundred years later to religious pilgrims, who carried home lustered display plates as souvenirs. Deruta's iridescent lusterwares, one of its specialties, were extolled by Leandro Alberti in 1550: "The earthenwares made here are renowned for being made to look as if they were gilt."[20] The ingenious technique that he referred to was a well-guarded secret restricted to only a few centers led by Deruta and Gubbio. Even there, production of lustered wares dropped off after mid-century, and the technique seems to have died out.

Certain shapes associated with Deruta's workshops included large display plates and ewer basins, along with such oddities as pinecone-shaped vases. Later in the seventeenth and eighteenth centuries, potters there also turned out charming votive plaques, which are still made today.[21] Some excellent *istoriato* wares were painted there by Giacomo Mancini (known as El Frate; fl. c. 1540; died c. 1581) and others, more often based on the compositions of familiar local painters like Perugino and Pinturicchio rather than on Raphael. But it was the ornamental wares, both lustered and polychrome, that dominated. The spectacular large albarello of 1501 with the bust of a Moor and two pharmacy emblems is a rare and early dated Deruta piece (cat. 10). It was part of an extensive set made for an unidentified ecclesiastical pharmacy. Most of the pieces feature a colorful wreath divided by a horizontal band that proclaims the jar's contents.[22] Despite its high level of production, Deruta remained quite isolated, and its works display a certain consistency and conservatism.

Farther to the north, in Emilia-Romagna, Faenza was well established as a ceramic town by the 1480s, and its very name later came to be applied to all European tin-glazed earthenware (faience). Larger than Deruta, it was a more innovative center and produced a great variety of wares. The spectacular tile pavement made by Faentine artisans in 1487 for the church

19. Wilson 1987b, p. 86.

20. Leandro Alberti, *Descrittione di tutta Italia* (Bologna, 1550), fol 85v.

21. A large collection of these plaques is installed in the walls of the church of the Madonna dei Bagni, a few miles south of Deruta.

22. One example in the British Museum, London, is unlabeled and bears an *istoriato* scene probably based on a woodcut; see Wilson 1987b, pp. 39–41, cat. 38. For more on the set, see Fiocco and Gherardi 1988.

CAT. 10

ALBARELLO WITH BUST OF A MOOR, DERUTA, 1501

of San Petronio in Bologna is a veritable compendium of the varied ornament for which the town became famous.[23] Derived from classical, Islamic, and medieval sources, many of those same decorative patterns are also found in the tablewares and pharmacy jars of Faenza and even in some of the small ceramic sculptures that were a local specialty. A classically Faentine plate depicts a bust portrait of a man in ancient garb surrounded by a border of wreathed medallions and swirling foliate ornament with dolphins (cat. 11). This sort of grotesque decoration, usually seen against a rich blue or orange ground, appears frequently in the wares of Faenza between about 1520 and mid-century. It later metamorphoses into the *a quartieri* (quartered, or compartmentalized) designs found on *crespine*, bowls formed in molds, through the end of the century (see cat. 66). Three border medallions on the Philadelphia plate contain profile heads of a man and two women *all'antica*, recalling ancient coins and medals. The revival of the medallic image was not restricted to maiolica and in fact became an important

23. Wilson 1987b, p. 34, fig. viii.

art unto itself in the Renaissance. Actual medals, usually bronze, were reintroduced in the fifteenth century as a means by which men and women could record and circulate portraits, often of themselves, but sometimes of revered figures from ancient history. These portable likenesses served as a kind of "currency of fame," conveying not only the image but the character and attributes of an individual.[24] The fourth medallion on this plate contains a pure landscape, an uncommon theme in mid-sixteenth-century Italy.

Faenza produced its share of *istoriato* wares as well, sometimes using a distinctive bluish glaze called *berettino* that was favored by the workshops of Baldassare Manara, Piero Bergantini, and the Casa Pirota (see cats. 75a,b). The famous *bianchi di Faenza*, or white wares of Faenza, were turned out from the mid-sixteenth through the seventeenth centuries by Virgiliotto Calamelli, Leonardo Bettisi, and others. Exported to Germany and France, they were also imitated in other centers like Deruta (see cat. 38). These thickly glazed white wares were often made in molds and became increasingly complex in shape as time progressed. They were traditionally undecorated or sparsely painted with figures, ornamental patterns, or coats of arms in what was known as the *compendiario,* or sketchy, style.

The difficulty of attributing maiolica to one center or another is illustrated by the so-called Orsini-Colonna wares, once assigned firmly to Faenza because of stylistic affiliations.[25] With few exceptions, these distinctive ceramics were pharmaceutical in nature: albarelli, two-handled jars, tall-necked bottles, and dragon-spouted pitchers (cat. 12). However, systematic archaeological excavations in Castelli, a remote village in the mountainous Abruzzi region east of Rome, have proven that the more than 280 identified pieces were made in the workshop of Orazio Pompei (c. 1510/20–after 1590) and his extended family in Castelli, not Faenza. The repetition of various drug names within the group (up to five times, in one case) and the use of both Gothic and Roman lettering suggests that there were multiple sets of jars made between about 1540 and the late 1550s. The Philadelphia pitcher probably dates from the earlier phase, to judge from the sharply pointed dragon spout, Gothic script, and highly stylized, caricaturelike figures typical of the shop's production.[26] One is led to wonder whether the dragon spouts favored by Castelli potters bear any significance beyond the purely decorative, or are descended from medieval bronze *aquamanilia* (ewers), which often take the form of

24. See Stephen K. Scher, ed., *The Currency of Fame: Portrait Medals of the Renaissance* (New York: Harry N. Abrams in association with the Frick Collection, 1994), and bibliography given there.

25. The group was originally given this name by Bernard Rackham after a large two-handled bottle in the British Museum decorated with a bear embracing a column and the words *ET SARRIMO boNI AMICI* (And we will be good friends), thought to signify a reconciliation between the rival Orsini and Colonna families; see Rackham (1940) 1977, p. 78.

26. See Poole 1995, pp. 439–41; Baldisseri 1989; and De Pompeis 1990.

CAT. 12
SPOUTED PHARMACY JAR WITH MALE HEADS, CASTELLI, WORKSHOP OF ORAZIO
POMPEI, C. 1540–50

imaginary beasts.[27] The dragon, a traditional symbol of vigilance, would be an appropriate attribute for jars holding prophylactic preparations.

In many ways, the ceramics of Sicily are as idiosyncratic as those from the remote town of Castelli. Although the technique of maiolica itself gained entry into Italy from this southern island by the twelfth century or possibly earlier, much of what is familiar about Sicilian ceramics today is based on the products of Messina, Palermo, Caltagirone, and Trapani from the seventeenth century and later. The study of island wares can also be deceiving because ceramics were actively imported from Venice, Montelupo, Naples, Faenza, and Castel Durante, and the styles of those centers were enthusiastically imitated by Sicilian potters and painters.[28] Often the wares of Sicily are less accomplished than those of the mainland craftsmen. Sicilian artisans emphasized color and quick, linear execution over painterly finesse and three-dimensionality. A large and well-executed example, however, is an albarello signed by Andrea Pantaleo (cat. 13). A native of nearby Monreale, Pantaleo (fl. 1582–1620) was working in Palermo by 1582, where he signed and dated pharmacy jars from 1601 to 1620. Documents attest to the fact that Castel Durante pharmacy jars decorated with Roman-style trophies—"alberelli pinti a trofei grandi e graziosi" (large and elegant albarelli painted with trophies)—were imported into Palermo from the mid-sixteenth century onward to supply the numerous hospitals and medical foundations around the island.[29] These wares had a great impact on local artisans like Pantaleo, who in this example combines an image of Saint Peter in a medallion surrounded by trophies and vigorous rinceaux that recall ancient sculptural motifs. In small plaquettes, the painter signed his name, the date of 1613, and SPQP, which signified its manufacture in Palermo.[30] Apothecary jars continued to be turned out in quantity in Sicily into the eighteenth century, although the quality of the painting declined. Another dated jar in the Philadelphia collection, this one from 1701 and from the town of Burgio in western Sicily, was also decorated with trophies (cat. 14). On one side, the maker depicted a young man in a sporty blue cap, and on the other a cursorily drawn Saint Eustace with his customary attribute, the deer. Also from Sicily, but made in the southeastern town of Caltagirone, is an eighteenth-century rounded jar with a helmeted soldier (cat. 15).

Urbino, the seat of a court under the della Rovere dukes, was a flourishing ceramic center whose wares found a ready market in the area and well beyond. Nearby Pesaro, Duke

27. Fifteenth-century German metalwares with similar spouts are illustrated in Ravanelli Guidotti 1990, p. 202.

28. Sicilian potters are known to have migrated north as well. Poole (1995, pp. 468–69), for example, cites the case of Andrea da Palazzo Adriano, who was working in Montelupo in 1556.

29. Raffaelli 1846, p. 140.

30. SPQP signifies "Senatus Populusque Panormitanus"; see Ragona 1975, p. 62.

Guidobaldo II's preferred residence closer to the sea, had its own prosperous maiolica industry.[31] The high point of Italian ceramic production comes with the flowering of *istoriato* maiolica in those two cities as well as Castel Durante and other towns of the Metauro River valley, between the late teens and the middle of the sixteenth century. The production of *istoriato* ceramics, the first true narrative wares since Greek vase painting died out in the third century B.C.E., was accompanied by the emergence of complex workshops and of painters as definable personalities. The practice of inscribing, signing, and dating works became more common and revealed clues about workshop, individual artisans, and the often-fascinating interactions among them. The link that already existed between ceramics and the major arts became even more apparent as maiolica painters adapted not only decorative motifs, but paintings and even sculpture and architecture in their own designs. The growth of printmaking and the production of individual prints and illustrated texts played crucial roles in the transmission of both images and themes. In Piccolpasso's drawing of painters at work (see fig. 6), prints or drawings are tacked up on the wall behind them, a tradition that was also followed by goldsmiths and other artisans, and is still practiced today.[32] With these visual references and the guidance of a learned adviser, a maiolica painter, though not highly educated himself, could turn out ceramics to suit discriminating clients with a taste for Ovid or Virgil.

Nicola di Gabriele Sbraghe (fl. 1520–37/38), also known as Nicola da Urbino, was one of the first artisans to specialize in *istoriato* wares, beginning around 1520. The preeminent painter of the genre, he appears to have spent his entire career in his native city, and was one of several Urbino shop owners who banded together in 1530 to oppose a group of employees agitating for higher wages.[33] One of those upstarts, Francesco Xanto Avelli da Rovigo, would later become one of the most influential *istoriato* painters of the time. The earliest known works by Nicola include seventeen pieces from an exquisite service dating to the beginning of the 1520s. This set, now in the Correr Museum in Venice, is one of three major services by him.[34] Painted in an unusual pale palette and based on a figural style that evokes Raphael, the Correr service is perhaps the most striking example of the early, truly narrative wares that changed the course of maiolica decoration forever. Before his death in the winter of 1537–38, Nicola created some of the finest examples of Italian Renaissance maiolica, including a magnificent

31. The wares of Pesaro have become better understood in recent years, thanks to new scholarship in this area.

32. Dean Walker has noted the differing ages of the painters in Piccolpasso's drawing; the youngest of them may well be an apprentice learning the trade from the older masters. See also a painting by Alessandro Fei (1543–1591) in the Palazzo Vecchio, Florence, which shows working drawings tacked on the wall near the goldsmith's bench.

33. F. Negroni, "Nicolò Pellipario: Ceramista fantasma," *Notizie da Palazzo Albani*, vol. 14 (1985), pp. 13–20. The article is summarized in Mallet 1987, p. 286.

34. For the Correr service, see Wallis 1905. For the Calini service, made in the mid-1520s, see Watson 1986, pp. 112–14; and Curnow 1992, pp. 59–63. Good summaries of Nicola's career are given in Wilson 1993; and Poole 1995, pp. 306–7.

CAT. 13

ALBARELLO WITH SAINT PETER, SICILY, PALERMO, ANDREA PANTALEO, 1613

CAT. 14
GLOBULAR JAR WITH SAINT EUSTACE AND A YOUNG MAN, SICILY,
BURGIO, 1701

CAT. 15
GLOBULAR JAR WITH HEAD OF A SOLDIER, SICILY, CALTAGIRONE,
EIGHTEENTH CENTURY

plate depicting the death of Saint Cecilia, signed with an ornate monogram and the inscription "made in the workshop of Guido of Castel Durante in Urbino 1528."[35] Not only did he direct his own *bottega*, but at least on this occasion, Nicola painted an *istoriato* work in the shop of Guido Durantino (fl. 1519; died c. 1576), as the inscription indicates. Good painters were in demand and could move from shop to shop as studio owners competed for their services.

In the 1520s, Nicola—working in his own *bottega*—was commissioned to provide a ceramic service for Isabella d'Este (1474–1539), the marchioness of Mantua and cultivated patron of Leonardo da Vinci, Titian, and other major painters.[36] As the wife of Duke Francesco Gonzaga (1466–1519), Isabella attracted a glittering circle of humanists and literary figures who served as advisers on artistic undertakings that ranged from the decoration of her famous *studiolo*—that quintessentially Renaissance room that symbolized intellectual status and urbanity—to the complex iconography of the paintings she ordered.[37] Twenty-two pieces from the Este-Gonzaga service, all bearing her arms and *imprese* (personal symbols), have survived in collections around the world.[38] With the exception of two Biblical scenes, the subjects were all derived from classical mythology and history. This piece draws upon Ovid's tale of Hippolytus, son of King Theseus of Athens (cat. 16). In the story, the goddess Venus causes Phaedra, Hippolytus's stepmother, to fall in love with him. But Hippolytus spurned her advances, and fearing that he would reveal her impropriety to Theseus, Phaedra claimed that Hippolytus had tried to rape her. After hearing the story, Theseus banished his son and had him killed. By the time he learned the truth, Hippolytus was dead and Phaedra had hanged herself. Here Nicola chose to represent one version of the story in which the goddess Diana sent Asclepius, the god of healing, to revive Hippolytus.

Although Nicola was known to copy figures from the illustrated 1497 Venetian edition of the *Metamorphoses*, a primary source for other maiolica painters, none of the figures has yet been paired with a specific print. Nicola had a particular talent for painting gentle receding landscapes, using both line and color to full effect, and here he punctuates the idyllic setting with a classically inspired building. His fantastic architectural creations appear to be inspired by such ancient monuments as the Pantheon in Rome and contemporary buildings as Donato Bramante's Tempietto. This gifted artist exerted a long-lasting influence on other maiolica painters and was a central figure in the development of Italian narrative wares.

35. Now in the Museo Nazionale del Bargello, Florence; see Mallet 1987, figs. 1, 1a, and corresponding discussion.

36. The uninscribed suite may have been given to Isabella in 1524 by her daughter, Eleanora, duchess of Urbino; see chapter 7.

37. Thornton 1997, p. 165. Dora Thornton provides an excellent, thorough treatment of the *studiolo*, its functions, meaning, and attributes.

38. For a complete list, see Rasmussen 1989, pp. 110–14, 246–51, cats. 66–67; and Ravanelli Guidotti 1991, with an extensive bibliography for the service. A ewer from the set is illustrated in Palvarini Gobio Casali 1987, pp. 184, 186, 188–89.

The ambitious Francesco Xanto Avelli da Rovigo (c. 1500–after 1542) gained renown through the signatures that adorned the reverses of many of his works (cat. 17, appendix 1). Despite his flair for self-promotion, he evidently preferred to remain an artist-for-hire and never directed his own workshop. A very prolific artisan, Xanto turned out services or individual pieces for at least fourteen families whose heraldry appears on at least ninety-three examples.[39] While he may not have been the most gifted of all maiolica painters, he was surely among the most imaginative. Xanto's style is characterized by a firm line, an interest in anatomy and architecture, and a dynamic palette sometimes using *colori cangianti*. His compositions were frequently assembled piecemeal taking figures from different prints (sometimes in quite hilarious ways), although he would occasionally borrow an entire scene. Like other *istoriato* painters of the 1530s and 1540s, Xanto treated the curving ceramic surface as if it was a canvas, painting adroitly across the undulations. In 1530 he began to sign and annotate his works, which he did until the end of his career twelve years later. This practice may have been an effort to reclaim credit after Maestro Giorgio Andreoli (before 1489–1555) began to initial the wares when luster was added in his Gubbio shop. The tradition of signing and inscribing ceramics proved fruitful for artists' reputations and useful for patrons wanting to know the precise subjects and literary sources of the narratives.

"Dirty and unglamorous" is how one contemporary writer described the potter's profession, even though his creations were designed to make life more civilized for others.[40] Unlike colleagues who may have been satisfied with an artisan's life, Xanto had social and intellectual ambitions that went far beyond those of a mere potter. Social status in the Renaissance was dependent upon occupation, among other things, and rank was measured by one's distance from or proximity to physical labor.[41] Xanto, however, aspired to be a poet, perhaps even a courtier, and wrote a series of expansive sonnets in praise of Francesco Maria della Rovere, duke of Urbino (1490–1538). He also signed plates with the Latin terms *pinse* or *pittor*, which signified his status as a true painter, rather than a mere decorator of ceramics.[42] Xanto was evidently familiar with the writings of Petrarch, Ovid, Virgil, Ariosto, and others, to judge from his choice of secular and religious subjects. It is likely that he, like most other artists, read them in the vernacular rather than in Latin. However, he was clearly familiar enough with

39. See Triolo 1996, p. 8. Thirty-seven pieces remain from the service he made for the Pucci family of Florence. He appears to have collaborated with other artisans from time to time, as for example in the "Three Crescents" set (c. 1529–30) that he shared with the Milan Marsyas Painter; see ibid., pp. 258–78.

40. See Tomaso Garzoni, *La piazza universale di tutte le professioni del mondo*, eds. Giovanni Battista Bronzini with Pina de Meo and Luciano Carcereri (Florence: Leo S. Olschhki, 1996), vol. 1, pp. 563–65; and Lincoln 2000, p. 156.

41. See Joanna Woods-Marsden, *Renaissance Self-Portraiture: The Visual Construction of Identity and the Social Status of the Artist* (New Haven and London: Yale University Press, 2000), especially pp. 1–12.

42. Ibid., p. 14. Regarding Xanto's ambitions as a courtier or court-connected artist, see Triolo 1996, p. 89; Talvacchia 1994; and Cioci 1987.

CAT. 16
DISH WITH DEATH OF HIPPOLYTUS, URBINO, NICOLA DI GABRIELE SBRAGHE
(NICOLA DA URBINO), C. 1524

CAT. 17
PLATE WITH ARETHUSA FLEEING ALPHEUS, URBINO, FRANCESCO
XANTO AVELLI DA ROVIGO, 1531; LUSTERED IN GUBBIO,
WORKSHOP OF MAESTRO GIORGIO ANDREOLI

the literary sources to use them knowledgeably and cleverly.[43] Occasionally he also depicted contemporary events in rather sophisticated allegorical forms.

Xanto and Nicola da Urbino were only two of the numerous maiolica painters who worked in the *bottega* of Guido Durantino (documented 1516–76).[44] Although Guido was a principal figure in Urbino's thriving ceramic industry, it now appears that he was not an artist himself. From 1527 onward he is referred to in documents and on maiolica as "maestro" or "magister," signifying not that he was a master painter, but the *capo-bottega*, or head, of the shop.[45] Numerous plates marked "in the workshop of Guido Durantino" are clearly by different hands and none is actually *signed* by him as maker. Indeed, the relationships among the painters and workshops in Urbino form a tangled web that is complicated by this disjunction. A prime example is a plate portraying the favorite Ovidian story of Apollo and Daphne (cat. 18). In this tale, the god amorously pursued the young woman until she escaped by being changed into a laurel tree by her father, the river god Peneus. Here an anonymous painter worked in a style that owes much to that of his contemporary Nicola da Urbino, and to Nicola's close but unnamed associate, the so-called Milan Marsyas Painter.[46]

We may never know how many painters worked for Guido Durantino, but there must have been many, since his shop produced both *istoriato* and white wares well into the 1560s. The venture was successful enough that he was able to attract the most talented painters of the time and to pay them competitively. His sons Camillo and Orazio and his nephew Flaminio joined him in the business, all using a new surname, Fontana, which Guido adopted in or before 1553.[47] In 1565 Orazio Fontana (died 1571) formed a separate *bottega* in Urbino, dividing the assets of the original shop with his father. His new workshop gained renown for its pharmacy vases (see cats. 78a,b, 79) and for its white-ground grotesque wares, a fashion that both he and Guido exploited to great advantage. A spectacular snake-handled vase, one of the treasures of the Philadelphia Museum of Art (cat. 19), was made in one of the Fontana workshops, perhaps by Orazio, sometime in the 1560s. It is contemporaneous with a celebrated service that Vasari says was commissioned by Duke Guidobaldo II for King Philip II of Spain.[48] The dazzling white surface is covered with elegantly drawn grotesques based on ancient wall paintings discovered around 1500 in the underground ruins of Rome. The narrative scenes are

43. Julia Triolo, conversation with the author, June 2001.

44. The hands of at least six major painters have been discerned by John Mallet; see Mallet 1987, for a thorough treatment of Guido's workshop.

45. Ibid., p. 286.

46. See Mallet 1980.

47. For documents relating to Guido Durantino and the Fontana, see Poole 1995, p. 366.

48. An excellent summary of this service is given in Poole 1995, pp. 378–90; see also Gere 1963. Olivar (1953) notes that an examination of Philip II's inventory of the late-sixteenth century includes no Italian ceramics and to date, no extant pieces can be connected with the Zuccaro service that was sent to Spain in 1562.

from a famous fourteenth-century chivalric romance, *Libro de caballeria Amadis de Gaula* (first published in 1508). Inscriptions in Spanish indicate that it was destined for yet another patron or recipient in Spain. The taste for grotesques continued unabated, carried on by Flaminio Fontana, who took over Orazio's shop after his death in 1571, and by members of the prolific Patanazzi family workshop of Urbino from the 1560s onward. It has been recently discovered that the two families were in fact related, which explains the close stylistic connections and their common use of certain printed material.[49]

At least four Patanazzi family members, Antonio, Alfonso, Francesco, and Vincenzo, were active in the making of maiolica through the 1630s. A fine example of their *istoriato* ware from the 1580s depicts a scene from the Trojan War taken from Virgil's *Aeneid* (cat. 20). The coat of arms on the rim also appears on several major architectural monuments in Rome and can be identified as that of the distinguished cardinal Anton Maria Salviati, a grandnephew of Pope Leo X Medici (1475–1521).[50] The Salviati were dedicated patrons of maiolica-makers in the sixteenth century, not only in Urbino, but in Tuscany and Faenza as well. This plate was made around the time that Anton Maria was elevated to the cardinalate (1583) and would have been an appropriate gift for such an occasion, its theme a fitting one for a highly educated cleric who would have been familiar with the literature.

In Urbino and elsewhere in the Marches, the interactions among painters and workshops were such that stylistic differences began to melt away into what John Mallet has called the "all too general style of istoriato painting" that was practiced there by the 1540s.[51] The narrative mode developed by Nicola, Xanto, and Guido Durantino's painters in the 1520s and 1530s spread to Venice, Pesaro, and other centers. Many examples of maiolica cannot be more precisely connected with individual artists, thus the designations "in the circle of Nicola da Urbino" or "Fontana workshop" must suffice. However, some artisans, like Francesco Durantino (fl. 1543–75), stand out by virtue of their highly individualistic manner. Francesco was one of the most prolific painters of his time, working in a style characterized by painterly fluidity, with complex figural poses and architectural elements, unusually imaginative compositions, and a lively palette. Livy's *History of Rome* is the source of a dramatic scene from the life of the Roman general Scipio (cat. 21, appendix 2), as noted on the reverse of the plate in the

49. See Negroni 1998; and Gardelli 1991, p. 131. See Poke 2001, for a detailed study of Italian maiolica painters' use of Jacques Androuet I Ducerceau's grotesque prints.

50. The coat of arms of his mother, Costanza Conti, is impaled with that of his father, Giuliano Salviati, and topped by a cardinal's tasseled hat. The arms of the Salviati are illustrated in the Cartari-Febei manuscript, Archivio di Stato di Roma, busta 166, 14v; and in Spreti 1928–35, vol. 6 (1932), pp. 72–74; see also Wilson 1996a, p. 372. For the arms of the Conti of Rome and Ferrara, see Crollalanza 1886–90, vol. 1, p. 347.

51. John Mallet, conversation with the author, June 2000.

CAT. 18
PLATE WITH APOLLO AND DAPHNE, URBINO, WORKSHOP OF GUIDO DURANTINO, 1535

SIDE ONE

CAT. 19

SNAKE-HANDLED VASE WITH SCENES FROM *AMADIS DE GAULA*, URBINO, WORKSHOP OF
GUIDO DURANTINO OR ORAZIO FONTANA, C. 1560–70

SIDE TWO

CAT. 20
DISH WITH AENEAS AND ANCHISES, URBINO, PATANAZZI WORKSHOP, C. 1580S

painter's recognizable script. The rich palette and meticulous execution—like that of eight others belonging to this same service—are consistent with the artist's earlier work. Later in the 1540s, he began to paint more rapidly, using paler hues dominated by yellows. Inscribed and dated pieces help to chart Francesco's career, which accelerated after he moved from Castel Durante to Urbino. There he worked collaboratively with Guido di Merlino (fl. c. 1523–58), the owner of the second largest workshop, and exerted a profound effect on other painters in the city and probably in Pesaro as well.[52] By 1547, we find Francesco in Monte Bagnolo, across the Appenines in Perugia, where he ran a pottery business that ended around 1554. Later, the painter surfaces in Rome, where he established a workshop that he eventually sold to another Castel Durante potter in 1575.[53]

A rare interior scene on another plate in the Philadelphia collection (cat. 22) was painted by Sforza di Marcantonio (fl. c. 1540–81), whose style was shaped by both Xanto and Francesco Durantino. A contemporary of Francesco's, Sforza was also a Durantine by birth and received his training in Urbino. Throughout his career, he drew consistently and deeply upon Xanto's work, basing many of his creations on the same print sources, and inscribing them in the manner of his artistic mentor. The plate shown here is a dynamic rendering of an episode involving the unfaithful Clytemnestra, wife of King Agamemnon of Mycenae, and Cassandra, the king's concubine. It bears the date of 1551, by which time Sforza had moved from Urbino to the coastal town of Pesaro. Evidently, however, he retained his memories of Francesco Durantino's earlier style, and the distinctive faces and pointing gestures of the Scipio dish appear in Sforza's work throughout the remainder of his career. Pesaro was the site of several potteries whose works are only now being distinguished from those of Urbino's. Duke Guidobaldo II's preference for his country villa near Pesaro and the frequent presence of his court there must account in part for the success of the local ceramic industry.

Piccolpasso commented that "a great part of the masters who work in Urbino are from the town of Durante [Castel Durante.]"[54] But despite this migration, the level of production in Castel Durante was very high, including not only *istoriato* wares but pharmacy jars that were exported as far away as Sicily.[55] The close proximity of the two towns ensured regular interchange between them and some inevitable confusion between their wares today. A series of

52. See Wilson 1993, pp. 223, 224 n. 8; see also Timothy Wilson in Elena Parma, ed., *Perino del Vaga: Tra Raffaello e Michelangelo* (Milan: Electa, 2001), pp. 195, 214–15.

53. See Fiocco and Gherardi 1988, pp. 136–39.

54. Piccolpasso 1980, vol. 2, p. 61.

55. Among the best of Castel Durante's painters were Giovanni Maria, author of the spectacular 1508 bowl with the arms of Pope Julius II della Rovere (see Rasmussen 1989, pp. 100–104), and the "in Castel Durante" Painter (see Watson 1986, cat. 41). Documentary evidence shows large orders of pharmacy jars coming from merchants in Palermo around 1550. Sometimes the commissions were so extensive that they had to be shared between potters; see Antonino Ragona, "Maioliche casteldurantine del secolo XVI per un committente siculo-genovese," *Faenza*, vol. 62 (1976), p. 108.

CAT. 21
DISH WITH SCIPIO AND HIS TROOPS, URBINO, FRANCESCO DURANTINO,
C. 1544–45

CAT. 22

PLATE WITH DEATH OF CASSANDRA, PESARO, SFORZA DI MARCANTONIO, 1551

REVERSE

CAT. 23
LIDDED GLOBULAR JAR WITH GROTESQUES, CASTEL DURANTE,
WORKSHOP OF MAESTRO SIMONE DA COLONELLO, 1562

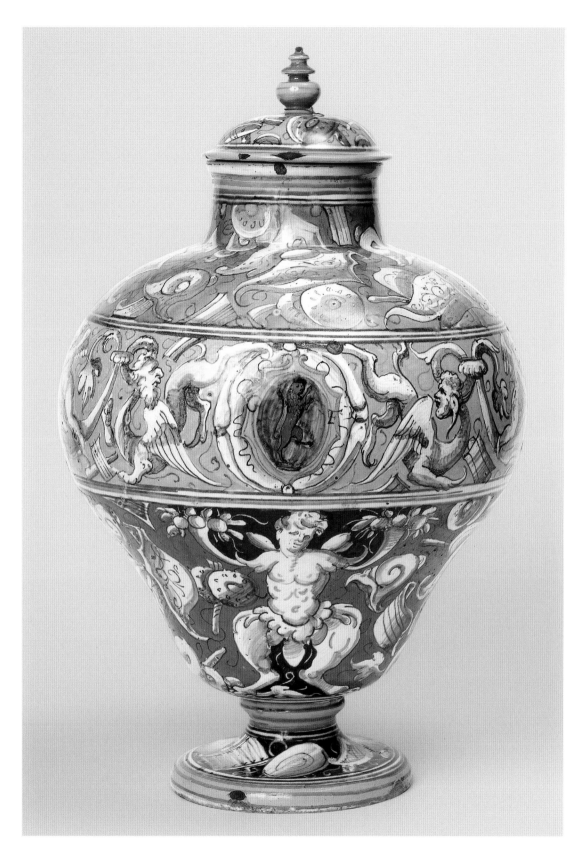

CAT. 24
LIDDED GLOBULAR JAR WITH GROTESQUES, CASTEL DURANTE,
WORKSHOP OF MAESTRO SIMONE DA COLONELLO, C. 1562

famous *belle donne* (beautiful women) plates decorated with charming images of lovely ladies and young warriors still remains to be assigned to one town or the other. Firmly attributable to Castel Durante, however, are two of the most spectacular pieces in the Philadelphia collection (cats. 23, 24). These two handsome pear-shaped covered jars are adorned with registers of grotesques, coats of arms, trophies, and festoons of foliage—an encyclopedic display of the decorative motifs most popular in Italian Renaissance maiolica. The coat of arms must represent their unidentified owner or pharmacy, but the date, 1562, on one fixes them in time. A signed vase in the Fanfani collection makes it possible to assign the Philadelphia vases to Maestro Simone da Colonello, master of a *bottega* that continued for generations and provided wares to the growing medical centers of Sicily.[56]

Maiolica craftsmen of the sixteenth century traveled not only from one Italian center to another, but to Spain, France, the Low Countries, and central Europe as well. The *istoriato* style also found its way north, and was produced in quantity in Lyon and Nevers after mid-century.[57] A French plate in the Philadelphia collection shows yet another interior scene—unusual in maiolica—with an unfaithful female protagonist. While Sforza di Marcantonio's compositionally related plate (see cat. 22) depicts the classical tale of Clytemnestra and Cassandra, the French artist portrays the Biblical episode of Joseph pursued by the wife of Potiphar, the Egyptian pharaoh's captain of the guard (cat. 25). Both stories occurred in the distant past, but are set by their painters in sumptuous rooms that are decidedly Renaissance in character. Although the Italian plate may be based on an unidentified graphic source, the French example appropriates imagery from a woodcut by Bernard Salomon in Claude Paradin's *Quadrins historiques de la Bible,* first published 1553 by Jean de Tournes in Lyon, and a principal source for maiolica.[58] Compared to Italian wares, the painting lacks finesse, and the perspective in French compositions is often inexpertly handled, as if it were more of an effort for these artisans to transform rectangular compositions into the circular format. Apart from stylistic considerations, the brief note on the reverse that describes the Biblical source—*Genese XXXIX / joseph*—is evidence of the plate's French manufacture. In the later sixteenth and early seventeenth century, however, certain French wares came to resemble those of Urbino, Pesaro, and Venice, making it difficult to distinguish between them.

56. The Fanfani collection is now part of the Museo Internazionale delle Ceramiche, Faenza; see Ravanelli Guidotti 1990, pp. 211–13, for an excellent summary of the literature on Maestro Simone da Colonello.

57. For concise summaries of the diffusion of Italian maiolica abroad, see Wilson 1987b, p. 164; and Giacomotti 1974, pp. 384–85. For one piece whose mark may refer to Lyon, see Wilson 1987b, cat. 257.

58. Norman 1976, pp. 318–19.

59. See David Bull, *The Feast of the Gods: Conservation, Examination, and Interpretation* (Washington D.C.: National Gallery of Art, 1990).

60. For information on Medici porcelain, see Wilson 1987b, pp. 157–59, and bibliography cited there.

Tin-glazed earthenware continued to dominate the ceramic market in Europe throughout the seventeenth century. But the original desire to create hard, translucent white wares that resembled porcelain continued unabated. Imported Chinese wares—like the treasured blue and white bowls depicted by Giovanni Bellini in his painting *The Feast of the Gods* (1514–26)[59]— had always been expensive and difficult to obtain. Experiments to create porcelain in Venice and Ferrara appear not to have been successful. It was only in Florence in the 1560s and 1570s that the Medici potters succeeded in turning out a very limited number of delicate soft-paste wares with blue and white patterns derived from Chinese models.[60] By the second half of the eighteenth century, however, the new English white earthenwares and fine true porcelain—first produced at the Meissen factory in Saxony Germany, around 1710—overtook maiolica and spelled an end to its supremacy in Europe.

The art of designing ornaments, in which one must take account of surfaces and volumes . . . is much more difficult than that of making figures.

—Ottaviano Ridolfi, 1603[1]

CHAPTER 4

The Art of Embellishment: Designs and Decoration

Whether or not his statement about the relative challenges of decorative versus figural design is true, Ottaviano Ridolfi was in a position to have seen the vast explosion in the use of ornament in his lifetime. The Renaissance cultivation of beauty and luxury encouraged the proliferation of nonfunctional embellishments everywhere in the new "empire of things," from churches to domestic settings, from dining rooms to pharmacies, from clothing to wall coverings, from armor to tablewares. Hardly a surface remained untouched. One need only to look at Ghirlandaio's frescoes in Santa Maria Novella in Florence (1485–90), or at Pinturicchio's Piccolomini Library in Siena (1502–8)[2] to appreciate the sophisticated detail in the decorative arts and paintings of the time. Following Vasari's key ideas of the "remarkable," the "inexpressible," and the "admirable,"[3] Renaissance patrons and artists placed great value on the notions of "complexity rather than economy, on copiousness and abundance, on the capricious, the bizarre."[4] The value of an object was cued not merely to its inherent materials, but to the *difficultà* and virtuosity of its facture, and to the innovative and surpassing qualities of its design—as Vasari's friend and fellow theorist, Vincenzo Borghini, termed it the *meraviglia*, or marvelous.[5]

1. From the *Aggiunta* to the Venetian edition of Vignola's *Li ordini di architettura* (1603); cited in Gruber 1994, p. 363.

2. Alessandro Cecchi, *The Piccolomini Library in the Cathedral of Siena*, trans. Andrew McCormick (Florence: Scala, 1982).

3. Vernon Hyde Minor, *Art History's History*, 2nd ed. (Upper Saddle River, N.J.: Prentice Hall, 2001), p. 70.

4. Shearman 1979, p. 22.

5. See Summers 1981, p. 172–73.

A variety of factors, including the intersection of the major and minor arts, the transmissive role of the graphic arts, and even the physical proximity of artists and artisans were crucial for the development of decorative motifs used on maiolica. Another key influence was the adaptation of design elements from ancient, medieval, Islamic, and Chinese traditions. As Greek vasemakers did before them, Renaissance artisans quickly developed a vocabulary of ornament that they tailored to an evolving set of pottery shapes. The most obvious of the early outside influences came from imported Spanish lusterwares. At the same time, stimulated by the underlying spirit of the Renaissance, ceramic artisans looked to their own heritage for inspiration, resurrecting motifs from the remnants of ancient buildings and sculptures that littered the landscape, or to the prints that depicted them. Works of art based on antique precedents were just what Renaissance rulers needed to project an image of confidence and establish their legitimacy.

An early sixteenth-century vase from the della Robbia workshop exemplifies this trend (cat. 26). Molds were used by the della Robbia to turn out vases and sculptures alike, and vessels like this reflect a Florentine's notion of what ancient metalwares—or pottery imitating metal—looked like. Crisply adorned with meanders, palmettes, imbrications, gadroons, and dolphins, this rich blue vessel could have conceiveably been gilded originally, further likening it to expensive metalwares. Some of these vases have retained their original molded lids, which resemble fanciful bouquets of fruits and flowers. Probably intended only for display, they were used in both sacred and domestic settings.[6] The earlier marble sculptures of Luca della Robbia, like his *Cantoria* (1431–38)[7] for the Florence duomo, incorporated ancient motifs as a matter of course, and his graceful figures have been likened to those on the Augustan Ara Pacis in Rome.[8] It should, therefore, come as no surprise that antique influences pervaded the ceramics from the family's workshop.

Interestingly, an amphora with a related shape forms the primary decoration on a mid-sixteenth-century Montelupo albarello (cat. 27). Part of an extensive group of apothecary jars, the vase is covered with daisylike flowers on stems that sprout from the ocher-colored amphora, undoubtedly meant to represent gold. The artisans who produced this set limited their palette to blue, yellow, and orange, despite the fact that by this time a wide range of

6. A similar pair adorn the bed-head in a relief of the *Birth of Saint John the Baptist* (1511) by the della Robbia workshop; see Thornton 1991, fig. 107.

7. Now in the Museo dell'Opera del Duomo, Florence; see Adams 2001, p. 127, fig. 6.7.

8. David Castriota, *The Ara Pacis Augustae and the Imagery of Abundance in Later Greek and Early Roman Imperial Art* (Princeton: Princeton University Press, 1995).

CAT. 26
VASE WITH CLASSICAL ORNAMENT, FLORENCE, WORKSHOP OF
GIOVANNI DELLA ROBBIA, C. 1515–20

CAT. 27
ALBARELLO WITH FLORAL PATTERN, MONTELUPO, MID-SIXTEENTH CENTURY

CAT. 28
PHARMACY BOTTLE WITH TROPHIES, EMILIA-ROMAGNA, PROBABLY FAENZA,
C. 1520—30

colors was readily available. Perhaps seeking to economize, they also looked back to drug jars

of the Quattrocento that used similar, very popular color schemes. Technically, this albarello

is interesting because the decorator used the *graffito* technique, which meant he scratched

through the blue pigment atop the tin glaze to produce white curling tendrils.

Other blue and white wares, one probably made in Faenza around 1520–30 (cat. 28)

and the other probably in Castel Durante in 1562 (cat. 29), illustrate the fashion for ancient

Roman "trophy" motifs (see fig. 4). Piccolpasso illustrates not one but two trophy designs

for maiolica, and comments, "these are in use everywhere; though it is true that 'trophies' are

made more often in the state of Urbino than elsewhere."[9] Originally, trophies consisted of a

staff hung with arms and armor that were the spoils of victory. They were carried in proces-

sions, set up as stationary monuments, or represented in stone, like the first-century marble

9. Piccolpasso 1980, vol. 2, p. 111.

pair that adorn the top of the staircase of the Capitoline Hill in Rome. As a decorative design, the trophy metamorphosed over time and eventually included musical instruments and other attributes of the arts and sciences. Printmakers did a brisk business in engravings of trophies, candelabra, grotesques, masks, foliage, and related ornaments that were used by Renaissance artisans in the same way that their predecessors had used modelbooks. Nicoletto da Modena (fl. c. 1500– 1520), Antonio da Brescia (c. 1460–c. 1520), and Zoan Andrea (fl. c. 1475–19), for example, had flourishing careers specializing in these sorts of prints, while artists like Marcantonio Raimondi (c. 1480–c. 1534) reproduced the narrative works of Raphael and others that were adapted for *istoriato* maiolica.

Even after maiolica designers ceased emulating the Spanish wares from which they had drawn their early inspiration, they continued to look beyond their own borders for ideas. Persian palmettes and peacock-feather patterns entered the decorative vocabulary, probably based on Asian and Middle Eastern textiles. Vigorous curling leaves derived from Gothic sculpture and manuscript illuminations were also popular. Islamic blue and white wares and Ming Dynasty (1426–35) porcelain imported from China through Venice also had a significant impact on the industry, not only in finely made individual pieces, but in the more mass-produced containers manufactured to meet the demand of Renaissance pharmacies and hospitals. These two albarelli are decorated with a pattern called *alla porcellana*, after blue and white Chinese porcelain (cats. 30, 31). Piccolpasso calls these designs "universal," and suggests that they were made in many centers, not only in Faenza, as was once thought.[10] Marchigian in origin, but with a completely different design sensibility, is a finely potted bowl dating to around 1500 (cat. 32). Its exterior is covered with bands of rich polychrome ornament similar to an important series of tiles in the Victoria & Albert Museum.[11] It exemplifies how by this time maiolica painters had created a panoply of motifs very much their own and of the Renaissance, but informed by their knowledge of ancient and medieval decoration.

The Umbrian hilltown of Gubbio, halfway between Urbino and Deruta, became prominent in the sixteenth century for its specialization in gold and ruby metallic lusters, like those seen on a particularly fine *tondino* (small plate) (cat. 33, appendix 3). Its borders are adorned with classical anthemia, and the central well contains a winged putto playing a drum. It is one

10. Piccolpasso 1980, vol. 2, p. 118.

11. See Rackham (1940) 1977, no. 220.

CAT. 30
SHORT ALBARELLO, PESARO OR FAENZA, C. 1480–1500

CAT. 31
SHORT ALBARELLO, FAENZA OR VENICE, FIRST QUARTER OF THE SIXTEENTH
CENTURY

of many examples that have been linked to the workshop of Maestro Giorgio Andreoli, the

chief practitioner of the secret medium, who may have been responsible for introducing it

into Gubbio around 1498. The limitation of the luster technique to only a few centers was

a decisive factor in the success of Gubbio's workshops. Both Duke Guidobaldo I of Urbino

(died 1508) and Pope Leo X granted special privileges to Maestro Giorgio's studio, as the

pope noted, "in consideration of the honour which redounds to the city . . . from the popu-

larity of these wares, in whatever land they are taken, and in consideration of their great

profitableness and revenue."[12] Piccolpasso described the application of metallic lusters, which

he called "gold maiolica": "They leave the places where it is to be put on without laying any

sort of colour on them . . . an Arabesque . . . or else a Grotesque will be executed on a plate,

and the leaves that would properly be done in green are left blank, only the outlines are

12. Quoted in Piccolpasso 1980, vol. 2,
p. xii n. 6. A summary of the important
bibliography on Maestro Giorgio
Andreoli is given in Poole 1995, pp.
219–21.

drawn. The wares are then fired to a finished state like other wares, and after firing these blanks are filled with maiolica. . . ."[13] It was also, in his words, a "treacherous" technique, with only six or so successful pieces for every hundred fired.

Piccolpasso's annotations on his sample designs underscore the fact that some centers were particularly renowned for certain styles, and this was especially true of Deruta. Although brilliant polychrome wares were made there, Deruta may be best known for its luster technique, which was introduced sometime around 1496.[14] Impressive display plates were a prime product of the town, but other shapes were produced as well, like two-handled jars (cat. 34), ewers, footed dishes (cats. 35, 36), and idiosyncratic pinecone jars. Many of these bore Deruta's characteristic stylized floral or abstract designs in a blue, white, and gold luster palette. Often they imitate metalware, with fictive gadroons or other originally three-dimensional forms.

13. Piccolpasso 1980, vol. 2, pp. 86–90.

14. The first dated example found so far was made in 1501; see Rackham (1940) 1977, no. 437.

Like the large plates with idealized portraits of young women and banderoles bearing their names, these ceramics were associated with betrothal or marriage rituals. Smaller examples, like a footed *tazza* (dish), could also be personalized as gifts—in this case, for a woman named Diana (see cat. 36).

The use of molds to form pieces with complex shapes was described in detail in Piccolpasso's treatise, and added another dimension to the decorative vocabulary of maiolica. A rare Deruta ewer basin belongs to a group of five made from a single mold. Each has identical grotesques of the type described by Piccolpasso, but different central images (cat. 37).[15] They were intended to resemble repoussé metalwares, with the reflective gold adding to the effect. The medallion on the ewer emplacement is of interest for its subject as much as for

15. For two in the Robert Lehman Collection, the Metropolitan Museum of Art, New York, see Rasmussen 1989, cats. 42–43, and additional pieces listed there; see also Rackham (1940) 1977, no. 489; Giacomotti 1974, cats. 663–64; Kube 1976, cat. 42.

CAT. 35
FOOTED DISH WITH THE LETTER *N*, DERUTA, C. 1500–1530

CAT. 36
FOOTED DISH WITH THE NAME *DIANA*, DERUTA, C. 1500–1530

the quality of the painting. The Biblical heroine Judith, a popular figure in Renaissance art in general, was traditionally associated with classical ideals of patriotic self-sacrifice, not unlike the Roman hero Marcus Curtius. In the Renaissance, Judith also represented the virtue of chastity, and was seldom depicted unclothed.[16] Here, however, a heroic nude Judith holds the head of Holofernes, having accomplished the deed by which she saved her people.[17]

After 1546, there were few dated lusterwares as the taste for them waned. By the 1560s, other decorative styles had taken over, like the white *compendiario* wares developed in Faenza and copied elsewhere, and the enormously successful Urbino-style grotesques on a white ground. A Deruta plate with a stylized garland and quickly sketched viol player is a typical example of the *compendiario* style that continued well into the seventeenth century (cat. 38). Less labor-intensive and more porcelainlike in appearance, these wares enjoyed enormous popularity. Many of them were also made in molds, with the glistening white glaze applied thickly over their articulated surfaces. Perhaps referring to such ceramics during his travels in Tuscany in 1581, the French author Michel de Montaigne remarked: "In looking at the earthenware of these parts, which resembles porcelain, and is white, and clean, and very cheap, I thought it would be far more appetising for table use than the pewter used in France, which in the inns is especially disagreeable."[18]

An Urbino plate, probably made around 1560–70, shows the story of Marcus Curtius, and combines the love of dramatic *istoriato* scenes with encircling ornament drawn from antiquity (cat. 39). Following the directive of an oracle, the mythical hero leaped, fully armed and on horseback, into a chasm in the Roman Forum in order to save his county. This episode from Livy's *History of Rome* was a favorite theme on maiolica, and appealed to Renaissance viewers both for its exaltation of civic virtue and for its action. The border—and virtually the entire surfaces of other objects in the collection (see cats. 19, 52, 53)—is filled with bizarre grotesques that are distributed liberally over the white ground. In the 1480s, curious artists and antiquarians began to explore the overgrown Roman ruins and discovered remarkable ceiling frescoes and stuccoes with fantastic imaginary creatures, ribbons, foliage, and festoons. These ornaments acquired the name *grottesche* from the place of their discovery, the *grottoes* of ancient Rome.[19] Vasari described grotesques as "a type of quite licentious and ridiculous

16. Compare Donatello's *Judith and Holofernes* (c. 1446–69), at the Palazzo Vecchio, Florence; see Adams 2001, figs. 10.3–4.

17. See Elena Ciletti, "Patriarchal Ideology in the Renaissance Iconography of Judith," in Marilyn Migiel and Juliana Schiesari, eds., *Refiguring Woman: Perspectives on Gender and the Italian Renaissance* (Ithaca and London: Cornell University Press, 1991), pp. 35–70. There, Ciletti remarks, "One might well wonder if the conceptual impropriety of a woman's killing a man could account for the rarity in Italian Renaissance art of depictions of Holofernes' actual decapitation" (p. 68).

18. Michel de Montaigne, *The Journal of Montaigne's Travels in Italy . . . in 1580 and 1581*, trans. and ed. W. G. Waters (London: John Murray, 1903), vol. 3, p. 154.

19. See Dacos 1969; and Gruber 1994.

CAT. 37
MOLDED EWER BASIN WITH JUDITH HOLDING THE HEAD OF HOLOFERNES,
DERUTA, C. 1530–40

painting, used by the ancients to fill up empty spaces, and some places look as if they are

floating in the air. There are all sorts of monsters, their size depending on the available space,

and their forms depending on the imagination of the painting. There are no particular rules

for making them, and thus hanging from the thinnest thread is a weight it could not possibly

bear, or a horse with legs of leaves, or a man with crane's legs, along with many small ribbons

and birds. And he who possesses the strangest imagination is considered the best painter."[20]

Grotesques were first taken up by Andrea Mantegna in the early 1470s in Mantua, but it was

not until the early decades of the Cinquecento that Pinturicchio and then Raphael created

the most influential painted versions. Only in the 1560s did maiolica painters adopt them,

long after they had entered the decorative repertoire of the major artists (cat. 40). Adding

to the mystery is Piccolpasso's comment about this sort of ornament: "Grotesques have

almost fallen out of use, and I do not know why; it is a delicate style of painting; I do not

know whence its use derives."[21] Between the grotesques on the plate with Marcus Curtius

(see cat. 39) the rim is studded with figural medallions that recall Roman coins, famous

20. Giorgio Vasari, *Le vite de' più eccellenti pittori scultori e architettori,* eds. Rosanna Bettarini and Paolo Barocchi (Florence: Sansoni, 1966), vol. 1, pp. 143–44; see also Dacos 1969. Some sketches of grotesques, possibly by a maiolica artisan, are in the Civico Museo e Biblioteca Comunale, Urbania (formerly Castel Durante); see Filippo Trevisani, ed., *Le ceramiche dei duchi d'Este* (Milan: Federico Motta, 2001), p. 21.

21. Piccolpasso 1980, vol. 2, p. 113.

CAT. 39
LARGE PLATE WITH MARCUS CURTIUS, URBINO, C. 1560–70

sculptures like the Apollo Belvedere, and ancient engraved gems that were of great interest to Renaissance collectors.

At the same time in Venice, foliate patterns on a blue ground prevailed, often with enframements containing heads of women or men, saints and martyrs, or putti (cats. 41, 42). Piccolpasso's note on the page showing a plate with flowers and fruit relates that "these designs are truly Venetian, very pretty things."[22] Perhaps the lack of terra firma in the lagoon city engendered a particular taste for the foliate ornament that was very popular there and widely copied by Sicilian painters.

The ceramics discussed here provide some idea of the breadth of decorative programs found in Italian maiolica from the fifteenth to seventeenth centuries. Many more, of course, can be seen in other examples in the Philadelphia collection. Rinceaux, strapwork, heraldic

22. Piccolpasso 1980, vol. 2, p. 115.

CAT. 41
SHORT ALBARELLO WITH SAINT CATHERINE
AND A MALE HEAD, VENICE, CIRCLE OF
MAESTRO DOMENEGO DA VENEZIA, SECOND
HALF OF THE SIXTEENTH CENTURY

CAT. 42
ALBARELLO WITH SAINT LUCY, VENICE,
POSSIBLY WORKSHOP OF MAESTRO
DOMENEGO DA VENEZIA, THIRD QUARTER
OF THE SIXTEENTH CENTURY

imagery, arabesques, interlace, grotesques, and other design motifs were the foundations upon which all of the decorative arts of the Italian Renaissance were created. Through them, objects of daily use were transformed into elegant works of art, with style often taking precedence over function.[23]

The infinite possibilities of ornament gave ceramic painters the means to fulfill the desires of Renaissance consumers for beauty, abundance, and caprice, not to mention humor and wit. With the introduction of *istoriato* wares and their narrative subject matter, however, maiolica moved beyond the level of pure decoration toward a new engagement with Renaissance intellectual currents.

23. See Holman 1997, pp. 43–44.

The eminent painter Phidias used to say that he had learned from Homer how best to represent the majesty of Jupiter. I believe that we too may be better endowed and more accomplished painters from reading our poets. . . .

—Leon Battista Alberti, 1435–36[1]

CHAPTER 5

The Art of Erudition

For Renaissance humanists, the ancient writers Horace and Plutarch were fundamental sources for the theoretical basis of painting. Horace's famous simile *Ut pictura poesis*—"As is painting, so is poetry"—grew out of Plutarch's "Poetry is a speaking picture; painting is a silent poem." Leon Battista Alberti emphasized this crucial linkage between word and image in his treatise *De pictura* (1435–36), where he stated unequivocally that the greatest work of the painter is the *istoria*, or narrative.[2] Maiolica, too, was a painter's medium, and the development of the *istoriato* style eventually followed the prevailing trends in painting.[3] Although narrative subjects began to appear on Italian ceramics in the later Quattrocento, it was only in the 1520s that the genre came into its own. Subjects needed to be chosen and designs "invented," all conforming to the desires of the buyer. For maiolica painters—as for painters, sculptors, architects, and other decorative artists—the notion of *disegno* was a fundamental one. First articulated by Alberti in his treatise, this important concept signified not only "drawing" but also "design" in the broadest sense, or even "intention." Federico Zuccaro, a sixteenth-century Roman artist, who with his more famous brother Taddeo, created drawings specifically for maiolica, wrote that *disegno* encompassed two notions under a single rubric: *disegno esterno*, the physical manifestation of *disegno interno*, the intellectual idea or design.[4]

A maiolica painter could both invent and execute a design idea, or take guidance from a

1. Leon Battista Alberti, *On Painting*, trans. Cecil Graydon (London: Phaidon, 1972), p. 89. Alberti erroneously refers to the great fifth-century B.C.E. Athenian as a painter. Phidias, in fact, was best known for his sculptures, which included the so-called Lemnian Athena, and a colossal statue of the seated Zeus for that god's temple at Olympia.

2. Ibid., p. 71.

3. *Istoriato* wares were much more time-consuming than purely decorative pieces and made up only a tiny proportion of a shop's business.

4. Holman 1997, p. 2.

patron or adviser. He might draw upon images or works of art by other artists or from the past. Thanks to the invention of printing and the subsequent development of the woodcut and engraving, artistic ideas could be easily transmitted. To what extent maiolica workshops actually owned original prints and illustrated books is not known, but they surely had access to such materials through their patrons. Independent prints (like the mid-fifteenth-century *Tarocchi,* or tarot card series), reproductive images (like Marcantonio Raimondi's engravings after Raphael's paintings), or prints in books (such as emblem books or illustrated editions of Ovid), all became essential tools in the hands of maiolica painters. In a few exceptional circumstances, major artists were called upon to make drawings specifically for maiolica. An unexpected result of the use of prints or drawings was the overshadowing of maiolica-makers by the painters whose work had influenced them. As early as the seventeenth century, artists' biographer Carlo Cesare Malvasia, for example, referred disparagingly to Raphael as a "potter of Urbino," giving credence to the notion that the great artist had actually painted maiolica himself.[5] That misapprehension—based on maiolica artisans' use of prints after his compositions —persisted into the nineteenth century, when maiolica was often referred to as "Raphaelware."

The narrative subjects that appear on maiolica accurately reflect the intellectual tenor of the time. The aspirations of Renaissance individuals to inhabit a cultivated environment characterized by beauty and elegance was balanced by their desire for an intellectual life based on classical models. By the mid-fifteenth century, the major cities and courts of Rome, Naples, Venice, Milan, Mantua, Ferrara, Urbino, and Rimini were bursting with humanists deeply immersed in classical languages, history, and literature, and they in turn brought forth their own remarkable works. They advocated the study of classical achievements through the liberal arts—history, moral philosophy, grammar, poetry, and rhetoric—and the application of the lessons of antiquity to modern life, whether for the purposes of statecraft, the waging of war, or the creation of art. It was thought that through the emulation of illustrious men and women of the ancient past, the human character could be enhanced, perhaps even perfected. Along with literary studies (made easier by the invention of the printing press) came other intellectual activities that were hallmarks of the Italian Renaissance: archaeological investigation, the creation of libraries, and art collecting.

5. Carlo Cesare Malvasia, *Felsina pittrice: Vite de pittori bolognese* (Bologna, 1678), vol. 1, p. 471; cited in Wilson 1996a, p. xvii. François Misson (*A New Voyage to Italy* [London: R. Bentley, 1714], vol. 2, part 1, p. 102) took issue with these apochryphal stories: "Perhaps I should not have taken the liberty singly, to attack the common prejudice that puts the Reputation of Raphael in a three-penny dish, which he never saw or touch'd; tho' I am pretty well acquainted with the history of that artist, and had several good arguments to confute that opinion. But having had the fortune to discourse with the famous Carlo Maratti on the same subject, I dare confidently assure you, that Raphael never drew a stroke on any of these dishes, notwithstanding the very great value that is set upon 'em, and the commonness of the contrary opinion."

Style, of course, was not an end in itself, even in the decorative arts. The content of works of art was important to Renaissance patrons as well. Books, along with fine works of art, were considered an essential part of a well-furnished gentleman's home. As the mid-sixteenth-century writer Sabba da Castiglione noted: "If you were to ask me which ornaments I would above all desire for my home, I would without much thought reply Arms and Books . . . the books by grave, mature, approved and authentic authors, yet oft used with the pages turned . . . since having books and not using them is like not having them at all."[6] Ancient history and the classics provided a treasure trove of themes, many of which encompassed the all-important moral or allegorical messages that were the foundations of the humanistic movement—Livy's *History of Rome*, Homer's *Iliad* and *Odyssey*, Virgil's *Aeneid*, and Ovid's *Metamorphoses*.[7] By the middle of the Cinquecento another major literary source, the Bible, became widely available in inexpensive illustrated editions thanks to French and German publishers. In addition, contemporary writings like Francesco Colonna's *Hypnerotomachia polifili* (1499) or Ludovico Ariosto's epic poem *Orlando furioso* (1516) were important as well.

In the Renaissance, Ovid's *Metamorphoses*, containing vivid tales from classical mythology, was a favorite source for artists. It was not one of the rediscoveries of the Renaissance, as has been thought, but had been widely read throughout the Middle Ages. The embedding of philosophical truths in allegorical form allowed it to be associated with Christian principles and therefore acceptable to the Church. The *Ovide moralisé*, a French fourteenth-century reinterpretation of the original text, was redrawn as a series of simplified didactic lessons about how to avoid pitfalls and lead a virtuous life. In the Renaissance, Ovid's work was a central feature of a humanistic curriculum for students, along with Cicero, Horace, Virgil, and others.[8] No longer seen as a mere recounting of the tales of ancient pagan gods, the *Metamorphoses* was reinterpreted within a classicizing context as a metaphor for the cosmic universe. In 1497 the Venetian printer Zoane Rosso published an edition of the moralized text from the 1370s. To it he appended his own allegorical interpretations and, more importantly, illustrative woodcuts that became essential tools of the maiolica painter's trade. The first widespread Italian translation was issued in 1522, and after mid-century, there was an explosion in the popularity of Ovid, with many new translations into the vernacular.[9] A number

6. Sabba da Castiglione, *Ricordi overo ammaestramenti*, with new material (Venice: Paolo Gherardo, 1560); cited in Gentilini 1993, p. 26.

7. For treatment of print sources in maiolica, see Ravanelli Guidotti 1993.

8. See Paul F. Grendler, *Schooling in Renaissance Italy: Literacy and Learning, 1300–1600*, The Johns Hopkins University Studies in Historical and Political Science, 107 series (Baltimore and London: Johns Hopkins University Press, 1989).

9. Gentilini 1993, pp. 20–22.

CAT. 43
PLATE WITH DEATH OF NARCISSUS, URBINO OR POSSIBLY PESARO, C. 1530–40

CAT. 44

LOW-FOOTED DISH WITH NARCISSUS AND ECHO, URBINO, POSSIBLY FRANCESCO
DURANTINO, C. 1545

of examples in the Philadelphia Museum of Art's collection can be linked to those works.

The death of Narcissus, a favorite Ovidian moralizing tale, appears on two pieces. The beautiful youth Narcissus had toyed with the affections of several admirers, including the nymph Echo, who wasted away until only her voice remained. Finally, one of those whom he had spurned asked the gods for revenge. Narcissus was condemned to fall in love with his own reflection, pined away, and was transformed into the flower that bears his name. In the earlier of the two works (cat. 43), the scene unfolds in two episodes, as it is also shown in the woodcuts of the 1497 edition of Ovid: Narcissus gazes into the water at left, and is mourned by the nymphs at right. The kneeling Narcissus is modeled after a figure of Achilles in one of the Venetian woodcuts. In the later example (cat. 44), possibly by Francesco Durantino, the nymphs in the background recall female figures in Marcantonio Raimondi's engraving after Raphael's famous painting of *Mount Parnassus* in the Vatican.[10]

Other favorite episodes from Ovid are seen on two plates of the 1540s from the Urbino area, one with the birth of Adonis (cat. 45) and the other showing Leto with her twins Apollo and Artemis (cat. 46). The story of Adonis and his mother Myrrha is one compounded by tragedies relating to ill-fated love. Myrrha, having refused to honor the goddess Aphrodite, was made to fall in love with her own father, with whom, while in disguise, she conceived Adonis. Her father killed himself out of shame when he realized the truth, and Myrrha was changed into a tree, from which Adonis was born. On the plate, nymphs cluster around the anthropomorphic tree at the moment of birth, a mythological version of contemporary birth scenes that we find in maiolica sets given to expectant mothers. Although Adonis's birth appears often in maiolica, it is his tragic death that is depicted in the paintings of Raphael, Giulio Romano, Baldassare Peruzzi, and Giorgione. This difference may be due to the maiolica painters' familiarity with Bernard Salomon's well-known print from the *Metamorphoses*, versus the major artists' interest in the poetic tragedy that provided an irresistible opportunity to paint the beautiful goddess and her handsome lover.[11] In the second plate, Leto holds her twins Apollo and Artemis, who were conceived during a secret liaison with Zeus. When Hera, Zeus's jealous wife, learned of the pregnancy, she punished Leto by threatening to destroy any land that would allow her to give birth there. After reaching safe

10. James Beck, *Raphael: The Stanza della Segnatura, Rome* (New York: George Braziller, 1993), pp. 62–63.

11. Jane Davidson Reid with the assistance of Chris Rohmann, *The Oxford Guide to Classical Mythology in the Arts, 1300–1990s* (New York: Oxford University Press, 1993), pp. 25–40.

CAT. 45
PLATE WITH BIRTH OF ADONIS, URBINO,
CIRCLE OF FRANCESCO DURANTINO,
1540–45

CAT. 46
PLATE WITH LETO, ARTEMIS AND
APOLLO, URBINO OR PESARO,
C. 1540–50

haven on the island of Delos, Leto's twins were born. Forced to continue her flight, she was prevented by the peasants of Lycia from drinking the water or washing her children, and as retribution, she changed them into frogs.

Yet another example from Ovid's *Metamorphoses* in the Philadelphia collection is a large, finely painted plate that lacks an identifying inscription (cat. 47). Although it has been described in the past as the abduction of Helen of Troy, the dramatic moment that sparked the Trojan War, it more likely depicts Pluto carrying off Persephone to the underworld. Maiolica painters did not always adhere precisely to texts, but in this case Ovid's words seem to have dictated the artist's interpretation. The scene takes place in a pastoral setting on a lake, with Persephone, her mother Ceres, and her companions picking flowers: "Almost at one and the same time, Pluto saw her, and loved her, and bore her off . . . the terrified goddess called to her mother and to her comrades . . . she rent and tore the upper edge of her garment, till the flowers she had gathered fell from its loosened folds . . . her captor urged on his chariot, called each of his horses by name."[12]

As the familiarity with classical subjects from myth, legend, and history grew, so did the desire for works of art based on them. One can easily imagine a patron displaying his *istoriato* ceramics to guests, not only for their inherent beauty, but for the admiration he would gain by owning such erudite works of art. Captions marked on many of the pieces also made it easier to recall the texts from which scenes were drawn. Legends from the Trojan War—the *Iliad*, the *Odyssey*, the *Aeneid*—were central themes for Renaissance artists, who responded to patrons' demands for objects with lofty intellectual content. Climactic events from the end of the Trojan War appear on two dishes in the collection: the death of Achilles and the suicide of Ajax (cats. 48, 49). While both are faithful to the stories, the inscriptions are erroneous, obviously written by craftsmen unfamiliar with the literature, perhaps even illiterate. In the first, a dish from Guido Durantino's workshop, Paris kills Achilles by shooting an arrow into his vulnerable heel, fulfilling the prophesy of the dying Hector. In the second, from the workshop of Maestro Domenego da Venezia, the action continues after the death of Achilles, when a dispute ensued over whether the Greek warrior Ajax or his rival Odysseus should be given the armor of the dead hero. Unable to bear the humiliation when the Greek leaders

12. Ovid 1980, p. 126.

CAT. 47
PLATE WITH PLUTO ABDUCTING PERSEPHONE, URBINO, CIRCLE OF NICOLA DA
URBINO, C. 1525–35

awarded it to Odysseus, Ajax went mad and took his own life, which is depicted here by him falling onto his sword. On the first plate the figures of the two protagonists and the statue being venerated in the aedicula are lifted directly from the Ovid woodcut of the same episode.[13] Like Nicola da Urbino and Francesco Durantino, this anonymous artist displays his talent for creating imaginary classical architecture. *Istoriato* maiolica is filled with such fascinating flights of architectural fancy, some of it based on actual buildings like Bramante's Tempietto or his great choir apse for Santa Maria delle Grazie in Milan.

Few maiolica craftsmen—perhaps only Xanto—were as literate as contemporary Renaissance painters, and they sometimes supplemented original texts with simpler, moralized versions published in the vernacular. The visual evidence of Xanto's compositions shows that he probably consulted the work of the second-century mythographer Hyginus and others to obtain more detailed descriptions of subjects that were treated only briefly in Ovid. This is the case in a scene of Amphiaraus, who foresaw the disastrous outcome of Polyneices's campaign of the Seven against Thebes—that none would return alive except his brother-in-law Adrastus (cat. 50, appendix 4). Eriphyle, bribed by Polyneices with the necklace that she holds at right, persuaded her husband, Amphiaraus, to participate. This story, portrayed numerous times by Xanto, shows Amphiaraus hiding to avoid the campaign that would end in his death.[14] As he habitually did, Xanto pieced together this composition by using figures from three different prints, resulting in a rather disjointed appearance.

Military initiatives geographically closer to home though equally distant in time were treated in *istoriato* wares based on the exploits of the Roman general Scipio (see cat. 21) and his Carthaginian nemesis, Hannibal (cat. 51, appendix 5), whom he ultimately defeated in 202 B.C.E.[15] Both of these admired military men were included in Livy's *History of Rome*, which graced the bookshelves of all self-respecting Renaissance intellectuals. Part of a service of at least thirty-three pieces depicting Hannibal's campaigns of the Second Punic War, the plate shows him crossing the River Ebro in Spain to acquire more territory for his African empire. Cohorts of armed soldiers range through a deep landscape dotted with whimsical towns and castles, while the river, represented both allegorically and literally, occupies the foreground.

A pair of elaborate snake-handled vases are supported by triangular bases inscribed

13. See Biscontini Ugolini and Petruzzellis Scherer 1992, p. 38.

14. Watson 1986, p. 130. Another example of the same story by Xanto is on a plate whose present whereabouts is unknown; see Triolo 1996, p. 272.

15. See Drey 1991.

CAT. 50
PLATE WITH ERIPHYLE AND AMPHIARAUS, URBINO, FRANCESCO XANTO
AVELLI DA ROVIGO, 1531; LUSTERED IN GUBBIO, WORKSHOP OF MAESTRO
GIORGIO ANDREOLI

CAT. 51
PLATE WITH HANNIBAL CROSSING THE RIVER EBRO, URBINO, WORKSHOP
OF GUIDO DURANTINO, C. 1540–60

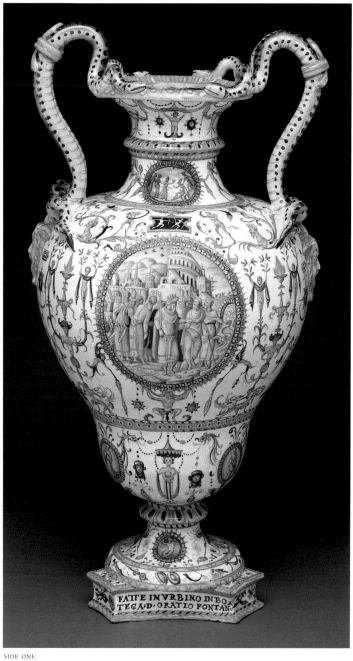

SIDE ONE

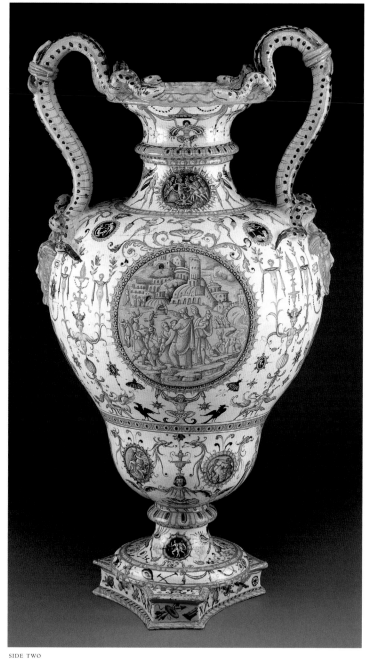

SIDE TWO

SIDE ONE

SIDE TWO

CAT. 53
SNAKE-HANDLED VASE WITH BIBLICAL SCENES, URBINO, WORKSHOP OF
ORAZIO FONTANA, C. 1560–71

"made in Urbino in the workshop of Orazio Fontana," who was described by the contemporary Urbino writer Bernadino Baldi (1553–1617) as "the noblest among those who make vases in terracotta" (cats. 52, 53).[16] Although questions have been raised about these pieces over the years, scientific and scholarly analysis supports their authenticity and their attribution to Orazio's workshop. Additional weight is added to that argument by the recent discovery of the maiolica artists' reliance upon the Frenchman Jacques Androuet I Ducerceau's grotesque prints from the mid-sixteenth century.[17] Medallions set into a background of grotesques contain scenes from the Old Testament, which were undoubtedly drawn from woodcut illustrations.[18] Between 1467 and 1530, about 7,500 illustrated books were published in Italy, including numerous editions of the Bible that often contained as many as four hundred images each.[19] These printed resources could be circulated with considerable ease and were enthusiastically taken up by ceramic artisans and artists in other media. A preference for subjects from the Old Testament (cat. 54, appendix 6), as opposed to the New, may be tied to the desire of Renaissance patrons, especially those from noble families, to associate themselves with the distant past, with ancient ancestors, and sometimes even with mythological gods, from whom they could borrow authority and bolster their social status.

Like most artists of the sixteenth century, maiolica painters were fond of allegory. Xanto, for example, was one of the few artists in any medium to depict the disastrous 1527 Sack of Rome, which he did by combining figures in complex symbolic scenes. In some of the compositions he slyly inserted figures derived from *I modi,* the notorious erotic prints of Giulio Romano and Marcantonio Raimondi, which illustrated various sexual postures and earned the ire of Pope Clement VII.[20] Pietro Aretino wrote lascivious sonnets to accompany the prints, which gained them an even greater notoriety. Xanto's utilization of these charged figures added another layer of meaning to his images for those who recognized them, especially in the case of his political narratives.[21]

An allegorical plate in the Philadelphia collection carries with it some of the most perplexing questions that challenge maiolica scholars today (cat. 55). We know that important sixteenth-century painters like Battista Franco and the Zuccaro brothers (Taddeo and Federico) made drawings for maiolica, and provided them to the artisans who then executed

16. Bernadino Baldi, *Encomio della patria di Monsignor Bernardino Baldi da Urbino . . . al serenissimo Principe Francesco Maria II* (Urbino: Angelo Monticelli, 1706), pp. 130–31.

17. The difference between the two vases indicates that there was more than one painter involved. For details on the Ducerceau prints and their relationship to Urbino maiolica, see Poke 2001. A comprehensive study of the pair will be given in a forthcoming publication by Dean Walker and Melissa Meighan.

18. The issue of decorum in the mixing of pagan and religious motifs has been discussed by Hall (1999, p. 147), who notes that the issue remained open to interpretation. Following the Council of Trent, in the 1560s some cardinals converted decorations in their villas from pagan to religious stories, but continued to accompany them with rich enframements of grotesques.

19. Gentilini 1993, p. 11.

20. Most of the prints from the series, made around 1524, were destroyed. For a detailed study of *I modi,* see Lawner 1988.

21. This follows Vincenzo Borghini's notion of pleasure obtained from a work of art based on the recognition of its *concetto* (concept); see Summers 1981, p. 172.

CAT. 54
PLATE WITH THE QUEEN OF SHEBA
BEFORE KING SOLOMON, PROBABLY
FRANCE, LYON OR NEVERS, LATE-
SIXTEENTH CENTURY

the paintings on clay. Several of these rare designs survive and can be matched to extant plates,
like those commissioned by Duke Guidobaldo II. The Philadelphia plate's sophisticated artistic program, with its complex allegorical narrative and border decoration, hints at the partici-
pation of a major artist and perhaps the involvement of an erudite adviser. To date, however,
no related drawings have been discovered that can be connected to it. A hypothesis about
its theme originates with the *impresa* on the right rim: a mountain being struck by lightning.
This symbol was adopted by Vespasiano Gonzaga (1531–1591), a member of the elite ruling
family of Mantua and the surrounding areas. The Latin motto that usually accompanied the
image—*Feriunt summos* (they hit the high, or lightning strikes only the highest), derived from
Horace's *Odes*—was meant as a stark reminder of the responsibilities and perils of rulership.[22]
The date painted on the elaborate reverse (appendix 7) places this work at the crucial

22. Mario Praz, "The Gonzaga
Devices," in Chambers and Martineau
1981, p. 72.

moment in Vespasiano's life in 1555. Having returned from a series of successful military campaigns, he was embarking on the transformation of the small village of Sabbioneta into an ideal Renaissance city, with state-of-the-art fortifications, a magnificent palazzo and summer residence, a library, theater, mint, gallery of antiquities, and Hebrew-language press.

The imagery on the rim contains references to Juno (the peacock) and Jupiter (the eagle),[23] and to love, marriage, and time. The second *impresa*, on the left border, may be that of Vespasiano's first wife, Diana de Cardona, who died young under mysterious circumstances. Perhaps the plate was commissioned by her, or another member of the Gonzaga family, to mark this important moment for Vespasiano. The work at Sabbioneta may well be allegorized in the scene that reflects a crucial turning point in the *Aeneid*. Sleeping beside the Tiber, Aeneas has a dream in which the river god foretells Aeneas's role in the founding of the Roman empire, saying: "In times to come, my waves shall wash the walls of mighty Rome!"[24] Awakening, Aeneas forms an alliance with King Evander and a vision of armed forces (provided with the aid of his mother Venus) appears in the sky who will help realize his destiny. For Vespasiano Gonzaga, whose very name harkened back not only to his grandfather but to the first-century Roman emperor and military hero, an association with Rome and its founder would be a momentous one. Indeed, his grand plans for Sabbioneta eventually came to fruition, and the town was referred to by contemporaries as a "new Athens" and a "new Rome," with Vespasiano as its new Aeneas.[25]

23. The eagle was also a prominent symbol of the Gonzaga family.

24. Virgil, *Aeneid*, trans. John Dryden (New York: Heritage Press, 1944), book 8, p. 249. Although it is highly unusual in maiolica, the scene is found in woodcuts of the illustrated editions of the *Aeneid*. The only other example of maiolica with a similar subject is a plate from the workshop of Guido Durantino (dated 1535), illustrated in J. P. Palmer and Meredith Chilton, *Treasures of the George R. Gardiner Museum of Ceramic Art* (Toronto: George R. Gardiner Museum of Ceramic Art, 1984), p. 23.

25. My forthcoming article on this work will provide a detailed examination of the plate, its attribution, and its possible design by a major painter.

CAT. 55
PLATE WITH ALLEGORY RELATING TO VESPASIANO GONZAGA, POSSIBLY MANTUA, 1555

Master potter, take my advice. If you wish to sell your wares fast, you should depict on them the women whom I honour here [in my poem], who have come down to us from heaven. —Andreano da Concole, 1557[1]

CHAPTER 6

Daily Life and Contemporary History

Italian Renaissance maiolica decorated with themes from ancient mythology and literature reveals a great deal about the educated elite and their intellectual lives. Far rarer are those wares that depict or symbolize events from contemporary history, like those showing the loading of a ship (c. 1510–20) supervised by Doge Agostino Barbarigo of Venice, the coronation of Emperor Charles V in Bologna in 1530, the Battle of Mühlberg in 1547, the opening of the Holy Door at Saint Peter's in Rome for the Jubilee Year of 1550, or allegories about the 1527 Sack of Rome.[2] Although current historical narratives are unusual in maiolica, other themes and images related to daily life are more common and introduce us to less-elevated aspects of the Renaissance world. Documents such as inventories and letters supplement the concrete evidence about the objects themselves and complete a picture that would otherwise remain indistinct. Different sorts of wares were made both for everyday use and for elegant banquets. In addition, there were ceramic objects intended for more personal, private applications as opposed to those meant as declarations of an individual's social and economic status. A dish given as a love token by a young man to his intended bride, for example, was something quite different from a maiolica service with Ovidian themes designed to impress one's dinner guests.

Aspects of private life are revealed in many objects in the Museum's collection, beginning

1. Quoted in F. Briganti, *Le coppe amatorie del secolo XVI nelle maioliche di Deruta* (Perugia, 1902), pp. 13–15; cited in Ajmar and Thornton 1998, p. 140.

2. Illustrated respectively in Poole 1995, cat. 326; Liverani 1958, figs. 19–20; Norman 1976, p. 146; Wendy Watson, "Taddeo Zuccaro's Earliest Drawings for Maiolica," in Wilson 1991a, fig. 1; Kube 1976, cat. 76; and Cioci 1987, pp. 33–41.

with those that present images of Renaissance Italians. Accurate likenesses are by far the exception in ceramics, although an extraordinary Cafaggiolo *boccale* (pitcher) records the profile of Pope Leo X, and a group of Neapolitan albarelli bear portraits of Aragonese nobles.[3] More common, however, are idealized images like that of Orsella, who commands our attention on a dish from Deruta (cat. 56, appendix 8). Here the border is embellished with classic Deruta ornament alternating with medallions that contain a pierced heart, a young man in modern dress, a monogram, and a warrior in armor (perhaps Saint George, to judge from the halo-like object atop his helmet and the rays above). Ceramics of this type have usually been interpreted as love gifts relating to courtship and marriage. In his 1752 book on the maiolica of Pesaro, Giovanni Battista Passeri uses, perhaps for the first time, the adjective *amatorii* (amatory) in describing some small basins or bowls (*bacinetti*) "on which admirers used to have painted from life their loved one with their own name . . . as a sign of constancy."[4] Other wares with similar associations are the *belle donne* (beautiful women) plates—and there were those that depicted young men as well—that were made in various centers, notably Castel Durante and Deruta. Conventional female heads on maiolica signal the concerns with courtly standards of beauty, virtue, and behavior found in contemporary treatises. At first glance, these depictions appear to contradict the general notion that Renaissance portraiture was based on individuality. But new research into medallic and ceramic images suggests that the relationship between these ideal heads and contemporary women is made through the addition of their names and other more subtle details rather than straightforward likenesses. The longstanding tradition of idealized portraiture seems to have rendered actual physical resemblance less important.[5]

A few decades later in Deruta, monumental plates with idealized women and men came into fashion (cat. 57). A banderole personalized with a name or favorite motto customarily winds its way through the background, although these representations are, if anything, even more formulaic and generalized than those of Castel Durante. A few examples have been found with blank ribbons, probably shop samples that would show how a buyer might tailor an item to his or her needs.[6] The garb of our two subjects provides a glimpse of contemporary style, although one suspects that Orsella's drapery, held at the shoulder by a jeweled

3. For the Leo X *boccale*, see Bojani et al. 1985, cat. 393, color plate XXI. For the Neapolitan jars, see Watson 1986, cat. 23; and many examples in Donatone 1970. The likenesses can be confirmed through a comparison to contemporary medals and painted portraits.

4. Passeri (1752) 1980, p. 63; cited in Ajmar and Thornton 1998, pp. 138–39.

5. For further information, see Ajmar and Thornton 1998.

6. One example is at the Los Angeles County Museum of Art (inv. 50.9.22); see Watson 1986, p. 88.

CAT. 56
LARGE DISH WITH ORSELLA, DERUTA, C. 1500–1510

CAT. 57
LARGE DISH WITH FEMALE HEAD, DERUTA, C. 1520–30

fibula, owes more to antique precedent than to contemporary Renaissance fashion. The unnamed Deruta lady on the lustered plate wears a structured headdress called a *balzo* that covers most of her hair, and is topped by a veil.[7] A typical linen chemise, or *camicia*, is worn under her pleated overdress, or *gamurra*. At the same time in Deruta, painters were also turning out quantities of similar plates decorated with images of the Virgin and female allegorical figures with winged headwear—all bearing a marked resemblance to the timeless women of Perugino and Pinturicchio, two favorite local artists.[8]

In Venice, vases embellished with heads of women and men proliferated in the second half of the sixteenth century, especially those by the workshop of Maestro Domenego da Venezia (cat. 58; see also cat. 5). His fair-haired women, repeated over and over with remarkable consistency, became a hallmark of maiolica from this city, like the foliate patterns that Piccolpasso called "truly Venetian."[9] Venice was renowned for its beautiful women, thus it is not unusual that they should occupy a prominent place in maiolica made there. It has been said that the images on these vases represent the lagoon city's famed courtesans, but since such women often mimicked the dress and hairstyles of upper–middle-class ladies, this hypothesis would be difficult to support. Here the depiction, which is not a true likeness but more a type, replicates the ideal blonde of perfect complexion found in the paintings of Paolo Veronese and Titian. Cesare Vecellio reveals the secret of these pale tresses in his 1590 book on the clothing of Venetian men and women. He describes and illustrates how the women sat on rooftop terraces "devoting themselves intensely to the art of dyeing their hair blond . . . in the hottest moment of the day . . . enduring great discomfort in order to achieve the desired result."[10] The popular coiffure of the day, seen here in a modest version, involved braiding and piling up the hair to form two "horns" above the temples (sometimes as much as six inches high) with a widow's peak over the forehead.

Love, of course, was a major iconographic theme, symbolized by the putti, pierced hearts, and clasped hands that are ubiquitous in maiolica. Certain shapes like the Orsella plate have been called *coppe amatorie* (literally, love cups), based on the assumption that they were given by lovers as presents. And many *istoriato* wares show amorous themes from myth and legend, some so blatantly erotic that they drew disapproving comments from the clergy.

7. See Rasmussen 1989, cat. 44, for a woman wearing a similar headdress.

8. See Fiocco and Gherardi 1988, pp. 92–93. It has been said Pinturicchio's wife was herself the daughter of a Deruta potter; see Bojani 1982, p. 36.

9. Piccolpasso 1980, vol. 2, p. 115.

10. Cesare Vecellio, *Habiti antichi e moderni di tutto il mondo* (Venice, 1590); cited in Lawner 1987, pp. 18–19; see also Giacomo Franco, *Habiti delle donne venetiane* (Venice, 1600). For a 1589 print illustrating this custom, see Thornton 1991, fig. 192.

CAT. 58

ALBARELLO WITH FEMALE AND MALE HEADS, VENICE, WORKSHOP OF

MAESTRO DOMENEGO DA VENEZIA, C. 1550–75

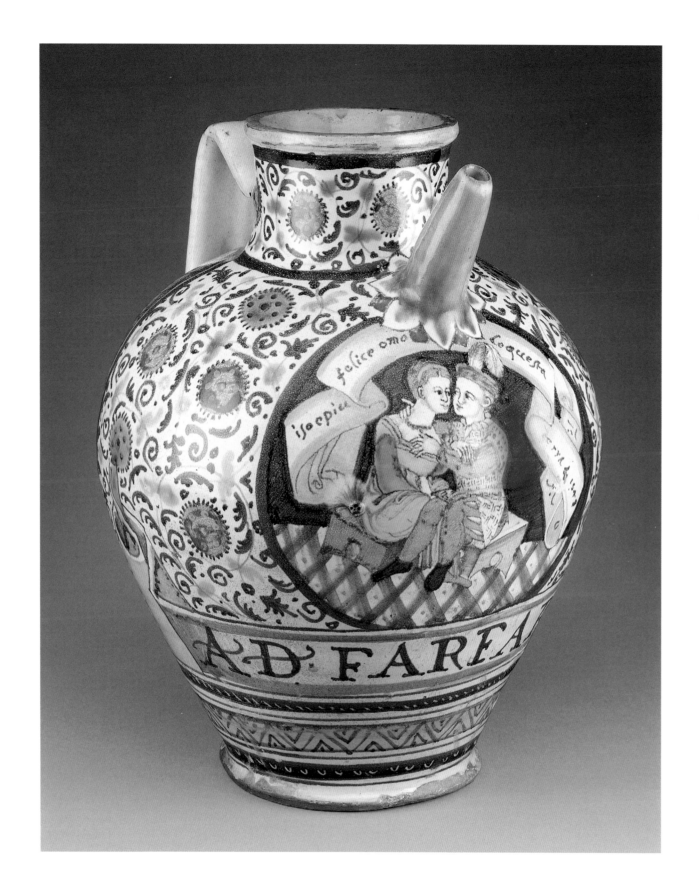

CAT. 59
SPOUTED PHARMACY JAR WITH EMBRACING COUPLE, CASTELLI, 1548

Occasionally, we find a piece like a 1548 spouted drug jar from Castelli (cat. 59), where an instance of secular love is featured. The unusual pitcher, made for the pharmacy whose initials and symbols appear on the reverse, is in the *porcellana colorata* style, meaning that it resembles Chinese blue and white porcelain but with added colors. A young couple sit cozily on low stools embracing each other. The inscription above proclaims, "I am the happiest man in the world." Such banderoles provide an opportunity to identify a subject, or to repeat a popular adage or proverb. Several Deruta plates depicting a man and a donkey are accompanied by sayings like "He who washes the head of an ass wastes his effort."[11] Allegorical scenes of this sort—and those with a biographical overlay, like the Gonzaga plate (see cat. 55)—enlighten us about the regional customs and daily life of both the lower and upper classes, if only in an indirect manner.

The well-appointed interior of a private home is depicted in a lidded bowl from Urbino made specifically for a woman in childbirth (cats. 60a,b). Childbirth sets were made for the personal use of an expectant or new mother, and they were both functional and symbolic. Large families were important for economic and political reasons, and the birth of children was a central event of what Jacqueline Musacchio calls a "post-plague, pro-natalist society."[12] Multipart ceramic sets contain a wealth of information about everyday life, and almost without exception are the pure inventions of maiolica painters, free from the influence of prints.[13] The comfortable bedchambers in paintings by Ghirlandaio (see fig. 2), Paolo Uccello, and Pinturicchio are furnished with other works of the fine and decorative arts, and have much in common with the interior seen on this bowl.[14] On the lid a draped bed with a flowered cover is remade by two servants, while other women and children (or putti) cuddle the swaddled baby, plump up the cradle cushion, and warm linens by a blazing fire.[15] A *cassone* (chest), convex mirror, and painted grisaille frieze adorn the room, underscoring the family's favorable economic status. Inside the bowl, the new mother receives visitors, including her fashionably dressed husband at right.[16] Her nudity, unusual in these depictions, implies that she is nursing the baby herself, as was advocated by contemporary moralists, despite a popular preference for wet nurses. On the tabletop are plate, bowl, and saltcellar—perhaps the elements of another birth set—as well as a glass drinking vessel and flasks. As is often the case, a landscape wraps

11. Pringsheim 1994, fig. 129. For additional details on this proverb, see Rasmussen 1989, pp. 84–85.

12. Musacchio 1997, p. 42; see also Musacchio 1999.

13. While the animal-leg table inside the bowl may have been inspired by the Marcantonio Raimondi print after Raphael's *Quos Ego* (see Poole 1995, p. 313), the rest is pure invention. A childbirth plate quoting a Bernard Salomon print is illustrated in Claudia Silvia Däuber, "La tazza da parto nella Collezione Pringsheim," *CeramicAntica*, vol. 6 (1994), figs. 9–10.

14. See Paolo Uccello's *Birth of the Virgin* (Prato Cathedral) and Pinturicchio's *Birth of John the Baptist* (Baptistry, Siena Cathedral) in Musacchio 1999, figs. 40 and 35, respectively.

15. A 1623 inventory describes "una rimbocchatura da donne di parto bianca agiglietti" (a coverlet for a woman in childbirth, white, with lilies); see Musacchio 1999, p. xiii.

16. See Musacchio 1997, chapter 2, for references to the tradition of new mothers receiving guests in their bedrooms.

CATS. 60A, B

CAT. 60B

CAT. 60B, REVERSE

CATS. 60A, B
FOOTED BOWL AND LID OR TRAY FROM CHILDBIRTH SET, THE MARCHES,
PROBABLY URBINO, FRANCESCO DURANTINO, MID-1540S

around the exterior of the bowl, and under the lid a winged putto hovers with quiver, bow

and arrow. Another winged cherub on a Venetian albarello (cat. 61) plays with a pinwheel, a

toy popular throughout history. Numerous depictions of children with pinwheels show up in

works of art ranging from paintings and prints to maiolica and painted wooden birth trays,

although only boys appear with them in ceramics.[17] The emphasis on boys in these depictions

is related to the strong preference for male children, who would become heirs and carry on

the family name.

Domestic settings were also a locus for devotional objects. These usually took the form

of small religious paintings, relief sculptures, statuettes, or inexpensive prints, according to

the economic status of the owner.[18] Deruta's brisk business in display plates with the Virgin

or such popular saints as Francis and Jerome conveys a special sense of religious fervor, and

the pierced footrings indicate that the wares were meant to be hung on walls like other art

17. For a painting by Bernardino di
Antonio Betti, see Klapisch-Zuber 1985,
pl. 14.3; for a print with playing putti,
see Lutteman 1981, p. 113; for maiolica,
see Poole 1995, cat. 370, and Gardelli
1999, cat. 46; for a *desco da parte*, see
Musacchio 1999, p. 3, color plate 2. In
1390 Jehan de Vivier is said to have made
a pinwheel out of gold with pearls and
rubies for Isabelle of France; see *The
Encyclopedia of World Art*, vol. 6, p. 6, col. 2.

18. For a detail of Vittore Carpaccio's
Saint Ursula cycle (Galleria dell'
Accadémia, Venice) with a small paint-
ing of this type in a bedroom, see
Thornton 1991, fig. 38.

objects (cat. 62).[19] Saint Jerome (c. 340/42–420) was one of the four doctors of the early Church. He studied in Rome and became a close associate of Pope Damasus, who elevated him to the cardinalate. The Latin translation of the Bible, known as the Vulgate, was among Jerome's greatest contributions. The notable preference in Deruta for Saints Jerome and Francis above all other saints may stem from their shared devotion to prayer, asceticism, repentance, and virtuous obedience—their imitation of the life of Jesus himself. Through them, laymen were able to participate more directly in religious life, an aspiration that was one of the most profound spiritual demands of the age.[20] Following the dictates of the church fathers at the Council of Nicaea in 787, the saints were to be represented, venerated, and emulated. Maiolica display plates thus served as devotional tools in the service of these two important role models: Saint Francis, the gentler and more loving of the two, and Saint Jerome, the more stern and demanding. The very image of Saint Jerome was thought to be apotropaic, and it was said that demons feared to enter the cell of a nun who kept his picture on the wall.[21] Protection of the same kind may have been ascribed to the large plates and to wall plaques or tiles like one with the letters *IHS*, the monogram of Christ, which Saint Bernard of Siena (1380–1444) used in his preaching and took as his personal symbol (cat. 63). This populist preacher ascribed to similar ascetic strictures, turning down the bishoprics of Siena, Ferrara, and Urbino in order to remain a simple friar. A dish of monumental size (cat. 64), painted in a more popular and less refined style, reproduces Federico Barocci's famous altarpiece (c. 1567–69) for the cathedral of Perugia.[22] It too may have served a devotional function, hanging on the wall of a private residence.

An object decidedly more secular in tone is an eighteenth-century *scaldamani*, or hand-warmer (cat. 65), that probably belonged to a woman. Filled with hot water from an opening in the back, it could retain heat for some time and bring relief from the cold interior of a stone palazzo. It has also been suggested that such flasks held spirits, another means of "warming" the body. This example is particularly charming and informative. *Scaldamani* were produced in various shapes, including books, shoes, and boots. Latchet-tie shoes like the one represented here were worn by both men and women. They came into vogue around 1610 and remained in style well into the eighteenth century. In a watercolor by Jan II van Grevenbroeck

19. See Watson 1986, cat. 32; Bojani 1982, fig. 11. One Deruta plate even shows a monk preaching to his congregation from a raised pulpit; see Gardelli 1999, cat. 183. For a plate in Lyon with the combined iconography of Saints Francis and Jerome, Christ, and the sacred monogram, see Fiocco and Gherardi 1994, p. 113. For a 1505 Deruta votive plaque, see Watson 1986, cat. 27.

20. Eugene F. Rice Jr., *Saint Jerome in the Renaissance* (Baltimore: Johns Hopkins University Press, 1985), p. 81.

21. Ibid., p. 59.

22. S. J. Freedberg, *Painting in Italy, 1500 to 1600* (Harmondsworth, Middlesex: Penguin Books, 1970), pl. 286.

CAT. 62
LARGE DISH WITH SAINT JEROME, DERUTA, FIRST HALF OF THE SIXTEENTH CENTURY

CAT. 63
PLAQUE WITH EMBLEM OF SAINT
BERNARD OF SIENA, EMILIA-ROMAGNA,
PROBABLY FAENZA, MID- TO LATE-
SIXTEENTH CENTURY

CAT. 64
LARGE DISH WITH DEPOSITION OF
CHRIST, POSSIBLY MONTELUPO OR
VITERBO, SEVENTEENTH CENTURY

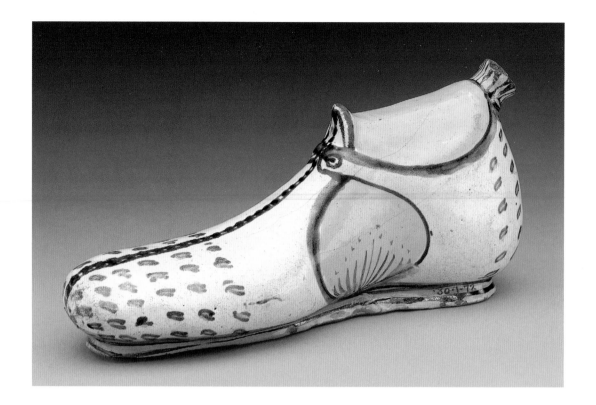

(1731–1807), an elegantly dressed Venetian courtesan wears shoes nearly identical to those copied for the hand-warmer.[23] The ceramic painter has reproduced precise details, like the slashing of the leather for both decorative and functional purposes, and the gathers of the bias-cut stocking under the arch of the foot.

From the domestic, personal world of the Renaissance individual, we move outside to the landscape itself, the subject of a Faentine *crespina*. The circular field in the center shows a view of an unpopulated countryside, almost like a window into the out-of-doors viewed through the bowl's ornamental frame (cat. 66, appendix 9). Landscape as an independent artistic subject was in its infancy in Italy in the sixteenth century, and yet it occasionally makes an appearance on maiolica from Faenza, Urbino, and Venice.[24] In spite of the dearth of surviving pieces, Piccolpasso illustrates one of these *paesi* (landscapes), noting that "these are done at Venice and at Genoa and nowadays among us [meaning in the Urbino region]."[25] Inspired by passages in the writings of ancient Roman authors like Pliny the Elder (23/24–79) and Vitruvius (fl. later first century B.C.E.), this genre was reborn in the Renaissance, and Alberti himself recommended the use of landscape painting in villas and palaces. An often-repeated description of Giorgione's famous but still-puzzling painting

23. Lawner 1987, p. 30.

24. See Burke (1986, pp. 166–67) about the increasing awareness of the backgrounds of paintings and the shift toward considering landscape as the true subject.

25. Piccolpasso 1980, vol. 2, p. 117.

The Tempest (c. 1510),[26] emphasizes the importance of the setting rather than the figures, calling it "a small landscape on canvas, with a thunderstorm, a gipsy and a soldier."[27] This statement underscores Venice's important and slightly ironic role—given its lack of any sort of traditional landscape—in the development of the genre.[28] In this mid-sixteenth-century Faentine dish, the view resembles one of those imaginary environments into which *istoriato* painters often placed their actors. Arching bridges, round buildings, sharp steeples, and peaked roofs are seen in the distance, which reflect the influence of the imagery of northern prints as much as those landscapes closer to home.

Also derived from the natural landscape are the flowers and other botanical elements that were favorite decorative motifs in the Renaissance, as they had been in antiquity. The leafy rinceaux of the Faentine *crespina* are subsidiary to the main landscape, but sometimes a plant itself becomes the prime subject in maiolica. A number of jars made in Deruta took the shape of pinecones, originally with pointed lids (cat. 67). Charged with symbolism since antiquity, pinecones were associated with Dionysus and Cybele, the ancient gods linked to fertility and immortality. These jars may have been used to hold the pine nuts or sweetmeats that were traditionally exchanged during courtship and marriage rituals.[29] Then, as now, pine nuts were an expensive delicacy (with medicinal powers as well), their cost tied to the difficulty of harvesting them from the cones. Mario Equicola (1460–1540) saw them as symbols of industry and virtue: "He who desires the fruit of the pine must labor to open the tightly closed cover."[30] The fifteenth-century humanist Platina, on the other hand, describes Lenten sweetmeats made from sugar and pine nuts, sometimes gilded "for magnificence . . . and for pleasure."[31]

In addition to these more immediate aspects of daily life—love, marriage, children, clothing, landscape, and culinary customs—maiolica included themes that hinted at larger issues. In the first decades of the sixteenth century, Deruta's painters sometimes chose equestrian Turks as their subjects (cat. 68). The ever-present threat of the Turk hovering just beyond the borders of Italy was never far from the Italian consciousness. The Ottoman empire had gained enormous momentum in the 1400s, overrunning Constantinople and, by the century's end, defeating a Venetian fleet off the western coast of Greece in the Ionian Sea.

26. Adams 2001, fig. 17.3.

27. Written by Marcantonio Michiel in 1521; quoted in E. H. Gombrich, *Norm and Form: Studies in the Art of the Renaissance* (London: Phaidon, 1978), p. 109.

28. See Patricia Fortini Brown, *Art and Life in Renaissance Venice* (New York: Harry N. Abrams, 1997), pp. 138–39, where she discusses the role of Venetian artists in transforming the literary notion of the pastoral into a visual one.

29. Poole 1995, p. 187.

30. Quoted in Ladis 1989, p. 56.

31. Platina 1998, p. 177.

CAT. 66
MOLDED DISH ON LOW FOOT, FAENZA, C. 1550–70

CAT. 67

VASE IN SHAPE OF A PINECONE, DERUTA, C. 1500–1530

CAT. 68
LARGE DISH WITH EQUESTRIAN TURK, DERUTA, FIRST HALF OF THE
SIXTEENTH CENTURY

By 1529, when the Ottoman Sultan Süleyman the Magnificent laid siege to Vienna, his political control extended around the Mediterranean, from Tunisia to the Balkans. A wary coexistence was negotiated with this relentless imperial force, which, on other levels, held a magnetic attraction for Europeans. Its cultural and intellectual achievements made the Islamic empire the equal of any Western power, and the empire's high-quality luxury goods were an irresistible incentive for strategic trade agreements. Turkish riders on Renaissance ceramics, in paintings, and on bronze medals, were immediately recognizable as representations of Ottoman power, while at the same time they revealed the Italian predilection for goods and images from the East.

At your villa, you should have—according to your means—several spoons and forks of silver and some plates of beautiful maiolica in order always to retain a measure of civility and to show that you are well born.

—Giovanni Battista Barpo, 1634[1]

CHAPTER 7

Patrons and Uses

Museum visitors, encountering maiolica for the first time, often ask, "Was Renaissance maiolica ever actually *used* at the dining table?" This seemingly simple question has paradoxically been one of the most difficult to answer. Accounts of upper-class banquets mention the use of silver or even gold tablewares, and contemporary paintings show glittering arrangements of metalwares stacked up on sideboards. Simple ceramics appear with some regularity in fifteenth-century paintings of the Last Supper, and Caravaggio (1573–1610) includes late-sixteenth-century maiolica in at least three of his works.[2] The British Pre-Raphaelite John Everett Millais (1829–1896) boldly paints banqueters eating from detailed *istoriato* plates in his 1848–49 canvas *Isabella*,[3] but no Renaissance painting has been found that documents their use at table. A better understanding of Renaissance dining customs and documentary evidence, however, now seems to point in that direction.[4] The absence of wear on the plates is probably attributable to their careful handling and to the fact that fewer metal utensils were employed at the time. Personal forks did not become customary in Italy until after the mid-sixteenth century, and it was not unusual in polite company to convey food from plate to mouth with one's fingers.[5] Erasmus's handbook of 1530, *De civilitate morum puerilium* (On Good Manners for Boys) confirms that practice, but advises: "To lick greasy fingers or to wipe them on your coat is impolite. It is better to use the tablecloth or the napkin."[6] He also offers an alternative to soiling the host's linens: "The guest holds out his hands and a page pours water over them. The water is sometimes slightly scented with chamomile or rosemary."[7] Giulio Romano depicts this action in his fresco, which includes a credenza of precious metalwares as would

1. Giovanni Battista Barpo, *Le delitie e i frutti dell'agricoltura e della villa. . . .* (Venice: Presso il Sarzina, 1634), pp. 12–13.

2. See John Varriano, "Caravaggio and the Decorative Arts in the Two Suppers at Emmaus," *Art Bulletin*, vol. 68 (1986), pp. 218–24.

3. Now in the Walker Art Gallery, Liverpool, England; see Geoffroy Millais, *Sir John Everett Millais* (London: Academy Editions, 1979), p. 35.

4. See Goldthwaite 1989, pp. 19–23.

5. The fork was still viewed with suspicion by some northern Europeans, including a German preacher who called it a "diabolic luxury"; cited in Goldthwaite 1989, p. 26.

6. Quoted in Norbert Elias, *The History of Manners* (New York: Random House, 1978), p. 90; see also Leon Kass, *The Hungry Soul: Eating and the Perfecting of Our Nature* (Chicago: University of Chicago Press, 1999).

7. Quoted in Elias, *History of Manners*, p. 90.

befit a mythological scene (see fig. 1). But ewer basins and pitchers were produced in maiolica workshops as well (cats. 69, 70). The very proliferation of shapes and the quantities in which they were ordered provide additional indications of use and reflect the evolving state of Renaissance cuisine.[8] In the mid-sixteenth century, Bartolomeo Scappi, chef to Pope Pius V, demonstrates the level of innovation in Italian cooking by this time in his monumental 1570 book on gastronomy. In it he lists extensive menus and notes the exact numbers of plates used for particular banquets.[9] This was the moment when, as Richard Goldthwaite has noted, "The preparation of food, along with manners, entered into the game of competition for status in a society increasingly conscious of hierarchy."[10]

In a letter of 1528, the Medici pope Clement VII was described as using "piatti di terra . . . depinti a figure" (ceramic plates with figural decoration) only when dining with cardinals, though it is unclear whether this was the common practice or his personal preference.[11] And four years earlier, Eleanora Gonzaga, duchess of Urbino, wrote to her mother Isabella d'Este in Mantua: "Thinking of visiting Your Excellency and bringing some product of these lands . . . I have had made a service of earthenware pottery . . . since the *maestri* of this land of ours have some reputation for good workmanship. I shall be pleased if Your Excellency likes it and if you will make use of it at Porto, since it is something suitable for a villa (per essere cosa da villa)."[12] These tantalizing lines imply that Nicola da Urbino's famous Este-Gonzaga service to which this letter apparently refers was deemed appropriate for a country setting, her more private retreat, rather than her urban palazzo in Mantua, the center of more formal court life.[13]

Services were commissioned by or for distinguished Italian individuals like Isabella d'Este (see cat. 16) or cardinals of the church, as well as important families like the Gonzaga (see cats. 55, 75a,b), the Orsini, and the Medici (cat. 71). Many were dedicated patrons of the maiolica workshops, as the appearance of their coats of arms on many works attests. While some wares were made for the family itself, others were intended as gifts for weddings, births, and other important occasions, or for diplomatic exchange, as in the case of the Spanish-inscribed vase (see cat. 19). The courtly culture of gift giving was closely tied to the Aristotelian definition of magnificence—making the appropriate gesture on a great occasion—combined with the decorum stressed by Pontano in his treatises. In the highly competitive

8. Piccolpasso's descriptions of various shapes—as meat platters, fruit salvers, comfit bowls, porringers, salts, drinking bowls, and so forth—would be pointless were they not intended for use. A payment record of 1518 for maiolica ordered by Clarice Strozzi specifies three sizes of plates along with porringers, bowls, and pitchers—a total of eighty-four pieces; see Marco Spallanzani, "Un 'fornimento' di maioliche per Clarice Strozzi de' Medici," *Faenza*, vol. 70 (1984), pp. 381–87.

9. Bartolomeo Scappi, *Opera dell'arte del cucinare: Testi antichi di gastronomia* (Bologna: Arnaldo Forni, 1981).

10. Goldthwaite 1989, p. 24.

11. Spallanzani 1994, p. 129.

12. Quoted in Palvarini Gobio Casali 1987, p. 211. Kidwell (1991, pp. 273–74) describes Giovanni Pontano's invitation to a friend to join him at his villa for a convivial meal served on earthenware dishes. Although this was to take place in the country, it was to be "elegant" and with "no rusticity."

13. Scholars continue to debate the meaning of this phrase, along with the issue of whether *istoriato* wares were used at the table. Few documents providing firsthand information have been discovered, however, and additional concrete evidence is needed for the clarification of such points.

CAT. 69

EWER BASIN WITH COAT OF ARMS, DERUTA, C. 1520

CAT. 70
EWER, DERUTA, FIRST HALF OF THE SIXTEENTH CENTURY

CAT. 71

PLATE WITH ARMS OF POPE CLEMENT VII MEDICI, DERUTA, C. 1523–34

court society, one's standing depended upon ancestry and family status, as well as on strategic marriages, friendships, and political ties. And heraldry was a key signifier of rank.

A family's *stemma*, or coat of arms, was typically placed in a prominent location on the front of each piece in a service, but one made in or around Urbino for the Lanciarini family of Rome is emblazoned on its reverse, perhaps indicating their greater modesty (cat. 72, appendix 10). The themes selected for *istoriato* maiolica—whether mythological, religious, or historical—may have been dictated by the patron or adviser, or attuned to the recipient's taste. One can imagine that Isabella d'Este, a notoriously domineering art patron, would have wanted a direct hand in anything she commissioned. And a churchman would have favored Biblical subjects, like a scene of Samson and Delilah, rather than the more titillating tales of Ovid (cat. 73).

It was not only Italians who wished to possess these beautiful ceramics, of course. Orders came from abroad, especially from Germany and France, and gifts flowed in the other direction as well.[14] Venice and Urbino were particularly active in producing wares for northern clients, and the existing commercial links between Italy and Germany (in the spice trade, for example) nourished the market for maiolica. Some plates or services appear to have marked the nuptials of wealthy couples, like this plate from the Patanazzi workshop with the arms of the Böckhli and Christell families of Augsburg (cat. 74). The brilliantly colored wares had a special appeal for Germans, as indicated in a 1546 letter from Hieronymus Imhoff to a friend back in Nuremberg: "I have bought two more *maiolica* bowls than I had instructions from you for; there are two quite different from the rest, of green and red . . . I liked them so much I just had to buy them."[15]

Pharmacies were another major market for maiolica. Unlike tablewares whose use remains somewhat unclear, drug jars were an integral part of the daily business for hospitals and apothecaries (fig. 7).[16] Large numbers of containers were required by pharmacies that also sold spices (*spezie*) and sweet concoctions, just as drugstores still do today. In 1430, for example, the Florentine *spezieria* (spice shop), of the hospital of Santa Maria Novella ordered approximately a thousand jars from the local potter Giunta di Tugio. Some of these ceramics can still be seen today on the shelves of their original pharmacies in Rome, Florence, and

14. For more on the taste for maiolica in the north, see Crépin-Leblond and Ennès 1995.

15. Wilson 1987a, p. 186; see also Julia Fritsch, "Services destiné à l'Allemagne," in Crépin-Leblond and Ennès 1995, pp. 68–80. For more on maiolica and its German collectors, see Mallet 1998, pp. 39–43.

16. Drug jars also appear as accessories in contemporary paintings like Ghirlandaio's *Birth of John the Baptist* (see fig. 2) and his *Saint Jerome* (1480; Ognissanti, Florence), as well as in scenes of the Annunciation and the Nativity where albarelli function as flower vases; see Thornton 1991, figs. 35, 79. In the Portinari Altarpiece (c. 1474–76; Uffizi, Florence), Hugo van der Goes depicts a Hispano-Moresque albarello prominently in the foreground as a flower vase; see Watson 1986, p. 13.

CAT. 72
PLATE WITH LEGEND OF CIRCE,
URBINO AREA, C. 1540–50

CAT. 73
LOW-FOOTED DISH WITH SAMSON
AND DELILAH, URBINO, WORKSHOP OF
GUIDO DURANTINO, 1535

CAT. 74
PLATE WITH ARMS OF THE BÖCKHLI AND CHRISTELL FAMILIES, URBINO,
PROBABLY PATANAZZI WORKSHOP, LATE-SIXTEENTH CENTURY

Figure 7
View of the interior of an apothecary's shop, fresco. Castello d'Issogne, Valle d'Aosta, c. 1500
Scala/Art Resource, New York

17. Vintage wares can be seen, for example, on the shelves of a pharmacy active since 1552 adjacent to the Trevi Fountain in Rome.

18. See Mallet 1981a, pp. 39–43.

19. The heraldry most often used by the Dominican order is a simple shield in black and white, but the one on these jars has also been linked to the group. Ragona (1975, p. 76), for example, describes an early eighteenth-century Sicilian albarello with "the *stemma* of the Dominicans, a dog with a lighted torch in its mouth, and above which is a blue field with three stars."

20. See Thornton 1991, pp. 177–84. Several hypotheses have been advanced about the identity of the queen on these pieces, based on the fleur-de-lys on her scepter. One links her with Catherine de' Medici, while another suggests that she represents allegorically the city of Florence whose symbol was the *giglio* (lily). See Paolo Casati Migliorini's recent article that summarizes the various opinions: "Tra ipotesi storiche e suggestioni simboliche: Un corredo farmaceutico ancora in cerca della sua spezieria," *CeramicAntica*, vol. 11 (May 2001), pp. 12–27.

Venice, which attests to the longevity of the establishments and to the sturdiness of the wares.[17] The pharmacies of monastic orders, hospitals, and noble families sometimes marked their drug containers with insignias or coats of arms, as in two Faentine *berettino* (blue-tinged) flasks of the Gonzaga (cats. 75a,b).[18] Since few potteries in Mantua produced painted wares, the family often ordered them from Urbino, Ferrara, and Faenza. And although the Gonzaga arms are immediately recognizable, others, such as these on a white-ground albarello, are not so easily identified (cat. 76). At first glance, the arms on this piece resemble those of the Salviati, but the colors—blue and white—are not those associated with this family (see cat. 20). In the exacting world of heraldry, color is as important as form, and it would have been very unlikely for a maiolica painter to flout heraldic conventions.

Several jars in the Philadelphia collection were once part of very large sets. A pair of Venetian *berettino* albarelli may be linked to a Dominican medical establishment, as the coat of arms suggests (cats. 77a,b).[19] This set, like two other pharmaceutical suites in the Museum's collection, has a consistent decorative scheme throughout, with the names of the contents being the only variation. A famous Urbino group, sometimes known as the Queen set after the crowned allegorical figure that appears on each vase, has a similarly consistent decorative program, although it has yet to be associated with any specific pharmacy or hospital (cats. 78a,b, 79). Attended by winged putti, who hold up banners with drug names, the royal figure occupies a type of folding chair that is based on an ancient prototype and emphasizes her lofty rank.[20] The so-called Fortune group, named after the allegorical figures that form the main subject, was probably produced in a Pesaro workshop (cats. 80a,b). Trophy motifs serve as background decoration to the exuberant nudes, who hold aloft billowing draperies that act as "masts" for fantastic dolphin sailboats. A drug jar from Trapani on the west coast of Sicily shows a variation from the oft-repeated designs derived from Venetian

CATS. 75A, B
PAIR OF PHARMACY BOTTLES WITH ARMS OF THE GONZAGA FAMILY, FAENZA,
C. 1530–40

CAT. 76
ALBARELLO WITH COAT OF ARMS, CASTEL DURANTE, FIRST HALF OF THE
SIXTEENTH CENTURY

CATS. 77A, B
PAIR OF ALBARELLI WITH ANGELS AND COATS OF ARMS, VENICE, SECOND HALF
OF THE SIXTEENTH CENTURY

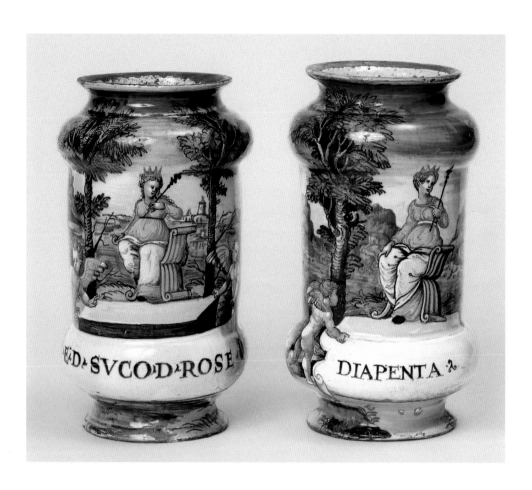

CATS. 78A, B
PAIR OF ALBARELLI WITH SEATED QUEENS, URBINO,
PROBABLY WORKSHOP OF ORAZIO FONTANA, C. 1565–71

CAT. 79
SPOUTED DRUG JAR WITH SEATED QUEEN, URBINO,
PROBABLY WORKSHOP OF ORAZIO FONTANA, C. 1565–71

CATS. 80A, B
PAIR OF ALBARELLI WITH TROPHIES AND FEMALE FIGURES REPRESENTING
FORTUNE, PESARO OR CASTEL DURANTE, C. 1580

and other mainland wares (cat. 81). Its somewhat crude but nonetheless charming decoration focuses on a coat of arms within a wreath, using a typically Sicilian ornamental frame around the shield. Trapani was renowned for its coral-work, which was exported to courts elsewhere in Italy, particularly Florence and Naples, cities whose ceramic workshops in turn exerted influence on the Sicilian wares.

Objects with other uses—neither for the pharmacy nor related to tablewares—include childbirth sets (also known as accouchement sets), which convey useful information about the domestic interiors of the time and the lives of women and families in the Renaissance.[21] Important painting cycles record the births of the Virgin or Saint John the Baptist, but there are myriad works of art—prints, painted wooden birth trays, and ceramics—that relate to the everyday realities of birth, a much-celebrated, but often perilous feature of Renaissance life. Piccolpasso illustrates accouchement sets with five pieces stacked one atop another, although he mentions that some had as many as nine elements. No complete set exists today, but one Urbino bowl, or *ongaresca*, from around 1560–70 shows the happy outcome of a pregnancy, the swaddled baby having been bathed in the basin and dried with towels warmed at the fireplace (cat. 82). Another bowl, this one with a related lid, shows another bedroom interior with the baby standing in a *bacino* (basin) attended by two women and a family dog (cats. 83a,b). In the background, a second naked child cavorts as a servant carries a bowl to the new mother, hidden in the bed at right. On the lid is a figure of Saint John the Baptist in the wilderness. Conceived in the old age of his parents, the saint was a symbol of fertility, and the playful male putti that abound in these wares have a talismanic role as well. In addition to scenes of childbirth and the care of newborns, accouchement sets sometimes were painted with subjects from mythology or the Bible, as well as allegories reflecting hoped-for qualities or virtues of the child.[22]

The world of Renaissance women is also reflected in maiolica items like rare inscribed beads that served as spindle whorls, or weights (cats. 84a–e). Like *bella donna* plates, many of these were personalized with the name of the recipient, and probably had a related function as love tokens or marriage gifts. Spindles were a common symbol of wifely responsibilities and would have been appropriate symbolic gifts to present to a bride at her wedding.[23]

21. See Musacchio 1999, for an extensive study of this topic; and Giovanna Bandini et al., *Da donna a madre: Vesti e ceramiche particolari per ornamenti speciali* (Florence: Scientific Press, 1996).

22. Poole 1995, p. 334.

23. See Musacchio 1999, pp. 94, 95 n. 23.

CAT. 81
DRUG JAR WITH COAT OF ARMS, SICILY, TRAPANI, FIRST HALF OF THE SEVEN-
TEENTH CENTURY

REVERSE OF BOWL

CAT. 83A, BOWL

CAT. 83A, REVERSE OF BOWL

CAT. 83B, LID OR TRAY

CAT. 83B, REVERSE OF LID OR TRAY

CATS. 83A, B
BOWL AND RELATED LID OR TRAY FROM CHILDBIRTH SET, URBINO, C. 1560—80

Small-scale ceramic sculptures, saltcellars, fountains, and inkstands graced the tabletops and desks in Renaissance households, and beautifully painted tiles were laid under foot. The *studiolo*—that all-important room within the Italian Renaissance palazzo—was the perfect place for the display of precious items of fine workmanship that showed one's learning and discriminating judgment.[24] Maiolica inkstands were often made in sections with molded figures on removable tops, like this one that shows two fisherman netting a catch (cat. 85a). Inside, one finds fictive pens, quills, knives, and related writing implements, as well as jewelry or other trinkets (cat. 85b). Wonderfully imaginative inkwells—like one with Saint George slaying the dragon and another with a sleeping knight[25]—were turned out by Faenza shops at the beginning of the sixteenth century, and the form came back into style in the 1580s. As might be expected, inkstands were prime symbols of literacy and erudition for the elite, and major artists like Francesco Salviati (1510–1563) and Giulio Romano supplied designs for them.[26] A 1609 inventory of the ducal palace in Urbino, for example, listed no fewer than eighteen maiolica inkstands decorated with religious or secular figures. These status symbols were not only functional, but proved to be excellent gifts: We know from a document stating that in 1575 Cardinal Ferdinando de'Medici presented to a fellow cleric "an inkwell made of earthenware from Urbino made in the form of a casket, in seven sections," by Flaminio Fontana.[27] Other items that might be displayed in one's *studiolo*, bedchamber, private chapel, or elsewhere in the home, were ceramic devotional sculptures made not only in the della Robbia workshop but in other areas of Italy. A tender Virgin and Child (cat. 86) made somewhere in Emilia-Romagna or the Marches around 1500 might have been such an object, as was a ceramic bust of Saint John the Baptist that Frate Francheschino da Cesena is said to have enjoyed in his study in the Malatesta library.[28]

24. Thornton 1997, p. 165.

25. Watson 1986, cats. 3–4.

26. See Holman 1997, cat. 13.

27. Poole (1995, p. 405) provides a list of other figural inkstands.

28. Thornton 1997, pp. 84–85, fig. 54.

CAT. 85A

CAT. 85A
INKSTAND IN FORM OF A BOAT
WITH FISHERMEN, URBINO,
PATANAZZI WORKSHOP, C. 1580–90

CAT. 85B
INTERIOR OF INKSTAND

CAT. 85B

CAT. 86

VIRGIN AND CHRIST CHILD, EMILIA-ROMAGNA OR THE MARCHES, C. 1487–1500

CAT. 87
TABERNACLE WITH THE GATHERING
OF MANNA, POSSIBLY VITERBO,
PROBABLY LATE-NINETEENTH CENTURY
IN THE STYLE OF THE SEVENTEENTH
CENTURY

An apparently unique ceramic tabernacle in the collection has yet to be precisely dated, although it bears a resemblance to seventeenth-century wares made in Viterbo, north of Rome (cat. 87). Probably created for a private chapel by one of that city's lesser-known ceramic workshops, its painting style is somewhat countrified in comparison to the more sophisticated products of Tuscany and the Marches. The narrative that wraps around the circular form tells the story of the Gathering of Manna, with God the Father appearing in the sky above the Israelites. Continuing beyond a fictive door at the rear, the scene becomes one of a priest at an altar with angels bringing forth the bread and wine that represent the sacrifice of the Mass. With a sense of wit belying his somewhat naive style, the painter repeats the manna scene in monochrome on the front of the altar itself, now a story within a story. The two images

FRONT

SIDE

CAT. 88
PUZZLE JUG WITH PHILYRA AND SATURN, URBINO, LATE-SIXTEENTH OR EARLY
SEVENTEENTH CENTURY

cleverly link the bread of the Old Testament with that of the New, and with the intended contents of the tabernacle itself.

The wit that surfaces in the Viterbo painter's work is not, in fact, unusual in maiolica or in Italian Renaissance art in general. Clever *vasi a inganno*, or puzzle jugs, were listed in Urbino household inventories, although few survive today (cat. 88).[29] Perforations encircling the neck ensure that the contents can never be poured from the jug into a glass, leaving the diner not only frustrated but thirsty. The trick involves hidden channels ingeniously constructed within the handle and the rim. One of the small spouts on the rim (and probably *only* one) had to be used like a straw to suck the wine out of the jar. Adding to the amusement is the erotic scene of the nymph Philyra being seduced by the god Saturn, here transformed into a horse. Other maiolica works meant for entertainment include table fountains and sculptures populated by drunken Bacchuses propped up by revelers, serenading musicians, and even an inebriated and half-naked acrobat with a trained bear.[30] Xanto, of course, habitually mined the sexual prints of Marcantonio Raimondi for his figures, sometimes using them as allegories of the degenerate city of Rome, and in other cases simply inserting them for the delectation of well-informed viewers.[31] And one only has to look closely at the grotesques on Urbino white-ground wares to detect risqué behavior among the creatures cavorting there. But this was not unusual fare in Renaissance culture, where wit, humor, and sly innuendo were often part of the artistic palette in every medium, from paintings and sculpture to ceramics and garden design.

Part of the great constellation of Renaissance possessions, maiolica speaks eloquently of that historical period. Whatever exoticism they may appear to have at first glance is leavened by an inevitable sense of familiarity. Pottery, after all, is the one medium that in some way touches nearly every life, both past and present. Half a millennium later, these works retain their fascination for us, and continue to inform, amaze, and delight those who pause to appreciate them. In company with the major arts and the other so-called minor ones, maiolica helps to complete the picture of both the private and public worlds of the Renaissance.

29. Spallanzani 1994, p. 112 n. 3.

30. Gardelli 1987, cats. 62–64, 66.

31. For more examples of erotic maiolica, see Catherine Hess, "L'enigma degli albarelli Bo," in De Pompeis 1990, pp. 46–55; and Hess, "Sex Pots," *Ceramic Review*, vol. 178 (1999), pp. 30–33. See Talvacchia 1999, for a discussion of eroticism in Renaissance culture.

APPENDIX OF REVERSES

APPENDIX I
REVERSE OF CAT. 17

APPENDIX 2
REVERSE OF CAT. 21

APPENDIX 3
REVERSE OF CAT. 33

APPENDIX 4
REVERSE OF CAT. 50

APPENDIX 5
REVERSE OF CAT. 51

APPENDIX 6
REVERSE OF CAT. 54

APPENDIX 7
REVERSE OF CAT. 55

APPENDIX 8
REVERSE OF CAT. 56

APPENDIX 9
REVERSE OF CAT. 66

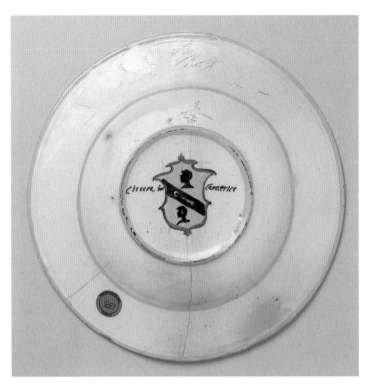

APPENDIX 10
REVERSE OF CAT. 72

CHECKLIST

CAT. 1

ALBARELLO WITH BRYONY FLOWERS

Spain, Valencia, probably Manises, c. 1430–70
Height 10½" (26.5 cm); width 5¼" (13.3 cm)
Philadelphia Museum of Art. Purchased with the
Thomas Skelton Harrison Fund, 1983-66-1
PROVENANCE: Arthur Sambon, Paris (his sale, Hirsch,
Mannheim, et al., Paris, May 25–28, 1914, lot 271);
Alphonse Kann, New York (his sale, American Art
Association, New York, January 6–8, 1927, lot 422);
Mrs. Walter C. Baker, New York (sale, Sotheby Parke-
Bernet, New York, May 30, 1981, lot 304); [Edward R.
Lubin Gallery, New York]
COMPARISONS: Mallet 1981a, no. 17; Ravanelli Guidotti
1992, fig. 16b
EXHIBITION: Philadelphia 1987

Lustered Spanish albarelli were imported into Italy for
use in pharmacies, but were also found in homes, as
Domenico Ghirlandaio's *Birth of Saint John the Baptist*
illustrates (see fig. 2). Treasured possessions, they also
appear in paintings like Hugo van der Goes's *Portinari
Altarpiece* (c. 1474–76), where an albarello serves as a
vase for flowers symbolic of the Virgin and Christ.
One late-fifteenth-century writer expressed his admiration for them, saying the "beauty of the golden
wares of Manises excels them all . . . so that the Pope
himself and the Cardinals and Princes of the world
all covet it, and are amazed that anything so excellent
and noble could be made from common clay."[1]

Drug containers without inscriptions would typically have had paper labels pasted onto them in order
to identify their contents on the apothecary's shelf.
Since they lacked ceramic lids, albarelli were covered
with a square of parchment, wrapped over the top
and tied below the rim.

CAT. 2

FOOTED JAR WITH COAT OF ARMS OF
THE PITTIGARDI FAMILY

Tuscany, probably Florence, second half of the
fifteenth century
Height 9⅞" (25 cm); width 8⅝" (21.9 cm)
The Howard I. and Janet H. Stein Collection
PROVENANCE: Possibly Johannes II, prince of
Liechtenstein, c. 1900; Emil Dreyfuß (Emile Dreyfus),
Switzerland (died 1966) (his sale, Galerie Fischer,
Lucerne, Switzerland, November 30, 1967, lot 75);
(sale, Sotheby Parke-Bernet, London, March 16, 1976,
lot 31); (sale, Sotheby's, London, October 17, 1988,
lot 253)

REFERENCES: Cora 1973, vol. 1, fig. 175c; Poole 1995,
p. 115 n. 24
COMPARISON: Cora 1973, vol. 2, fig. 240c

This vase belongs to a group Galeazzo Cora called
"Santa Fina" wares, after the hospital of the same
name in San Gimignano.[2] A set of jars found there
was decorated with the classic bryony pattern that was
derived from Hispano-Moresque sources, and transformed by Tuscan potters working around Florence
and Montelupo. Unique among the Santa Fina jars
for its shape, this footed vessel is very finely painted.
It is notable for the elegant garland surrounding the
coat of arms and the unusual ribbon motif around
the neck.[3] The arms, once said to be those of the
Gaddi family, can now be confirmed as belonging
to the Pittigardi family of Florence.[4]

CAT. 3

LARGE DISH WITH A LION

Deruta, first half of the sixteenth century
Height 3" (7.7 cm); diameter 16⅞" (41.6 cm)
The Howard I. and Janet H. Stein Collection
PROVENANCE: Raoul Tolentino, Rome (his sale,
American Art Association, New York, April 21, 1920,
lot 84a); private collector, San Francisco (sale,
Sotheby Parke-Bernet, New York, November 10, 1972,
lot 46)
COMPARISONS: Giacomotti 1974, cats. 560, 594; Bojani
1982, p. 97, fig. 8
THERMOLUMINESCENCE ANALYSIS: Oxford Authenti-
cation Ltd., Wantage, England, report dated May 9,
2000, estimated the last firing was between 350 and 550
years ago.

This large *piatto da pompa* was both made and lustered
in Deruta. It was common, however, for pieces painted
elsewhere to be shipped to the towns with specialized
luster workshops for the addition of the iridescent
tones.

Although lions have many allegorical associations
in the Renaissance, perhaps the most prominent of
them is with Saint Mark and, by association, the city
of Venice. Here the king of beasts strides confidently
through a stylized landscape in his role as ever-vigilant
protector. A Deruta plate with a Turkish rider (see
cat. 68) is linked thematically, and it may be that
such plates were intended to be hung in pairs. On a
sheet tacked to the wall in Piccolpasso's drawing of
painters, an allegorical poem describes Venice's role
in protecting Italy from the Ottoman incursion:

*Thou, great lion, whose valour resounds both where the day is
born and where it dies, thou, I say, on whom today peace depends,*

1. Quoted in Caiger-Smith 1973, p. 71.

2. See Poole 1995, pp. 113–14; and Wilson
1987b, cat. 24.

3. Cora (1973, vol. 2, fig. 240c) illustrates a
related piece that was altered by the removal
of its handles and neck.

4. Their heraldry is found in Rietstap 1887,
p. 446.

calm, for thou canst, the night and the day, guard thou and defend with thy holy hand afflicted Italy from all harm and despite and suffer not the impious foul monster to harm her and our native soil.[5]

CAT. 4
LARGE DISH WITH THE DESTRUCTION OF TROY

Venice, Francesco di Piero, 1546
Height 3" (7.6 cm); diameter 21¹⁄₁₆" (53.3 cm)
Philadelphia Museum of Art. Purchased with the John D. McIlhenny Fund, 1943-1-2
INSCRIPTIONS: (on reverse) *Roina d troia* [space] *1546 / fatto in venezia in chastello* (The destruction of Troy, 1546, made in Venice in Castello); (on reverse, incised) *af 23* [Andrew Fountaine collection mark]
PROVENANCE: Sir Andrew Fountaine I, Narford Hall, Norfolk, England (died 1753) (by descent, Fountaine collection sale, Christie's, London, June 17, 1884, lot 208); Lord Amherst of Hackney, Didlington Hall, Norfolk, England (his sale, Christie's, London, December 11, 1908, lot 14); [Lowengard, Paris]; William Salomon, New York (died 1919) (his sale, American Art Galleries, New York, April 4–7, 1923, lot 243); purchased, William Randolph Hearst, 1923 (his sale, Gimbel Brothers, New York, December 1942, lot 946-1)
REFERENCE: Wilson 1987a, pp. 186–87, figs. 7–8
EXHIBITIONS: New York 1923–38; Philadelphia 1944

Other images on maiolica that depict the destruction of Troy take full advantage of the textual description and show the city in flames. Here Francesco di Piero sets the scene in the countryside with only the barest indications of a city in the distance. Perhaps he was more captivated by Giulio Romano's battle scene in the print he had at hand than in an accurate rendering of the story. Francesco was one of those potters who moved freely between Venice and the Urbino area, working in both centers. As Timothy Wilson has noted, this mobility sometimes makes it difficult to distinguish between the products of the two areas.[6]

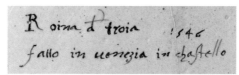

Cat. 4, reverse, detail of inscription

CAT. 5
GLOBULAR JAR WITH MALE HEADS

Venice, workshop of Maestro Domenego da Venezia, c. 1560–70
Height 15¼" (38.7 cm); width 12⅜" (31.5 cm)
The Howard I. and Janet H. Stein Collection
PROVENANCE: Private collector, New York (sale, Sotheby's, New York, May 20, 1988, lot 45)
COMPARISONS: Rasmussen 1984, cats. 159–60; Glaser 2000, cats. 212–13 (for foliage)

This large jar and related pieces from Maestro Domenego's active *bottega* illustrate the practice of artistic collaboration between painters within workshops. The foliate backgrounds were probably painted by one artisan, while another executed the more demanding portraits. Like most of Domenego's output, this piece is uninscribed, although there are a few examples from the 1560s in which he not only included his name, but the location of his workshop. Probably born in the 1520s, he seems to have died sometime between the last dated inscription in 1568 and 1574, after which a new register of deaths was established in his parish of San Polo.[7]

CAT. 6
CIRCULAR RELIEF OF THE ADORATION

Florence, circular relief attributed to Luca della Robbia, perhaps assisted by Andrea della Robbia; frame attributed to Andrea della Robbia, c. 1460–70s
Relief: diameter 41" (104.2 cm). Relief with frame: diameter 65¾" (169.5 cm)
Philadelphia Museum of Art. Purchased with the W. P. Wilstach Fund from the Edmond Foulc Collection, W1930-1-64a, b
INSCRIPTION: (on front, on banderole) *Gloria. in excelsis. De[o]* (Glory to God in the highest)
PROVENANCE: Palazzo Alberti, Florence, unconfirmed; [Stefano Bardini, Florence]; Edmond Foulc, Paris (died 1916); by descent, Foulc family; [Wildenstein & Co., Paris and New York, by 1927]
REFERENCE: Philadelphia 1995, p. 113
COMPARISONS: Gentilini 1998, pp. 137, 168–69, 174, 190–93, 214–15, 217
EXHIBITION: Philadelphia 1930

The tondo, or circular relief, we see today is the result of a collector's marrying of two works: the earlier central roundel attributed to Luca della Robbia, and the encircling frame of fruits and flowers probably by

5. Piccolpasso 1980, vol. 1, p. xxix.

6. Wilson 1987a, p. 187.

7. See Poole 1995, p. 415, regarding the inscriptions and possible locations of his workshop in Venice. The register of deaths in San Polo began in 1575. It is possible that he moved elsewhere in the city, but so far his name has not appeared in other documents after that year.

his nephew Andrea, a member of the workshop.[8] Edmond Foulc was not unjustified in joining them, since we know that such compositions were indeed turned out by the della Robbia *bottega*. The primarily blue and white palette of the narrative scene would have originally had a more brilliant effect, as it was highlighted with gold in the background and on the Virgin's hair and robe, many traces of which remain.[9]

CAT. 7
TWO-HANDLED PHARMACY JAR WITH DECORATIVE PALMETTES

Montelupo, c. 1500–1520
Height 11¹⁄₁₆" (28 cm); width 11⁹⁄₁₆" (29.3 cm)
Philadelphia Museum of Art. The Howard I. and Janet H. Stein Collection, in honor of the 125th Anniversary of the Museum, 1999-99-3
INSCRIPTIONS: (on body) *.DIE.SENA* (a laxative made from senna); (under each handle) *N*
PROVENANCE: Achille de Clemente, Florence; Whitney Warren, New York (died 1943) (his sale, Parke-Bernet Galleries, New York, October 7–9, 1943, lot 447); Dr. Robert Bak, New York, unconfirmed; Sydney N. Blumberg, Newtown, Connecticut (died 1972) (his sale, Sotheby Parke-Bernet, New York, April 26, 1973, lot 43)
REFERENCES: Conti 1971, cat. 147; Cora 1973, vol. 1, pp. 144–45, 471, no. 234C, vol. 2, no. M91
COMPARISON: Poole 1995, cat. 171

Excavations at Montelupo have unearthed numerous fragments related to this piece, undermining earlier attributions to Cafaggiolo. The *N* marks under the handles may be those of a maker or shop, although they have not yet been associated with a particular one.[10] The *palmetto persiano* motif had a long life, and appeared on similar shapes in the Sicilian ceramic center of Caltagirone later in the sixteenth century.[11]

Cat. 7, detail of *N* mark

CAT. 8
SPOUTED PHARMACY JAR WITH FOLIATE DECORATION

Montelupo, first quarter of the seventeenth century
Height 9¹⁵⁄₁₆" (25.2 cm); width (handle to spout) 7" (17.8 cm)
Philadelphia Museum of Art. The Howard I. and Janet H. Stein Collection, in honor of the 125th Anniversary of the Museum, 1998-176-13
INSCRIPTIONS: (on body) *AQ^A DI AC^ET^OSA* —(liquid made with vinegar); (on reverse, under handle) crescent mark
PROVENANCE: Sydney N. Blumberg, Newtown, Connecticut (died 1972) (his sale, Sotheby Parke-Bernet, New York, April 26, 1973, lot 50)
COMPARISONS: Pataky-Brestyánszky 1967, cat. 51; Conti 1971, cat. 146; Mallet 1981a, no. 82; Bojani et al. 1985, cat. 663; Berti 1986, cats. 102a, b, 104; Ravanelli Guidotti 1990, cats. 40, 42; Biscontini Ugolini 1997, cat. 12

Large numbers of similar pharmacy jars—some with lids—were produced in Montelupo in the late-sixteenth and early seventeenth centuries.[12] The marks on these Tuscan jars have, in some cases, eluded precise identification by scholars, even though the crescent moon was used frequently for almost two centuries from the late 1400s.[13] These marks were

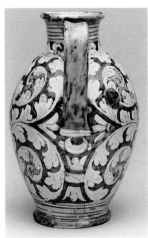

Cat. 8, reverse

sometimes connected to the hospitals that ordered them, like the crutch symbol of the hospital of Santa Maria Nuova in Florence. The compound held in this jar was a distillation made from the leaves and roots of the sorrel plant and was used by doctors for heart problems, jaundice, and eczema, among other things.[14]

CAT. 9
SPOUTED PHARMACY JAR WITH FOLIATE DECORATION

Montelupo, first quarter of the seventeenth century
Height 8¹¹⁄₁₆" (22.1 cm); width (handle to spout) 6¹¹⁄₁₆" (16.9 cm)

8. The tondo in the Musée National de la Renaissance, Ecouen, has a frame by Andrea della Robbia very similar to the one seen here; see Gentilini 1998, p. 214.

9. See Biavati 1987, for information about the gilding of della Robbia and other wares.

10. Examples that bear the letter *L* from the Fitzwilliam Museum, Cambridge, and elsewhere have not been identified either; see Poole 1995, cat. 171.

11. Donatone 1998, cat. 66.

12. Biscontini Ugolini 1997, p. 66.

13. See Cora 1973, vol. 2, cat. M262; Ravanelli Guidotti 1990, cat. 33; Bojani and Vossilla 1998, cats. 33–34.

14. Drey 1978, p. 182; and Platina 1998, p. 223.

Philadelphia Museum of Art. The Howard I. and Janet H. Stein Collection, in honor of the 125th Anniversary of the Museum, 1998-176-12

INSCRIPTIONS: (on body) *AQ^A DI MENTA* (liquid made with mint); (on reverse, under handle) *RA.* or *PA.*

PROVENANCE: Sydney N. Blumberg, Newtown, Connecticut (died 1972) (his sale, Sotheby Parke-Bernet, New York, April 26, 1973, lot 51)

COMPARISONS: (see cat. 8)

This spouted drug jar is similar to another in the Philadelphia collection (see cat. 8), but is inscribed below the handle on the reverse with the initials of another maker or owner, not yet identified. It was meant to hold a liquid distillation of mint leaves, a common compound sold by apothecaries. Platina noted that it was used to promote the appetite and

Cat. 9, reverse

the health of the heart, but was also effective against dog bites. Its popularity, however, may have been based on its traditional reputation as an aphrodisiac, or as Platina wrote, for "arousing dead passion on account of its inflammatory force."[15]

CAT. 10

ALBARELLO WITH BUST OF A MOOR

Deruta, 1501

Height 12 3/16" (31 cm); width 8 1/8" (20.6 cm)

The Howard I. and Janet H. Stein Collection

INSCRIPTIONS: (on body) *SEME.CoMUN^E* (common seed); *PAM*; (on reverse) *1501*

PROVENANCE: Philip, Lord Currie (his sale, Sangiorgi Gallery, Rome, April 30, 1903, lot 330); probably William Waldorf, 1st Viscount Astor, Hever Castle, Kent, England, to 1918–19; his son John Jacob V, 1st Baron Astor of Hever, Hever Castle (died 1971); his son Gavin, 2nd Baron Astor of Hever, Hever Castle (sale, Christie's, London, June 26, 1978, lot 175); [Cyril Humphris, London]; Dr. Arthur M. Sackler, New York (died 1987) (his sale, part 1, Christie's, New York, October 6, 1993, lot 7)

REFERENCES: Shinn 1982, cat. 12; Fiocco and Gherardi 1988, pp. 61, 70 n. 8, fig. 21; Fiocco and Gherardi 1994, cat. 54

COMPARISONS: Rackham (1940) 1977, no. 330; Giacomotti 1974, cat. 416; Wilson 1987b, cats. 38, 139, 150; Fiocco and Gherardi 1994, cats. 52–57; Bojani 2000, cat. 6

EXHIBITIONS: Washington, D.C. 1982–83, cat. 12; San Francisco 1986–88, no. 33

THERMOLUMINESCENCE ANALYSIS: The Research Laboratory for Archaeology and the History of Art, Oxford University, England, report dated December 1985, estimated the last firing was between 400 and 610 years ago.

The large group of apothecary jars to which this example belongs has been variously ascribed to Cafaggiolo, Faenza, and Siena over the years. Evidence from Deruta kiln sites, however, adds credibilty to the notion that the jars were made there, which would make them the earliest dated pieces from that center. The pharmacy connected with the monogram PAM or PAMQ, as it

Cat. 10, reverse

has also been read, remains unidentified.[16] The half-length grotesque figure above the label resembles one drawn by Piccolpasso, and was obviously a popular decorative convention used throughout the first half of the sixteenth century.[17]

CAT. 11

PLATE WITH HEADS AND A LANDSCAPE

Faenza, c. 1550

Height 1 5/8" (4.1 cm); diameter 9 13/16" (24.9 cm)

The Howard I. and Janet H. Stein Collection

INSCRIPTION: (on front, on banderole of portrait) *IVDITA* (Judith)

PROVENANCE: Thomas F. Flannery Jr., Chicago (died 1980) (sale, Sotheby Parke-Bernet, London, November 22, 1983, lot 178); [Cyril Humphris, London]; (Humphris sale, Sotheby's, New York, January 10, 1995, lot 35)

15. Platina 1998, p. 193.

16. See Fiocco and Gherardi 1988, pp. 59–63, 70 n. 8, for a list of other pieces in the series.

17. Piccolpasso 1980, vol. 2, p. 87.

COMPARISONS: Rackham (1940) 1977, no. 936; Giacomotti 1974, cat. 932

The female heads in the roundels, one of which is inscribed *Ivdita*—perhaps referring to the Old Testament heroine or to a patron or recipient—recall one drawn by Piccolpasso in the sample pages at the end of his treatise.[18] Although Piccolpasso describes that plate as typical of Urbino, these classically inspired busts appeared on maiolica from many pottery centers. Here the bust of Judith closely resembles the profile coin portraits of ancient empresses like Faustina, the wife of Antoninus Pius, whose image was circulated throughout the empire as an exemplar of female virtue.

Cat. 11, reverse

CAT. 12

SPOUTED PHARMACY JAR WITH MALE HEADS

Castelli, workshop of Orazio Pompei, c. 1540–50
Height 10%6" (27 cm); width (handle to spout) 9⅛" (23.1 cm)
The Howard I. and Janet H. Stein Collection
INSCRIPTION: (on body) *sy°.de.agresta* (syrup of grapes)
PROVENANCE: Sydney N. Blumberg, Newtown, Connecticut (died 1972) (his sale, Sotheby Parke-Bernet, New York, April 26, 1973, lot 42)
COMPARISONS: Baldisseri 1989, cats. 352–55; Ravanelli Guidotti 1990, cat. 110

Spouted containers like this one typically held syrupy liquids that were dispensed by pharmacists, spice-sellers, and hospitals. The *syropo de agresta* in this jar was a vinegarlike compound made from unripe grapes, intended as a general health tonic to support the immune system and ward off the plague.[19] A seventeenth-century apothecary treatise says it "strengthens the stomach, especially in pregnant women . . . is useful in cholerics, and for the warm intemperance of the

18. Piccolpasso 1980, vol. 2, p. 119.

19. Drey 1978, p. 183.

20. Donzelli 1686, p. 162; see also Platina 1998, p. 169.

21. Kremers and Urdang 1986, p. 28.

stomach, [and] it vehemently extinguishes bilious fevers and thirst. It is also useful against poisons."[20]

Cat. 12, side

CAT. 13

ALBARELLO WITH SAINT PETER

Sicily, Palermo, Andrea Pantaleo, 1613
Height 19½" (49.5 cm); width 12⅛" (30.8 cm)
Philadelphia Museum of Art. Gift of Mrs. John Wintersteen, 1965-149-2
INSCRIPTION: (on four tablets) *SPQP/1613; 1613/S.P.Q.P.; 1613; andria pa/ntaleo.f[ecit]* (Senatus Populusque Panormitanus, 1613, Andrea Pantaleo made this)
PROVENANCE: John D. McIlhenny, Parkgate, Philadelphia (died 1925); his daughter, Mrs. John Wintersteen, Philadelphia
COMPARISON: Ragona 1975, cat. 112

Sicily and Spain, both centers of Arabic culture from the ninth century, were the transit points through which Greco-Arabic medical knowledge arrived in the West.[21] The important medical establishments in Sicily acquired their pharmaceutical storage jars first from Spain, and then from mainland suppliers. It was only in the later sixteenth century that they began to support local workshops, which ultimately turned out great quantities of wares, often based on designs initiated elsewhere and less carefully executed. The dumbbell (*a rochetto*) shape of this albarello also appears in the ceramics of Venice (see cats. 77a,b), Urbino (see cats. 78a,b), Castel Durante, and Rome.

Cat. 13, reverse, detail of inscription

CAT. 14

GLOBULAR JAR WITH SAINT EUSTACE AND A YOUNG MAN

Sicily, Burgio, 1701
Height 14³⁄₁₆" (36.1 cm); width 10⅛" (25.7 cm)
Philadelphia Museum of Art. The Howard I. and
Janet H. Stein Collection, in honor of the 125th
Anniversary of the Museum, 1998-176-1
INSCRIPTION: (on body, on side in a trophy) *1701*
PROVENANCE: [B. Manheim, New Orleans, November
12, 1970]
COMPARISONS: Ragona 1975, figs. 49, 69; Biscontini
Ugolini 1997, cat. 70

Idealized images of men and women were quite prev-
alent on pharmacy jars, especially in Venice. The
export of those wares had an enormous impact on
Sicilian artisans, who took up the theme along with
others, such as figures of saints or putti, and the fruit
and foliage that Piccolpasso said was a specialty of
the lagoon city. The young man depicted on one side
of this vase wears a brimmed cap, and could be an
actual portrait rather than a generic figure. On the
other side, Saint Eustace is shown with a deer. As the
story goes, the saint had been a Roman general under
Emperor Trajan (98–117). While hunting one day,
Eustace had a vision of a stag with a luminous

crucifix between its antlers, and was converted to Christianity. Later, he was martyred for his beliefs. Although Saint Eustace appears often in Renaissance paintings, it now seems that he may be a ficti- tious figure based on folktales.

Cat. 14, reverse

CAT. 15

GLOBULAR JAR WITH HEAD OF A SOLDIER

Sicily, Caltagirone, eighteenth century
Height 12¹¹⁄₁₆" (32.2 cm); width 10⁷⁄₁₆" (26.5 cm)
Philadelphia Museum of Art. The Howard I. and
Janet H. Stein Collection, in honor of the 125th

Anniversary of the Museum, 1998-176-3
PROVENANCE: (Sale, O. Rundle Gilbert & Son,
Garrison-on-the-Hudson, New York, December 4,
1970, lot C 210)
COMPARISON: Baligand 1986, cat. 97

Sicilian jars were frequently decorated with the heads
of men wearing various types of parade helmets. This
one is embellished with a floral pattern that could
indicate either decoration engraved into the metal or
a textile covering over it.

CAT. 16

DISH WITH THE DEATH OF HIPPOLYTUS

Urbino, Nicola di Gabriele Sbraghe (Nicola da
Urbino), c. 1524
Height 1⅝" (4.1 cm); diameter 10¾" (27.4 cm)
Philadelphia Museum of Art. Purchased with the
John D. McIlhenny Fund, 1943-1-4
INSCRIPTIONS: (on front) coat of arms of Isabella
d'Este; two personal emblems, one with the motto
NEC SPE/NEC METV (Neither hope nor fear)
PROVENANCE: Countess Lauredana Gatterburg-
Morosini, Venice (her sale, Sambon and Mannheim,
Palazzo Morosini, Venice, May 17, 1894, lot 177);
[Charles Mannheim, Paris, 1894 to 1901]; purchased,
J. Pierpont Morgan, London and New York, 1901
(died 1913); [Duveen Brothers, New York]; purchased,
William Randolph Hearst, May 22, 1922 (his sale,
Gimbel Brothers, New York, December 1942, lot
947-2)
REFERENCES: Mallet 1981b; Brody 1997
COMPARISONS: Mallet 1981b, cats. 131–38; Brody 1997,
p. 51
EXHIBITIONS: New York 1914–16; New York 1923–38;
Philadelphia 1944

For many years, Nicola da Urbino was thought to
be Nicola Pellipario of Castel Durante, the father
of maiolica workshop owner Guido Durantino. The
once-shadowy figure has now been identified as
Nicola di Gabriele Sbraghe, who was not related to
Guido, but worked alongside him in Urbino and
sometimes painted in his studio.²² Nicola seldom
signed wares and never wrote identifying captions as
became common later. The Philadelphia plate has
been interpreted as an episode from the *Metamorphoses*
about the young beauty Chione, who was killed by
Diana for her excessive pride—a story that is told in
the 1497 edition of Ovid, but not illustrated. However, it seems more likely that the androgynous figure

22. Mallet 1987, pp. 284–85; Berardi 1984,
p. 17 n. 9.

at right represents the dead Hippolytus, whose tale is recounted twice in that edition of the *Metamorphoses* and illustrated with a woodcut that Nicola chose not to use here. While the figures cannot be connected to a print in the 1497 volume, the reclining youth recalls a figure in the 1505 edition that depicts Peleus and Thetis.[23] Another plate in the Este-Gonzaga service that treats the Hippolytus legend shows earlier moments in the story.[24]

At left, Isabella d'Este's coat of arms appears, and on the trees hang shields with some of her *imprese*. The batch of paper lottery tickets probably symbolizes Isabella's acceptance of reversals of fortune. The intertwined letters *Y* and *S* represent the first letters of her name, and the Latin motto *Nec spe nec metv* translates as "Neither hope nor fear."

CAT. 17

PLATE WITH ARETHUSA FLEEING ALPHEUS

Urbino, Francesco Xanto Avelli da Rovigo, 1531; lustered in Gubbio, workshop of Maestro Giorgio Andreoli
Height 1⅝" (4.1 cm); diameter 11¹³⁄₁₆" (30 cm)
Philadelphia Museum of Art. Purchased with the John D. McIlhenny Fund, 1943-1-3
INSCRIPTION: (on reverse; see appendix 1) *fra[ncesco]: xa[n]to, Auelli, R:pi[n]: / 1531 [in luster] / Alpheo ama[n]te, & Aretusa i[n] / fuga. / fabula y* (Francesco Xanto Avelli, from Rovigo, painted this 1531, Alpheus, the lover, and Arethusa in flight, y)
PROVENANCE: [Arnold Seligmann & Rey, New York]; purchased, William Randolph Hearst, October 1, 1930 (his sale, Gimbel Brothers, New York, December 1942, lot 362-10)
COMPARISONS: Lessmann 1979, cat. 142; Rasmussen 1989, cat. 83

In this episode from the *Metamorphoses*, the river god Alpheus came to life and pursued the nymph Arethusa, while she was bathing. The goddess Diana intervened and saved Arethusa by covering her in a cloud and transforming her into a brook that flowed underground and out to sea.

Xanto painted this story at least three times, inventing a different composition for each with figures taken from prints. In this case, he created a continuous narrative with Alpheus as the river, reclining at right, and then again in the center, pursuing the nymph. In Ovid's telling of the tale, Arethusa is nude, but Xanto uses a clothed figure from Giovanni Jacopo Caraglio's *Contest between the Muses and Pierides* after Rosso Fiorentino.[25] The central figure of Alpheus

comes from the *Battle of the Romans and Carthaginians* by Marco Dente da Ravenna after Raphael or Giulio Romano.[26] Both prints were favorites of Xanto, and he used them repeatedly, probably having traced figures that he particularly liked onto other pieces of paper. Ironically, he filled the background here with the imposing buildings of a city, even though the story took place in the sylvan countryside. Either he made a conscious decision to depart from the details given in Ovid's text, or had not read it thoroughly himself.

Xanto describes the story in his inscription, but does not provide a textual source or an indication that he was working in Urbino, where he had probably been since the 1520s.[27] The date, added in luster, confirms that both plates by him in the Philadelphia collection were made in 1531 (see cat. 50). Here the painter signed the plate with the *y* mark that he sometimes used in place of his name.[28]

CAT. 18

PLATE WITH APOLLO AND DAPHNE

Urbino, workshop of Guido Durantino, 1535
Height 1¼" (3.2 cm); diameter 10⁵⁄₁₆" (26.2 cm)
The Howard I. and Janet H. Stein Collection
INSCRIPTION: *fabula di phe/bo & Dafne / nella Botega d[i] M°/ Guido durantino / In urbino / 1535* (Fable of Phoebus Apollo and Daphne, made in the workshop of Maestro Guido Durantino, in Urbino, 1535)
PROVENANCE: George Ralph Ormsby-Gore, 3rd Baron Harlech (sale, Christie's, London, July 5, 1909, lot 52); Lady Godfrey Fawcett (sale, Sotheby's, London, June 18, 1946, lot 62); Robert Strauss, London (his sale, Christie's, London, June 21, 1976, lot 48)
REFERENCE: Mallet 1987, p. 297, cat. 27, figs. 5, 5a

In 1535 Guido Durantino received a prestigious commission for a service for the French soldier and diplomat Anne de Montmorency.[29] At least two painters were involved in that project, probably because of its magnitude.[30] In that same year, yet another artist from Guido's workshop painted the Apollo and Daphne plate, although it was inscribed by the same person who marked the Montmorency pieces as well as another work in this collection (see cat. 73).[31] The anonymous painter of this plate may have originally relied on graphic sources for some of his ideas, but in the process he combined and transformed them. The reclining river god Peneus is loosely based on a figure in Marcantonio Raimondi's *Judgment of Paris* after Raphael, and Apollo and Daphne both bear a strong resemblance to a figure at the right in another Marcantonio-Raphael print, *The Massacre of the Innocents*.[32] One can easily imagine a cache of prints

23. See Poole 1995, p. 306, fig. 14.

24. Rackham (1940) 1977, pp. 183–84 n. 547.

25. Bartsch, vol. 28 (15), no. 53 (89).

26. Bartsch, vol. 27 (14), no. 420 (316).

27. See Triolo 1996, p. 94 n. 26. Xanto is documented as having worked in Urbino between 1530 and 1542.

28. See Poole 1995, pp. 322–23.

29. Mallet (1987) lists nineteen surviving pieces from the Montmorency service.

30. Shared commissions occurred in other documented cases. For example, in a 1528 letter to Eleanora Gonzaga, duchess of Urbino, Giovanmaria della Porta encourages her to have a set of maiolica made as a gift for the pope: "Above all, the set should be made as quickly as possibly, so as to sieze the moment, and to speed the work even more one should give the commission to two master potters who should work on it at the same time"; cited in Spallanzani 1994, p. 129.

31. See Mallet 1987, p. 289, where he suggests a possible connection to the Milan Marsyas Painter, with whom this painter shares some characteristics. Another such link could be drawn between the maker of this plate and a painter influenced by Nicola da Urbino; see Fuchs 1993, cat. 153.

32. Shoemaker 1981, cats. 43, 26.

circulating in a shop, and being used in different ways by various painters.

Cat. 18, reverse with inscription

CAT. 19

SNAKE-HANDLED VASE WITH SCENES FROM *AMADIS DE GAULA*

Urbino, workshop of Guido Durantino or Orazio Fontana, c. 1560–70
Height 19¼" (48.8 cm); width 12⅞" (32.8 cm)
Philadelphia Museum of Art. Purchased with the Bloomfield Moore Fund and with other Museum funds, 1944-15-1a
INSCRIPTIONS: (on side one, in cartouche) *Despues de heridos en muchas / partes se reconoçen Amadis y / Galaor / .LXII.* (After multiple wounds, Amadis and Galaor recognize each other. LXII.); (on side two, in cartouche) *Corre Amadis tras Gasinan q [quein] / le havia hurtado una Donzella / q [quein] el hauia defendida de otro / Cauallero. / .LXIII.* (Amadis pursues Gasinan, who had stolen from him a maiden, whom he had defended from another knight. LXIII.)
PROVENANCE: Baron Adolphe de Rothschild, Paris (died 1900); Baron Maurice de Rothschild, Paris; [Duveen Brothers, Paris, by 1914–15]; purchased, William Salomon, New York, January 22, 1920 (his sale, American Art Galleries, New York, April 4–7, 1923, lot 245); Clarence H. Mackay, Harbor Hill, Roslyn, New York; [French & Co., New York]
REFERENCE: Olivar 1953, pp. 119–22, pl. 35
COMPARISON: Wilson 1987b, cat. 90
EXHIBITION: Philadelphia 1992
THERMOLUMINESCENCE ANALYSIS: Oxford Authentication Ltd., Wantage, England, report dated February 23, 1998, estimated the last firing was between 250 and 450 years ago.

Garci Rodriguez de Montalvo's chivalric romance tells the story of the knight Amadis de Gaula, his valiant feats, and his love for Oriane, daughter of the king of England. This popular epic was translated into many languages, including Italian in 1546, and provided inspiration for artists throughout Europe.

Two episodes are described in the Spanish inscriptions: The brothers Amadis and Galaor recognize each other in battle, and Amadis pursues Gasinan as he kidnaps a maiden. The second scene takes place at night, an extremely unusual occurrence in maiolica and in painting.[33] The numbers in the inscriptions on related works (the highest being 166) hint at the size of the service to which this vase belongs, perhaps fifty to one hundred pieces, since multiple scenes sometimes appear on a single work.[34] Although there are many woodcuts in the illustrated editions of the book, none has been found that relates to the set. The painters must have been supplied with drawings, as was the case with the service made for King Philip II of Spain around the same time.[35] At some point, a contemporary or slightly later hexagonal writing box with related grotesques was adapted to serve as a base for the vase (see cat. 90).

Cat. 19, details of inscriptions

CAT. 20

DISH WITH AENEAS AND ANCHISES

Urbino, Patanazzi workshop, c. 1580s
Height 2⅟₁₆" (5.3 cm); diameter 10⅗₁₆" (26.2 cm)
Philadelphia Museum of Art. The Howard I. and Janet H. Stein Collection, in honor of the 125th Anniversary of the Museum, 1999-99-6
INSCRIPTIONS: (on front) coat of arms of Cardinal Anton Maria Salviati; (on reverse) *Mostra suoi / desciendenzi Anchise / Al figllio / nel VI libro de / Eneida* (Anchises showing Aeneas his descendants, from book 6 of the *Aeneid*)
PROVENANCE: [Leo Kaplan Antiques, New York, 1975]
COMPARISONS: Mancini della Chiara 1979, cat. 318; Watson 1986, cat. 64

In this episode of the *Aeneid*, Aeneas visits the underworld and encounters the shade of his father, Anchises. His father points out a cohort of young

33. Another night scene from this same set is in the British Museum, London; see Wilson 1987b, cat. 90.

34. Remaining from this service, in addition to the present piece, are two large oval dishes, a vase, and three small plates; see Wilson 1987b, pp. 63–64.

35. In 1560 Duke Guidobaldo II of Urbino commissioned Taddeo Zuccaro to provide drawings for that service based on the life of Julius Caesar. The drawings, or copies of them, remained in circulation and continued to be used for maiolica until at least 1585; see Poole 1995, pp. 378–80; and Wilson 1996a, chapter 7.

soldiers and says, "Come, I shall now explain to you your whole destiny."[36] He identifies the youths as Aeneas's descendants, the future of the Roman race, and names each of the first five: Silius, Procas, Capys, Numitor, and Aeneas Silvius. Interestingly, the painter has shown a group of five young men, the first one holding a spear, precisely as in the text. Although no graphic source has been identified for this plate, it seems likely that there must have been one, or that the artist was given detailed instructions about the subject.

Cat. 20, reverse with inscription

CAT. 21

DISH WITH SCIPIO AND HIS TROOPS

Urbino, Francesco Durantino, probably in the workshop of Guido di Merlino, c. 1544–45
Height 1¹⁵⁄₁₆" (5 cm); diameter 10¾" (27.2 cm)
The Howard I. and Janet H. Stein Collection
INSCRIPTION: (on reverse; see appendix 2) *Come esendo in canusio / alcuni gintilomini disposti / d[i] abandonare la republica d[i] Roma / Scipione giovino co[n]la spada in / mano li constrinse agiarare [sic a giurare] d[i] / no[n] aba[n]donarla. / vedi titolivio / a libro deca[n] tertia: secundo [sic terzo] / a capitulo lxiiii [sic liiii]* (How it was in Canusium that some nobles were prepared to abandon the republic of Rome. Young Scipio, with sword in hand forced them to swear not to abandon it. See Titus Livius, third decade of the book: second [sic third] part, chapter 64 [sic 54])
PROVENANCE: [Alexander Barker, London]; (Barker sale, Christie's, London, June 8, 1874, lot 121); Sir Francis W. Cook, Baronet, Doughty House, Richmond Hill, Surrey, England (died 1901); his son Wyndham F. Cook, London (died 1905); his son, Humphrey W. Cook (his sale, Christie's, London, July 7–10, 1925, lot 3); [purchased, Durlacher Brothers, London, 1925]; (sale, Sotheby's, London, June 6, 1989, lot 6)
REFERENCES: Drey 1991, p. 54; Mallet 1996, pp. 45–61, figs. 19–20

COMPARISONS: Lutteman 1981, p. 97, cat. 6; Rasmussen 1984, pp. 184–86, cat. 127; Wilson 1987b, cat. 217; Drey 1991, figs. 12–13

Nine pieces remain from a service featuring episodes from the life of Scipio, although nothing is known of the patron who commissioned them. All are by the same painter, are inscribed in the same hand, and give precise references to Livy's *History of Rome*, a central text for Renaissance humanists. One dish in the Staatliches Museum, Schwerin, is marked as having been made by Francesco Durantino in the workshop of Guido di Merlino in 1544.

No prints have yet been found relating to the Philadelphia plate, but that would not be unusual for Francesco, who was more independent-minded than most of his contemporaries. The image here follows Livy's text quite closely: Wearing a winged helmet and raising his sword over the heads of the Roman nobility, as they sat in consultation, Scipio said, "I solemnly swear that even as I myself shall not desert the republic of the Roman people, so likewise shall I suffer no other Roman citizen to do so. . . . I call on you and the others who are present to swear after these terms and if any refuse to swear, let him know that against him this sword is drawn."[37] The importance of this dramatic episode resonated with humanists, who looked back at antiquity and took as their models historical figures like Scipio, a paragon of civic virtue.

John Mallet makes a still-controversial argument that two pieces in the Corcoran Gallery of Art, Washington, D.C., and the Museum für Kunsthandwerk, Frankfurt, marked with the Greek letters *phi* and *delta*, are early works of Francesco Durantino. As evidence, Mallet cites the close resemblance of a prominent sculpture on the Corcoran plate and this figure of Scipio.[38] In addition, Timothy Wilson has posited that ideas for the architecture in the maiolica painter's compositions may have sprung from his acquaintance with the work of the Urbino painter and architect Girolamo Genga (1476–1551).[39] Here the prominent round building recalls Bramante's Tempietto in Rome, probably known to Francesco through prints, drawings, or descriptions.

CAT. 22

PLATE WITH THE DEATH OF CASSANDRA

Pesaro, Sforza di Marcantonio, 1551
Height 1" (2.6 cm); diameter 8¾" (22.1 cm)
The Howard I. and Janet H. Stein Collection
INSCRIPTION: (on reverse) *Hor vedi & gisto . e . / [s?]empia clitennestra / 1551* (Take note [?] Aegisthus and the foolish, destructive [?] Clytemnestra, 1551)

36. Virgil 1962, p. 170.

37. Livy 1982, vol. 5, p. 375.

38. Mallet 1996, p. 57; see also Watson 1986, pp. 121–23.

39. Wilson 2001; see also Wilson 1991b. A 1528 letter from Giovanmaria della Porta to Duchess Eleanora Gonzaga refers to Genga, saying that he was apparently in charge of selecting, or perhaps helping to design maiolica for Pope Clement VII Medici ("altri piatti come parerà al Giengha nostro"); see Spallanzani 1994, p. 129.

PROVENANCE: (Sale, Sotheby Parke-Bernet, New York, May 30, 1975, lot 79)
REFERENCE: Lessmann 1979, cat. 465 (as art market)
COMPARISONS: Biscontini Ugolini 1979, pl. 4; Lessmann 1979, cat. 466; Bernardi 1980, cat. 34; Ravanelli Guidotti 1985, cat. 81

The inscription identifies the story as that of Clytemnestra, who in the absence of her husband King Agamemnon takes his cousin Aegisthus as a lover. After the king's return with his captured concubine Cassandra, the lovers murder them both. Clytemnestra's son Orestes later avenges his father's death by killing his mother and Aegisthus. The image appears to represent not the death of Clytemnestra, however, but that of Cassandra.[40] Aegisthus prepares to kill her as she gestures offstage toward Agamemnon. The co-conspirator Clytemnestra stands at right, uninvolved physically, but approving of the deed. The setting of the plate is nearly identical to another by Sforza in the Herzog Anton Ulrich-Museum, Braunschweig, that depicts a similar tale of love and murder from Herodotus. In both, the painter sets the action in a deep, perspectively accurate space. Here Aegisthus stands in the center, his gesture of unsheathing his sword cleverly following the arc of the plate's well.

Cat. 22, reverse with inscription

CAT. 23
LIDDED GLOBULAR JAR WITH GROTESQUES

Castel Durante, workshop of Maestro Simone da Colonello, 1562
Height (with lid) 16⁷⁄₁₆" (41.7 cm); width 10⅝" (26.9 cm)
The Howard I. and Janet H. Stein Collection
INSCRIPTIONS: (on front) unidentified coat of arms with a rampant lion facing right; the letters *G* and *F* at left and right; (on reverse) *15.62*
PROVENANCE: [Alexander Barker, London]; Sir Francis W. Cook, Baronet, Doughty House,

Richmond Hill, Surrey, England, c. 1870 (died 1901); his son Wyndham F. Cook, London (died 1905); his son, Humphrey W. Cook (his sale, Christie's, London, July 7–10, 1925, lot 87); [Rosenbach Company, New York and Philadelphia, 1925, acquired through Albert Amor, London]; The Philip H. & A.S.W. Rosenbach Foundation, Philadelphia, 1954 (sale, Sotheby Parke-Bernet, New York, March 2, 1974, lot 45)
COMPARISONS: Giacomotti 1974, cat. 971; Wilson 1989b, cat. 22; Ravanelli Guidotti 1990, cat. 117
EXHIBITION: London 1862, cat. 5,289

CAT. 24
LIDDED GLOBULAR JAR WITH GROTESQUES

Castel Durante, workshop of Maestro Simone da Colonello, c. 1562
Height (with lid) 16⁷⁄₁₆" (40.8 cm); width 10¹³⁄₁₆" (27.4 cm)
The Howard I. and Janet H. Stein Collection
INSCRIPTIONS: (see cat. 23 for coat of arms)
PROVENANCE: [Alexander Barker, London]; Sir Francis W. Cook, Baronet, Doughty House, Richmond Hill, Surrey, England, c. 1870 (died 1901); his son Wyndham F. Cook, London (died 1905); his son, Humphrey W. Cook (his sale, Christie's, London, July 7–10, 1925, lot 88); [Rosenbach Company, New York and Philadelphia, 1925, acquired through Albert Amor, London]; The Philip H. & A.S.W. Rosenbach Foundation, Philadelphia, 1954 (sale, Sotheby Parke-Bernet, New York, March 2, 1974, lot 46)
COMPARISONS: (see cat. 23)
EXHIBITION: London 1862, cat. 5,290
NOTE: The lid shown on cat. 24 is original, the other on cat. 23 is a contemporary replacement in a slightly different style, but also with trophies.

It has been suggested that these large containers were made for display in an apothecary rather than for actual use. Their robust decorative motifs are generally referred to as dark-ground grotesques, larger and more volumetric than the more delicate white-ground grotesques for which Urbino was famous. This may suggest that the artisan was looking more at the work of "painters on walls," as Piccolpasso called them, rather than that of his fellow maiolica craftsmen.[41] A related vase in the Fanfani collection (in the Museo Internazionale delle Ceramiche, Faenza), by the same

40. The same subject is treated by a Venetian maiolica painter; see Ravanelli Guidotti 1985, cat. 81. Although Ravanelli Guidotti suggests that the female figure at left is based on Caraglio's rendering of Roxanne in the *Marriage of Alexander and Roxanne* (Bartsch, vol. 28 [15], no. 62 [95]) the close comparison of these two plates may indicate that both were copied from a single print, yet to be identified. The inscription on the Venetian plate is identical to that on the Philadelphia piece as well.

41. Piccolpasso 1980, vol. 2, p. 101.

painter and obviously from the same set, provides additional documentation.[42] Along with the heraldic emblem and initials, there are four painted plaquettes on that vase that attest to its manufacture in the Castel Durante shop of "Maestro Simono" on the fifth of June 1562.[43] Similar in style are a group of earlier albarelli, probably from the same workshop, one marked made "in Castel Durante, 7 miles from Urbino" and dated 1555.[44]

CAT. 25
PLATE WITH JOSEPH AND POTIPHAR'S WIFE

France, probably Lyon or Nevers, last quarter of the sixteenth century
Height 1⅛" (2.8 cm); diameter 8⅞" (22.6 cm)
Philadelphia Museum of Art. Purchased with the John D. McIlhenny Fund, 1965-116-2
INSCRIPTION: (on reverse) *GENESE. XXXIX / joseph.*
PROVENANCE: (Sale, Sotheby's, London, November 20, 1962, lot 110); [purchased, Peel and Humphris, London, 1962]; [Cyril Humphris, London]
COMPARISON: Norman 1976, cat. C164
EXHIBITION: Philadelphia 1987

Although the Philadelphia plate and another in the Wallace Collection, London, are based on the same Bernard Salomon print of Joseph and Potiphar's wife, the two painters took liberties with the composition, adding certain elements and subtracting others.[45] Each, however, reproduces the elaborate bed with a *padiglione* (canopy) that is designed to hang from the ceiling (see cat. 22).[46] In Salomon's print, the top of the *padiglione* is cut off at the upper edge and does not show its means of suspension. The painter of this plate, not understanding the structure thoroughly, depicts the canopy as floating in midair.

Cat. 25, reverse with inscription

CAT. 26
VASE WITH CLASSICAL ORNAMENT

Florence, workshop of Giovanni della Robbia, c. 1515–20
Height 11⁄16" (28.1 cm); width 9⅜" (24.8 cm)
Philadelphia Museum of Art. Purchased from the Edmond Foulc Collection with Museum funds, 1930-1-66b
PROVENANCE: Baron Achille Seillière, Château de Mello, Paris (his sale, Chevallier, Château de Mello, Paris, May 5–10, 1890, lot 18 or 19); Emile Gavet, Paris (his sale, Galerie Georges Petit, Paris, May 31–June 9, 1897, no. 202 or 203); Edmond Foulc, Paris (died 1916); by descent, Foulc family; [Wildenstein & Co., Paris and New York, by 1927]
REFERENCES: Cora 1973, vol. 1, p. 188, A–V, nos. 31–34; Gentilini 1998, p. 277
COMPARISON: Gentilini 1998, cat. III.19a, b
EXHIBITION: Philadelphia 1930
THERMOLUMINESCENCE ANALYSIS: Oxford Authentication Ltd., Wantage, England, has analyzed two samples from this vase and two from its mate (1930-1-66a [not illustrated]), August 2000 and July 2001, with ambiguous results. At this time the age of the vases remains unclear. Both vases have been broken and repaired in the past. The visible gilding is ground or powdered gold leaf. In many areas this gilding was applied over glaze losses and restoration paint. At this time no evidence for earlier gilding has been found.

The della Robbia workshop produced a wide range of items, not only vases and large altarpieces, but also tabernacles, architectural elements, heraldic shields, mirrors, and small sculptures. Other contemporary Florentine artisanal products, most notably textiles and metalwork, had an influence on their output as well. Luca della Robbia had, in fact, been trained as a goldsmith, and the family had its origins in the textile industry; their name originated from the term for a particular red fabric dye. One can imagine stylistic influences flowing back and forth among different media, as artisans looked to each other, to common print sources, and to earlier works of art for inspiration. Countless ornament engravings of the period included candelabra patterns with images of metal repoussé wares similar to the della Robbia clay vessels.[47] In addition, similar vase shapes appear regularly in sixteenth-century Italian textiles.

42. Several views and the inscriptions are illustrated in Ravanelli Guidotti 1990, pp. 211–13.

43. Ibid., p. 211.

44. Giacomotti 1974, cat. 794; see also Wilson 1996a, cat. 123.

45. Norman 1976, p. 318, fig. 37. The Salomon woodcut illustrates the biblical story of Joseph and Potiphar's wife from Genesis, chapter 39, and appears in the illustrated Bibles of Claude Paradin (editions from 1553 onward) and Damiano Maraffi (1554).

46. See Thornton 1991, pp. 126–27.

47. Thornton (1991, fig. 356) illustrates three from a set of twelve such engravings by Giovanni Pietro da Birago from c. 1505–15.

CAT. 27

ALBARELLO WITH FLORAL PATTERN

Montelupo, mid-sixteenth century

Height 8¹⁵⁄₁₆" (22.8 cm); width 5" (12.7 cm)

Philadelphia Museum of Art. The Howard I. and Janet H. Stein Collection, in honor of the 125th Anniversary of the Museum, 1998-176-9

INSCRIPTION: (on body) *DIA PRVN¹S . S.* (Dia prunis s[emplice/simplex]; a compound made from plums or prunes, used to aid digestion)

PROVENANCE: Sydney N. Blumberg, Newtown, Connecticut (died 1972) (his sale, Sotheby Parke-Bernet, New York, April 26, 1973, lot 37)

COMPARISONS: Rackham (1940) 1977, no. 356; Ravanelli Guidotti 1990, pp. 70–71, cat. 35

A very large service, or perhaps more than one, was turned out in this pattern in Montelupo. It included tall and short albarelli, as well as ovoid two-handled jars. The *graffito* technique used in these wares also appears in earlier examples from this center, influenced perhaps by Moorish design, according to Carmen Ravanelli Guidotti.[48] An unusual sixteenth-century Neapolitan albarello also depicts a two-handled vase that is meant to represent silver rather than gold, as seen here.[49]

CAT. 28

PHARMACY BOTTLE WITH TROPHIES

Emilia-Romagna, probably Faenza, c. 1520–30

Height 8¾" (22.2 cm); width 5¹³⁄₁₆" (14.7 cm)

Philadelphia Museum of Art. The Howard I. and Janet H. Stein Collection, in honor of the 125th Anniversary of the Museum, 1998-176-11

INSCRIPTION: (on body) *.a . de . absenti* (an aqueous distillation of absinthe, made from the leaves and tops of wormwood)

PROVENANCE: Max Bondi, Rome; Sydney N. Blumberg, Newtown, Connecticut (died 1972) (his sale, Sotheby Parke-Bernet, New York, April 26, 1973, lot 39)

COMPARISONS: Ravanelli Guidotti 1987, cats. 35–36; Ravanelli Guidotti 1990, cat. 151

A blue and white flask similarly shaped but lacking a label, sits on the shelf in Antonello da Messina's painting of Saint Jerome in his study.[50] Like the albarello, this form persisted throughout the century and appeared in many centers from Venice to Sicily, probably because of its straightforward functionality. Small bottles of this type would have held liquid medical preparations such as the absinthe solution contained in this example. Platina asserts that the bitter herb was used from Roman times on, and that "it makes the stomach stronger and opens the fibers of the liver."[51] A 1795 list of drugs, the "Ricettario Senese," indicates that it was also useful in promoting menses in women and killing worms.[52] More recently alcoholic beverages made with absinthe have been outlawed for their dangerous and addictive qualities.

CAT. 29

PLATE WITH A WALKING BOY AND TROPHIES

The Marches, probably Castel Durante, 1562

Height 1⅛" (3.5 cm); diameter 9⅜" (23.8 cm)

Philadelphia Museum of Art. The Dr. Francis. W. Lewis Collection, 1903-24

INSCRIPTION: (on shield, on border at left) *1562*

PROVENANCE: Dr. Francis W. Lewis, Philadelphia (died 1902)

COMPARISONS: Hausmann 1972, cats. 184–87; Giacomotti 1974, cat. 761

Plates with trophy borders and varied central motifs were made in Castel Durante from at least the 1520s into the second half of the century. Although he seems to lack wings, the boy may represent one of Venus's cupids, or he might be linked to the custom of giving pregnant women images of baby boys to help them visualize the birth of a healthy male heir.[53] Naked boys also appear frequently on the backs of *deschi da parto* and on ceramic sets made specifically for women after childbirth (see also cats. 60a,b, 82, 83a,b).

CAT. 30

SHORT ALBARELLO

Pesaro or Faenza, c. 1480–1500

Height 7½" (19 cm); width 6" (15.2 cm)

Philadelphia Museum of Art. The Howard I. and Janet H. Stein Collection, in honor of the 125th Anniversary of the Museum, 1999-99-12

INSCRIPTION: (on body) *diapri[n]dio* (liquid compound including sugar)

PROVENANCE: Dr. Alfred Pringsheim, Munich, by 1914 (his sale, Sotheby's, London, July 20, 1939, lot 310); purchased, Bernard Rackham, London, 1934 (died 1964); by descent; (sale, Sotheby's, London, June 5, 1990, lot 173)

REFERENCE: Pringsheim 1994, vol. 1, pl. 17, no. 28

48. The term means that white patterns were made by scratching through the blue pigment.

49. Donatone 1998, pp. 52–53, cat. 5.

50. Thornton 1991, fig. 210.

51. Platina 1998, p. 209.

52. Biscontini Ugolini 1997, p. 168.

53. See Musacchio 1999, pp. 126–34.

COMPARISONS: Rackham (1940) 1977, no. 213; Ravanelli Guidotti 1990, cat. 93; Glaser 2000, cat. 124

Although this work and other related pieces have traditionally been attributed to Faenza, potsherds in a similar style have recently been excavated in Pesaro. It is possible, therefore, that the wares were made there rather than imported.[54] The inscription may refer to what Rudolf Drey describes as *penidiae* or *penidium*, a "confection made by melting sugar over a low heat, cooling and drawing out the product into strands, something akin to barley sugar."[55]

CAT. 31
SHORT ALBARELLO

Faenza or Venice, first quarter of the sixteenth century
Height 7¼" (18.4 cm); width 5" (12.7 cm)
Philadelphia Museum of Art. The Howard I. and Janet H. Stein Collection, in honor of the 125th Anniversary of the Museum, 1998-176-10
INSCRIPTION: (on body) *.benedeti[?]a./[?].*
PROVENANCE: Oscar Bondy, Vienna; Sydney N. Blumberg, Newtown, Connecticut (died 1972) (his sale, Sotheby Parke-Bernet, New York, April 26, 1973, lot 38)
COMPARISONS: Rackham (1940) 1977, no. 201; Pataky-Brestyánszky 1967, cat. 22; Hausmann 1972, cat. 118; Gardelli 1999, cat. 1; Glaser 2000, cats. 16–17

The *alla porcellana* leaves and flowers of this albarello are accompanied by a Gothic-style inscription so embellished by looping tendrils that it is difficult to decipher. Orthographic errors were common because maiolica painters were not always literate and could easily confuse a drug name from a list supplied by the pharmacist. The inscription here may refer to *unguentum benedictum*, an ointment made from mercury, white lead, frankincense, and lard,[56] or to an electuary made from an herbal plant that was used to treat gout or kidney ailments.[57]

CAT. 32
BOWL

The Marches, probably Pesaro, c. 1500
Height 2⅜" (6 cm); diameter 6½" (16.5 cm)
Philadelphia Museum of Art. The Howard I. and Janet H. Stein Collection, in honor of the 125th Anniversary of the Museum, 1998-176-18
PROVENANCE: [Charles Mannheim, Paris]; purchased, J. Pierpont Morgan, London and New York, 1901

(died 1913); Mortimer L. Schiff, New York, by 1917 (his sale, Parke-Bernet Galleries, New York, May 4, 1946, lot 6); David Goldman, New York (sale, Sotheby Parke-Bernet, New York, May 22, 1979, lot 345)
COMPARISONS: Rackham (1940) 1977, no. 220; Bojani 2000, cat. 128
EXHIBITIONS: New York 1914–16; New York 1917–19; New York 1937–41

This rare bowl can be compared to a set of tiles at the Victoria & Albert Museum, London, as well as to another related group of tiles illustrated in the recent collection catalogue of the Museo Artistico Industriale di Roma. All have been traditionally ascribed to Faenza, although recent scholarship supports a reassignment of many such wares to the coastal town of Pesaro.[58]

Cat. 32, interior of bowl

CAT. 33
PLATE WITH A PUTTO

Gubbio, workshop of Maestro Giorgio Andreoli, c. 1525
Height ⁹⁄₁₆" (1.5 cm); diameter 9⅝" (24.5 cm)
The Howard I. and Janet H. Stein Collection
INSCRIPTIONS: (on reverse; see appendix 3) five flourishes in luster
PROVENANCE: [Alessandro Castellani, Rome, by 1876]; (Castellani sale, Pillet, Paris, May 27–29, 1878, lot 81); Adalbert Freiherr von Lanna, Prague (his sale, Lepke, Berlin, March 21–28, 1911, lot 577); Walter von Pannwitz, Heemstede, Netherlands, unconfirmed; [Cyril Humphris, London]; Dr. Arthur M. Sackler, New York (died 1987) (his sale, part 1, Christie's, New York, October 6, 1993, lot 14)
REFERENCES: Shinn 1982, cat. 35
COMPARISONS: Rackham (1940) 1977, nos. 686–97; Giacomotti 1974, cats. 671–83; Bojani 1982, cat. 39; Watson 1986, cats. 36, 39
EXHIBITIONS: Philadelphia, Memorial Hall, *Italian*

54. Berardi 1984, figs. 28, 31–32.

55. Drey 1978, p. 221.

56. Drey 1978, p. 189.

57. Giorgio Melichio, *Avvertimenti nelle composizioni de' medicamenti per uso della spetieria* . . . . (Venice, 1660), p. 59; cited in Ravanelli Guidotti 1990, p. 165.

58. See Bojani 2000, pp. 72, 133–35, cat. 128; see also Claudio Giardini, ed., *Immagini dai piatelletti* (Fano: Grafo 5, 1996).

Maiolica, section 2, 1876, cat. 73; New York, The Metropolitan Museum of Art, *Castellani Collection: Maiolica, & c.*, 1877, cat. 81; Washington, D.C. 1982–83, cat. 35; San Francisco 1986–88, no. 51

THERMOLUMINESCENCE ANALYSIS: The Research Laboratory for Archaeology and the History of Art, Oxford University, England, report dated September 1985, estimated the last firing was between 400 and 620 years ago.

The drumming putto on this plate wears a coral necklace designed to ward off evil and disease—a tradition that was observed in the Renaissance, as it is today. Paintings of the Christ child often include coral amulets or necklaces as well. Documents show that in 1472 Nicolo Strozzi had a necklace made of ninety pieces of coral for Carlo, his six-month-old son. A particularly fine Ferrarese birth tray in the Museum of Fine Arts, Boston, shows a putto well-protected by his apotropaic coral necklace and bracelets.[59] It may be that a *tondino* such as this one was intended as a gift for an expectant or new mother.

CAT. 34
TWO-HANDLED JAR

Deruta, first half of the sixteenth century
Height 8⁵⁄₁₆" (22.8 cm); width (at handles) 7⁷⁄₈" (20 cm)
Philadelphia Museum of Art. The Howard I. and Janet H. Stein Collection, in honor of the 125th Anniversary of the Museum, 1999-99-10
PROVENANCE: Maurice Chabrières-Arlès, Paris (died 1897); Chabrières-Arlès collection, Paris; [purchased, Duveen Brothers, New York, 1916]; Carl W. Hamilton, New York; George R. Hann, Treetops, Sewickley Heights, Pennsylvania (his sale, part 2, Christie's, Treetops, Sewickley Heights, May 19, 1980, lot 95)
COMPARISONS: Giacomotti 1974, cats. 631–37; Fiocco and Gherardi 1988, p. 89, fig. 45; Rasmussen 1989, pp. 80–82, cat. 46; Fiocco and Gherardi 1994, cat. 127
EXHIBITIONS: Montclair 1925–26, cat. 41; Buffalo 1926–28, cat. 72; Newark 1929

Two-handled jars of this sort, originally with covers, survive in ample number and are said to have functioned as confectionary jars at banquets and weddings.[60] They were produced in great quantity in the sixteenth century, both in lustered and polychrome versions. Sometimes the jars bear portraits of young women or men or illustrate such love symbols as pierced hearts or clasped hands.[61]

CAT. 35
FOOTED DISH WITH THE LETTER *N*

Deruta, c. 1500–1530
Height 3⁹⁄₁₆" (9.1 cm); diameter 9⁷⁄₈" (25 cm)
Philadelphia Museum of Art. Purchased with the Elizabeth Wandell Smith Fund from the Edmond Foulc Collection, 1930-1-70
INSCRIPTION: (in center) *N*
PROVENANCE: Edmond Foulc, Paris (died 1916); by descent, Foulc family; [Wildenstein & Co., Paris and New York, by 1927]
COMPARISONS: Giacomotti 1974, cats. 546, 549; Lessmann 1979, cat. 89; Poole 1995, cat. 40
EXHIBITION: Philadelphia 1930

Cat. 35, interior of dish

CAT. 36
FOOTED DISH WITH THE NAME *DIANA*

Deruta, c. 1500–1530
Height 3⁷⁄₈" (9.9 cm); diameter 8¹³⁄₁₆" (22.3 cm)
Philadelphia Museum of Art. Purchased with the Elizabeth Wandell Smith Fund from the Edmond Foulc Collection, 1930-1-71
INSCRIPTION: (in center) *DIANA. BE* (Beautiful Diana)
PROVENANCE: Edmond Foulc, Paris (died 1916); by descent, Foulc family; [Wildenstein & Co., Paris and New York, by 1927]

Cat. 36, interior of dish

59. Musacchio 1999, pp. 131–33, fig. 129.

60. See Poole 1995, p. 173. For a related jar with its original cover, see Rackham (1940) 1977, no. 472.

61. Ibid., no. 460.

The motifs of pointed rays alternating with stemmed buds or flowers, visible on both of these footed dishes, appear in Deruta wares from the early sixteenth century onward.

CAT. 37

MOLDED EWER BASIN WITH JUDITH HOLDING THE HEAD OF HOLOFERNES

Deruta, c. 1530–40
Height 1⁵⁄₁₆" (3.3 cm); diameter 15⅜" (39.1 cm)
Philadelphia Museum of Art. Purchased with the Elizabeth Wandell Smith Fund, 1943-1-1
PROVENANCE: J. Pierpont Morgan, London and New York (died 1913); [Duveen Brothers, New York]; purchased, William Randolph Hearst, May 22, 1922 (his sale, Gimbel Brothers, New York, December 1942, lot 947-10)
REFERENCES: Rackham (1940) 1977, no. 489; Rasmussen 1989, p. 72; Poole 1995, p. 194 (in all three as "formerly in the J. Pierpont Morgan collection")
COMPARISONS: Rackham (1940) 1977, no. 489; Giacomotti 1974, cats. 663–64; Kube 1976, cat. 42; Rasmussen 1989, cats. 42–44; Fiocco and Gherardi 1994, cat. 156
EXHIBITIONS: New York 1914–16; New York 1923–38; Philadelphia 1944

This basin and two others in the Robert Lehman Collection at the Metropolitan Museum of Art, were once together in J. Pierpont Morgan's collection in New York. The central motifs on all three were executed by the same unnamed artist, who took special care on the Philadelphia piece, painting the raised central rim to look as though it were made of gold or silver. Four others from the same mold are in the Victoria & Albert Museum, the Louvre, and the Hermitage in Leningrad. The central figure here recalls Marcantonio Raimondi's well-known engraving of Dido.⁶² Scholars have traditionally associated this

Cat. 37, reverse

group with the polychrome tiles of 1524 from the church of San Francesco in Deruta. One of the Louvre examples, however, is dated 1546, providing an outside date range for the group's production.⁶³

CAT. 38

PLATE WITH A VIOL PLAYER

Deruta, late-sixteenth or early seventeenth century
Height 2¼" (5.7 cm); diameter 16½" (42 cm)
Philadelphia Museum of Art. The Sallie Crozer Hilprecht Collection, F1929-6-63
PROVENANCE: Herman V. Hilprecht, Philadelphia (died 1925); his wife, Sallie Crozer Hilprecht, Philadelphia (died 1929); City of Philadelphia, Commissioners of Fairmount Park
COMPARISONS: Fiocco and Gherardi 1990, cats. 96, 189; Fiocco and Gherardi 1994, cats. 186, 189; Salsi 2000, cat. 64

Allegorical figures and musicians were common motifs on *compendiario* wares, like this one and another in the Musée de la Renaissance, Ecouen, that has a similar border garland and figure of Saint Cecilia. However, the Ecouen dish is molded, decorated with gold luster, and dated 1587 in luster on the reverse. The viol player of the Philadelphia plate echoes the figural style of the Deruta workshop of Giacomo Mancini, known as El Frate.⁶⁴ Although here the handling is looser, which suggests a date in the late-sixteenth or early seventeenth century.

CAT. 39

LARGE PLATE WITH MARCUS CURTIUS

Urbino, c. 1560–70
Height 1¹⁵⁄₁₆" (4.9 cm); diameter 17¹⁄₁₆" (43.3 cm)
Philadelphia Museum of Art. Purchased with the Elizabeth Wandell Smith Fund, 1951-107-3
INSCRIPTION: (on reverse) *Marco Curtio Romano.* (Marcus Curtius, Roman)
PROVENANCE: E. C. Converse, Conyers Manor, Greenwich, Connecticut (his sale, American Art Galleries, New York, February 9, 1926, lot 81); [Dikran G. Kelekian, New York]
COMPARISON: Mancini della Chiara 1979, cat. 229

The story of Marcus Curtius, taken from Livy's *History of Rome*,⁶⁵ was one of several legends devised to explain the origin of the *Lacus Curtius*, a pond in the middle of the ancient forum. There a chasm had opened in the ground, which the oracle said could be filled only by casting into it something of the greatest

62. Bartsch, vol. 26 (14), no. 87 (153); see also Landau and Parshall 1994, fig. 112.

63. Rasmussen 1989, p. 72. For the San Francesco tiles, see Fiocco and Gherardi 1988, pls. 21–22.

64. See Fiocco and Gherardi 1994, cat. 183.

65. Livy 1982, book 7, chapter 6.

value. The brave young soldier Marcus Curtius interpreted this as a demand for a sacrifice of one of the city's finest youths and, in devotion, leapt with his horse into the abyss.

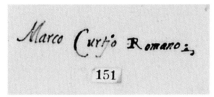

Cat. 39, reverse, detail of inscription

CAT. 40
BROAD-RIMMED DISH WITH TRITON

Urbino, possibly Patanazzi workshop, c. 1579 or later
Height 2¼" (5.7 cm); diameter 12⅝" (32.1 cm)
Philadelphia Museum of Art. The Howard I. and Janet H. Stein Collection, in honor of the 125th Anniversary of the Museum, 1999-99-1
PROVENANCE: Maurice Chabrières-Arlès, Paris (died 1897); Chabrières-Arlès collection, Paris; [purchased, Duveen Brothers, New York, 1916]; purchased, Thomas Barlow Walker, Minneapolis, July 15, 1920; T. B. Walker Foundation, Minneapolis (Foundation sale, Sotheby Parke-Bernet, New York, September 27, 1972, lot 388)
COMPARISONS: Curnow 1992, cat. 82; Poole 1995, cat. 429

The central figure, formerly described as Neptune, is more likely one of the youthful tritons who served as escorts for the sea god and his wife, Amphitrite. Marine deities often appeared on maiolica from the Fontana and Patanazzi workshops, on the reverses of platters or plates (see appendix 6), or on the interiors of basins and wine coolers meant to resemble more expensive silver examples.[66] Raphael's 1513 fresco *Galatea* in the Villa Farnesina, Rome (and related prints after his works), surely helped to inspire them.[67] The author of this wild-haired triton also painted the medallion on a plate in the Fitzwilliam Museum,

Cat. 40, reverse

Cambridge.[68] However, the grotesques on the Philadelphia dish, painted by another artisan, resemble those on some pieces of the *Ardet Aeternum* service made in the Patanazzi workshop to celebrate the marriage of Duke Alfonso II d'Este of Ferrara and Margherita Gonzaga in 1579.[69]

CAT. 41
SHORT ALBARELLO WITH SAINT CATHERINE AND A MALE HEAD

Venice, circle of Maestro Domenego da Venezia, second half of the sixteenth century
Height 6⅜" (16.1 cm); width 5³⁄₁₆ (13.1 cm)
Philadelphia Museum of Art. The Howard I. and Janet H. Stein Collection, in honor of the 125th Anniversary of the Museum, 1998-176-4
INSCRIPTION: (under foot, incised) >24
PROVENANCE: (Sale, O. Rundle Gilbert & Son, Garrison-on-the-Hudson, New York, December 4, 1970, lot C217)
COMPARISON: Salsi 2000, cat. 297

Saint Catherine of Alexandria (died early fourth century) can be identified by her palm of martyrdom and the wheel on which she was tortured. A learned woman from a noble family, who effected many conversions among those who heard her speak, Catherine was condemned to death by the Roman emperor Maximinus (died 313). However, the wheel on which she was to be broken (usually shown with spikes) was blown apart at her touch. She was subsequently beheaded and buried at Mount Sinai, where a monastery was established in her name.

CAT. 42
ALBARELLO WITH SAINT LUCY

Venice, possibly workshop of Maestro Domenego da Venezia, third quarter of the sixteenth century
Height 10⅛" (25.8 cm); width 5⁵⁄₁₆" (13.5 cm)
Philadelphia Museum of Art. The Howard I. and Janet H. Stein Collection, in honor of the 125th Anniversary of the Museum, 1998-176-15
PROVENANCE: Sydney N. Blumberg, Newtown, Connecticut (died 1972) (his sale, Sotheby Parke-Bernet, New York, April 26, 1973, lot 59)
COMPARISONS: Mazzucato 1990, p. 69; Gardelli 1999, pp. 54–55, cat. 24; Glaser 2000, pp. 254–58, cats. 219–25

Quickly painted figures of saints and other religious figures were among the most popular subjects for

66. For a maiolica basin at the Musée National de Cèramique, Sèvres, see Mallet 1996, p. 50, fig. 9.

67. Adams 2001, fig. 16.22.

68. See Poole 1995, cat. 429.

69. See Wilson 1987b, cats. 206, 242; and Ladis 1989, pp. 96–97.

Venetian and Sicilian albarelli. In this depiction, Saint Lucy holds a footed dish with her traditional symbol of two eyes. One legend relates that a young man was so smitten by the beauty of her eyes that he could find no rest, and to end his obsession, she tore them out. A more likely story is that Lucy was martyred for her faith, stabbed in the neck by Roman soldiers. The painted line on her neck probably represents the wound. Her name, Lucy, signified light, and the eyes may have become her symbol because of that association. It is possible that this albarello was intended to contain preparations for eye diseases. Since none of the Venetian foliate jars has painted labels, or even an appropriate space for a pasted paper label, one wonders whether some of these figures may have provided symbolic indications of their contents.

CAT. 43
PLATE WITH THE DEATH OF NARCISSUS

Urbino or possibly Pesaro, c. 1530–40
Height 1⅛" (2.7 cm); diameter 11¹⁄₁₆" (28 cm)
Philadelphia Museum of Art. The Howard I. and Janet H. Stein Collection, in honor of the 125th Anniversary of the Museum, 1998-176-7
INSCRIPTION: (on reverse, with lines above and below) *La morte De narciso* (The death of Narcissus)
PROVENANCE: Baron Adolphe de Rothschild, Paris (died 1900); Baron Maurice de Rothschild, Paris; [Duveen Brothers, Paris, by 1914–15]; purchased, Norton Simon Foundation, Los Angeles, 1964 (Foundation sale, Parke-Bernet Galleries, New York, May 7–8, 1971, lot 89)

Here the story of Narcissus is told in a continuous narrative: At left, the protagonist kneels over the pool, entranced by his own reflection; at right, Narcissus lies dead, attended by Cupid and a group of grieving nymphs. Echo is probably represented by the mourning figure in yellow with outstretched arms, a type seen also in a Narcissus plate by Francesco Durantino.[70]

Cat. 43, reverse with inscription

70. Alverà Bortolotto 1988, p. 55, cat. 12.

CAT. 44
LOW-FOOTED DISH WITH NARCISSUS AND ECHO

Urbino, possibly Francesco Durantino, c. 1545
Height 2⅜" (6 cm); diameter 8¹⁵⁄₁₆" (22.6 cm)
The Howard I. and Janet H. Stein Collection
PROVENANCE: Private collector, San Francisco (sale, Sotheby Parke-Bernet, New York, November 10, 1972, lot 48)
COMPARISONS: Rackham (1940) 1977, no. 858; Lessmann 1979, cats. 163–65, 171; Alverà Bortolotto 1988, cat. 14

This work was very likely painted by Francesco Durantino or by someone working alongside him. The treatment of the trees and the figures of nymphs in the center are characteristic of his individualistic style. But the lack of any inscription on the reverse is unusual for this painter, as is the straight, uninterrupted horizon line in the distance.

CAT. 45
PLATE WITH THE BIRTH OF ADONIS

Urbino, circle of Francesco Durantino, 1540–45
Height 1½" (3.8 cm); diameter 12¹⁄₁₆" (30.7 cm)
The Howard I. and Janet H. Stein Collection
INSCRIPTION: (on reverse) *Nasimento d[i] adonis* (Birth of Adonis)
PROVENANCE: Baron Adolphe de Rothschild, Paris (died 1900); Baron Maurice de Rothschild, Paris; [Duveen Brothers, Paris, by 1914–15]; purchased, Thomas Barlow Walker, Minneapolis, July 15, 1920; T. B. Walker Foundation, Minneapolis (Foundation sale, Sotheby Parke-Bernet, New York, September 27, 1972, lot 386)
COMPARISONS: Lessmann 1979, cats. 163–65

This plate resembles others of the same theme made by Francesco Durantino in Guido di Merlino's workshop in the 1540s. However, the painting seems less

Cat. 45, reverse with inscription

strong than some of Francesco's autograph works, and may have been produced by a younger artisan emulating his style. Timothy Wilson has suggested that Francesco was influenced by Girolamo Genga, who was responsible for the reconstruction and decoration of the della Rovere Villa Imperiale (c. 1529–32) near Pesaro. Genga's frescoes there of caryatids in a landscape are close enough to Francesco's composition of Myrrha to indicate that the maiolica painter may have known them first hand. Wilson makes a compelling argument that Genga himself may have made designs for maiolica, noting that he had close ties with other painters, like Battista Franco, who certainly did so.[71]

CAT. 46

PLATE WITH LETO, ARTEMIS AND APOLLO

Urbino or Pesaro, c. 1540–50
Height 1¹⁵⁄₁₆" (5 cm); diameter 12¹⁄₁₆" (30.7 cm)
The Howard I. and Janet H. Stein Collection
INSCRIPTION: (on reverse) *Ladea alatona / che fe conuertie. / inranochie* — (The goddess Latona who had them changed into frogs)
PROVENANCE: [Purchased, Rosenbach Company, New York and Philadelphia, possibly 1926]; The Philip H. & A.S.W. Rosenbach Foundation, Philadelphia, 1954 (sale, Sotheby Parke-Bernet, New York, March 2, 1974, lot 39)
COMPARISONS: Norman 1976, cat. C121; Fuchs 1993, cat. 119; Wilson 1993, pp. 230–31

Nicola da Urbino used the same subject in the Este-Gonzaga service of the 1520s where the peasants' hands have already changed into webbed appendages. Another version of the scene on a 1542 plate in the Fitzwilliam Museum is particularly imaginative, and shows figures immersed in a pool with their legs visible through the transparent water, as is also seen here.[72]

Cat. 46, reverse with inscription

CAT. 47

PLATE WITH PLUTO ABDUCTING PERSEPHONE

Urbino, circle of Nicola da Urbino, c. 1525–35
Height 1³⁄₁₆" (3.3 cm); diameter 12³⁄₈" (31.4 cm)
The Howard I. and Janet H. Stein Collection
PROVENANCE: Robert Stayner Holford, Westonbirt, Gloucestershire, and Dorchester House, London (died 1892); his son, Lt. Col. Sir George Lindsay Holford, Westonbirt and Dorchester House (died 1926) (his sale, Christie's, London, July 13–14, 1927, lot 27); [Rosenbach Company, New York and Philadelphia, 1927]; The Philip H. & A.S.W. Rosenbach Foundation, Philadelphia, 1954 (sale, Sotheby Parke-Bernet, New York, March 2, 1994, lot 37)
REFERENCE: Rackham (1940) 1977, no. 622
EXHIBITION: London 1921–22, p. 40, no. 7

The unknown painter of this plate was clearly influenced by Nicola da Urbino and his followers, and was probably working in their circle. The interpretation of the subject as Pluto and Persephone might be questioned because the male figure appears younger than the usual depictions of Pluto. However, the interpretation of it as Paris abducting Helen of Troy is much less convincing. That abduction is referred to only briefly in the *Iliad* and *Odyssey* and not described except in such later interpretations as Guido delle Colonne's *Historia distructionis troiae*, a thirteenth-century romance based on the classical texts. As it appears on maiolica, the scene is usually based on Marcantonio Raimondi's print after a lost Raphael painting that shows Helen being pulled onto a boat during a chaotic battle near a prominent temple of Venus.[73]

CAT. 48

LOW-FOOTED DISH WITH THE DEATH OF ACHILLES

Urbino, workshop of Guido Durantino, c. 1535
Height 1⅞" (4.8 cm); diameter 10⁹⁄₁₆" (26.8 cm)
The Howard I. and Janet H. Stein Collection
INSCRIPTION: (on reverse) *Il troiano Paris / ociso co[n] inganno / da Achille* (The Trojan Paris killed with deception, or being ambushed, by Achilles)
PROVENANCE: [Kate Foster Ltd., London, October 1974]
COMPARISON: Wilson 1993, pp. 219–22

This plate and another in the National Gallery of Art, Washington, D.C., with the Montmorency arms were probably painted by the same anonymous artist

71. See Wilson 1991b, pp. 157–62.

72. For the Fitzwilliam piece, see Poole 1995, cat. 401. See Rasmussen 1989, p. 251, no. 67.17, for a plate in the Museo Miniscalchi-Erizzo, Verona.

73. The Raphael painting was based on delle Colonne's text. For Marcantonio's print, see Bartsch, vol. 26 (14), no. 209 (170).

in Guido Durantino's workshop. Although the subjects differ in the two pieces, the same print from the 1497 edition of Ovid was used as the model for the kneeling youths.[74] The painter was one of at least two who shared the commission for the large Montmorency service made in 1535, which suggests a similar date for this piece. The inscription on the Philadelphia example—in a hand different from that of the National Gallery plate—confuses the subject: The author wrote that Paris is shown being killed by Achilles, when in fact the reverse is depicted.

Cat. 48, reverse with inscription

CAT. 49

FOOTED DISH WITH THE SUICIDE OF AJAX

Venice, workshop of Maestro Domenego da Venezia, 1569
Height 2½" (6.3 cm); diameter 10%6" (26.8 cm)
The Howard I. and Janet H. Stein Collection
INSCRIPTION: (on reverse) *La morte di achile. / 1569. setembrie* (The death of Achilles. 1569 September); [erroneous]
PROVENANCE: [Spanish Art Gallery]; [purchased, P. W. French & Co., New York, 1914]; purchased, Thomas Barlow Walker, Minneapolis, July 2, 1925; T. B. Walker Foundation, Minneapolis (Foundation sale, Sotheby Parke-Bernet, New York, September 27, 1972, lot 390)

Cat. 49, reverse with inscription

COMPARISONS: Lessmann 1979, nos. 731–34; Poole 1995, cats. 451–52

This scene painted in the *bottega* of Maestro Domenego da Venezia uses figures that appear and reappear in other plates from the same shop, perhaps taken from a print source not yet identified. This plate is unusual in that it is so precisely dated—September 1569—and the handwriting is quite similar to that of the master himself, who signed and dated a piece in the Herzog Anton Ulrich-Museum. The inscriber erroneously marked the plate with the legend "the death of Achilles," but it actually depicts the suicide of Ajax.

CAT. 50

PLATE WITH ERIPHYLE AND AMPHIARAUS

Urbino, Francesco Xanto Avelli da Rovigo, 1531; lustered in Gubbio, workshop of Maestro Giorgio Andreoli
Height 1¹¹⁄₁₆" (4.3 cm); diameter 11½" (29.3 cm)
The Howard I. and Janet H. Stein Collection
INSCRIPTION: (on reverse; see appendix 4) *.1531. L'avara & rea [?] moglier / di Amphiarao. / . historia . / fra[n]cesco Xanto, Avelli / da Rovigo, i[n] urbino / pi[n]se .* (1531. The avaricious wife of Amphiaraus. History. Francesco Xanto Avelli from Rovigo, painted this in Urbino); (on reverse, on rim) luster flourishes; (on reverse, on central inscription) luster flourishes over the artist's signature
PROVENANCE: Jakob Goldschmidt (his sale, Sotheby's, London, July 5, 1957, lot 59); John Scott-Taggart, Beaconsfield, Buckinghamshire, England (sale, Sotheby's, London, March 17, 1961, lot 7); [purchased, Alfred Spero, London, 1961]; Robert Strauss, London (his sale, Christie's, London, June 21, 1976, lot 45)
REFERENCES: Morley-Fletcher and McIlroy 1984, p. 74, no. 2; Watson 1986, pp. 130–31; Wilson 1987b, p. 58
COMPARISONS: Ballardini 1930, vol. 2, figs. 22–23, 88; Watson 1986, cat. 51

After having been painted by Xanto in 1531, this plate was sent to Gubbio for lustering in Maestro Giorgio Andreoli's *bottega*. The customary gold and red metallic foliate ornaments were added to the reverse, along with two prominent volutes that obscure Xanto's signature. This action, which is seen elsewhere on works by Xanto, has been interpreted as a vindictive effacement of his name by Maestro Giorgio, following the dispute between workshop owners and employees (including Xanto) that took place around the same time.

74. See Wilson 1993, pp. 219–22.

The deep colors on the front are characteristic of Xanto's works in the late 1520s. Giovanni Jacopo Caraglio's *Contest between the Muses and the Pierides* (after Rosso Fiorentino) served as the source for the two figures at left, who have been rather humorously transformed from nude nymphs into armed warriors. Amphiaraus is modeled after a figure in Marcantonio Raimondi's print *Isaac Blessing Jacob*,[75] and Eriphyle after a woman in the same printmaker's *Martyrdom of Saint Lawrence*.[76]

CAT. 51

PLATE WITH HANNIBAL CROSSING THE RIVER EBRO

Urbino, workshop of Guido Durantino, c. 1540–60
Height 2⅛" (5.4 cm); diameter 12¾" (32.4 cm)
The Howard I. and Janet H. Stein Collection
INSCRIPTION: (on reverse; see appendix 5) *Annibale passato il fiume Ibero, / Piu Terre acquista a l'Africano / impero.* (Hannibal crosses the River Ebro to acquire more territory for the African empire)
PROVENANCE: Robert Stayner Holford, Westonbirt, Gloucestershire, and Dorchester House, London (died 1892); his son, Lt. Col. Sir George Lindsay Holford, Westonbirt and Dorchester House (died 1926) (his sale, Christie's, London, July 13–14, 1927, lot 25); [purchased, Alfred Spero, London, 1927]; [Cyril Humphris, London]; Dr. Arthur M. Sackler, New York (died 1987) (his sale, part 2, Christie's, New York, June 1, 1994, lot 30)
REFERENCE: Shinn 1982, cat. 58; Drey 1991, p. 53 (as Sackler collection)
COMPARISON: Drey 1991, pp. 53–54, 58–60
EXHIBITIONS: London 1921–22, p. 40, no. 3; Washington, D.C. 1982–83, cat. 58; San Francisco 1986–88, no. 82
THERMOLUMINESCENCE ANALYSIS: The Research Laboratory for Archaeology and the History of Art, Oxford University, England, report dated September 1985, estimated the last firing was between 300 and 480 years ago.

At least thirty-three examples remain from this large and impressive service, all with rhyming couplets on the reverse of the plates that describe the scenes on the front.[77] A few also bear numbers, the last of which is 144, suggesting that the set might have been enormous. Shallow bowls, elaborate trilobe basins, and plates with rims comprise the variations in shape. On this plate and four others there is a circular area painted in a paler blue than the rest of the sky, where

a coat of arms was meant to be depicted. Rudolf Drey posited that the mysterious patron of both the Hannibal and Scipio services (see cat. 21) was a member of the ducal family of Urbino because of their iconographical complexity and evident cost. Expenses would have included not only the manufacture of the pottery itself, but also the hiring of a poet to compose the rhyming couplets.

CATS. 52, 53

PAIR OF SNAKE-HANDLED VASES WITH BIBLICAL SCENES

Urbino, workshop of Orazio Fontana, c. 1560–71
Cat. 52: height 21¼" (54 cm); width 11³⁄₁₆" (30 cm). Cat. 53: height 21⅝" (55 cm); width 12⅝" (32 cm)
Philadelphia Museum of Art. Purchased with the Bloomfield Moore Fund and other Museum funds, 1944-15-2, 1944-15-3
INSCRIPTIONS: (on one side of triangular base; cat. 52): *FATTE IN VRBINO IN BO / TEGA.D.ORATIO FONTAN^A.* (Made in Urbino in the workshop of Orazio Fontana); (on one side of triangular base; cat. 53): *FATTE.IN VRBINO IN BTEGA / .D. ORATIO FONTANA.* (Made in Urbino in the workshop of Orazio Fontana)
PROVENANCE: Charles Stein, Paris (his sale, Galerie Georges Petit, Paris, May 10–14, 1886, lot 83); Baron Adolphe de Rothschild, Paris (died 1900); Baron Maurice de Rothschild, Paris; [Duveen Brothers, Paris, by 1914–15]; purchased, William Salomon, New York, January 29 (?), 1920 (his sale, American Art Galleries, New York, April 4–7, 1923, lots 246–47); Clarence H. Mackay, Harbor Hill, Roslyn, New York; [French and Co., New York]
REFERENCES: Bojani 1988, pp. 135–36 (photographs confused); Tait 1991, pp. 272, 274–75, figs. 8a, b; Philadelphia 1995, p. 122; Poole 1995, p. 398; Poke 2001, pp. 334–35, 342–43
COMPARISONS: Conti 1971, cats. 6, 12; Poke 2001, figs. 1–2
EXHIBITION: Philadelphia 1992
THERMOLUMINESCENCE ANALYSIS: Oxford Authentication Ltd., Wantage, England, report dated February 23, 1998, estimated the last firing was between 250 and 450 years ago. Daybreak Archaeometric Laboratory Services, Guilford, Connecticut, report dated June 18, 1998, estimated the last firing was 500 (+/- 100) years ago. The samples were taken from the triangular bases.

75. Bartsch, vol. 26 (14), no. 6-I (7).

76. Bartsch, vol. 26 (14), no. 104-I (89).

77. This story was taken from Livy 1982, book 21, chapter 23.

Although they clearly belong together and were undoubtedly made in the same workshop, these vases were painted by different artisans; the quality of the grotesques and the narrative scenes on cat. 53 surpasses that of its mate. The elaborate ceramics of this period from the Fontana workshops are indebted to the more costly metalwares documented in drawings and prints by Francesco Salviati, Enea Vico, and others.[78] In addition, for the grotesque decoration seen here, painters in the Fontana workshops used prints as models, notably a set by the French designer, architect, and engraver Jacques Androuet I Ducerceau that was published in two editions (1550 and 1562).[79]

The full-bodied vases teeter on proportionally small bases. Too cumbersome to actually use, they were meant only for decoration and were probably displayed on a credenza or sideboard in the dining room of a prosperous patron. Biblical scenes are unapologetically set into a decidedly profane context filled with cavorting chimeras, nudes, and other fantastic grotesques based on Roman wall painting. The subjects in the medallions resemble prints in the numerous illustrated Bibles and represent stories including the building of the Tower of Babel and Solomon's temple, although not all the scenes have been securely identified. The subsidiary medallions contain miniature images styled after ancient cameos, gems, and coins—all favorite items of Renaissance collectors.

Cat. 52, detail of inscription

Cat. 53, detail of inscription

CAT. 54
PLATE WITH THE QUEEN OF SHEBA BEFORE KING SOLOMON[80]

Probably France, Lyon or Nevers, late-sixteenth century
Height (at knob) 2½" (5.7 cm); diameter 11" (27.9 cm)
Philadelphia Museum of Art. The Howard I. and Janet H. Stein Collection, in honor of the 125th Anniversary of the Museum, 1998-176-17
PROVENANCE: [Leo Kaplan Antiques, New York, 1975]

COMPARISONS: Lessmann 1979, cats. 920, 922–24; Poole 1995, cat. 426

This unusual flat plate was probably made in France in the late-sixteenth century. The painter modeled his image after one of Bernard Salomon's Bible illustrations.[81] The story is taken from the Book of Kings, and tells how the Queen of Sheba came to King Solomon with her retinue to test his wisdom. Left breathless by his magnificence, she said "Because the Lord loved Israel forever, he has made you king to execute justice and righteousness."[82] This biblical episode is one that would undoubtedly strike a special note with any Renaissance ruler seeking a perfect role model.

On the reverse of the plate, three dolphinlike creatures swim in a blue sea (see appendix 6). This sort of subsidiary decoration was common in maiolica from this date. It was normally found either on the reverses of plates or dishes or on the exteriors of basins or wine coolers. X-rays have revealed that the stem (not visible in this illustration) is original to the plate, strong evidence that the form was footed.[83]

CAT. 55
PLATE WITH AN ALLEGORY RELATING TO VESPASIANO GONZAGA

Possibly Mantua, 1555
Height 2¼" (5.7 cm); diameter 14⅝" (37.1 cm)
The Howard I. and Janet H. Stein Collection
INSCRIPTIONS: (on front) *impresa* at left: tree with orange fruit or flowers; *impresa* at right: lightning striking a mountain; (on reverse, in cartouche; see appendix 7) 1555
PROVENANCE: Baron Adolphe de Rothschild, Paris (died 1900); Baron Maurice de Rothschild, Paris; [Duveen Brothers, Paris, by 1914–15]; purchased, Norton Simon Foundation, Los Angeles, 1964 (Foundation sale, Parke-Bernet Galleries, New York, May 7–8, 1971, lot 83)
EXHIBITION: Florence, Palazzo Strozzi, *Mostra mercato internazionale antiquariato*, 1959

In addition to its style and iconography, three uncommon aspects of this plate are its complex figural border with scrollwork cartouches, the dramatic rinceaux patterns on its reverse, and the large cartouche that dates the plate to 1555. Borders of this type are somewhat infrequent in maiolica, first appearing in Urbino and Venice around the 1540s.[84] However, they were much more common in the major arts in the Renaissance, and in manuscript and book designs,[85] metalwares, embroideries and textiles, furniture, and jewelry.

78. Holman 1997, p. 44. Dora Thornton notes that in 1525 Duke Federico II Gonzaga of Mantua paid fifty-one ducats for a silver-gilt saltcellar designed by Giulio Romano—the equivalent price of about two hundred pieces of *istoriato* maiolica; see Syson and Thornton 2001.

79. Poke (2001 pp. 334–35, 342–43, and n. 46) notes that the painter of cat. 52 derived his grotesque decorations from two specific Ducerceau prints.

80. The missing foot on this plate was replaced with another one (since removed) in the twentieth century. A later restoration replaced the modern foot with a knob that is still attached. The resulting erroneous implication was that the plate was originally a lid. The foot would probably have been similar to one shown in Poole 1995 (cat. 430); another modern restoration to a plate with a missing foot can be seen in ibid. (cat. 409).

81. Claude Paradin, *Quadrins historiques de la Bible* (Lyon: Jean de Tournes, 1553), no. 86.

82. 1 Kings 10.1–10.

83. Compare Poole 1995, cat. 409.

84. See, for example, the work of Francesco Durantino in the 1540s (Rackham [1940] 1977, no. 860); the pieces made after Battista Franco's drawings (Wilson 1987b, cat. 240); and works from Maestro Domenego's shop and elsewhere in Venice (Gardelli 1999, cat. 19; and Lessmann 1979, cats. 776–78, 848–49).

85. Such enframements appear in Piccolpasso 1980 (vol. 2, pp. 4, 50, and 94).

In the ceramics based on Battista Franco's drawings, the designs are symmetrical as they are in metalwares, and therefore less time-consuming for the designer.

The decoration on the reverse of this remarkable piece is as unique as the allegorical subject on its front. The dramatic blue and yellow rinceaux were surely drawn by an artist different from the one who painted the narrative scene, and even suggest that the two painters may have learned their craft in different towns or were influenced by currents from those separate locales. While the reverse has a Faentine flavor about it, an attribution to Faenza seems unlikely.[86] The only remotely comparable decoration for the elaborate pattern on the reverse is found in some works by the independent-minded Coal-Mine Painter, who was active in Urbino in the 1540s.[87]

CAT. 56
LARGE DISH WITH ORSELLA

Deruta, c. 1500–1510
Height 2¼" (5.7 cm); diameter 15⁵⁄₁₆" (38.2 cm)
The Howard I. and Janet H. Stein Collection
INSCRIPTIONS: (on banderole, adjacent to central image) *ORSELLA.B[ella]* (Beautiful Orsella); (on rim, in medallion above) *EM*
PROVENANCE: [Alessandro Castellani, Rome]; (Castellani sale, Palazzo Castellani, Rome, March 17–April 10, 1884, lot 54); James Simon, Berlin, by 1898; Dr. Alfred Pringsheim, Munich, by 1914 (his sale, Sotheby's, London, June 8, 1939, lot 139); Robert Lehman, New York (died 1969), acquired through Goldschmidt Galleries, New York; his son, Robert Owen Lehman, New York (sale, Christie's, London, April 4, 1977, lot 35)
REFERENCES: Chompret 1949, vol. 2, fig. 284; Morley-Fletcher and McIlroy 1984, pp. 33–34; Fiocco and Gherardi 1988, pp. 73–74, fig. 32; Rasmussen 1989, p. 59 (with incorrect provenance)
COMPARISONS: Mallet 1970, figs. 2–3; Fiocco and Gherardi 1984, cats. 165–80; Rasmussen 1989, cats. 34–36; Fiocco and Gherardi 1994, cats. 34–43
EXHIBITIONS: Berlin, Kunstgeschichtlichen Gesellschaft, *Ausstellung von Kunstwerken des Mittelalters und der Renaissance aus Berliner privatbesitz veranstaltet von der Kunstgeschichtlichen Gesellschaft*, 1898; Cincinnati Art Museum, *The Lehman Collection*, 1959, cat. 383

This plate belongs to a group known as "petal-back wares," after the flowerlike linear decoration on their reverses (see appendix 8).[88] Unlike most of them, however, this example lacks the central initial that is thought to refer to the name of the owner or maker.

The prominent monogram on the front may have substituted for the mark on the reverse, which also supports the idea that it indicates the owner or perhaps the giver. Once again, the circular fields with figural busts highlight the popularity of profile portraits, derived from medals, in the late-fifteenth and early sixteenth centuries.

CAT. 57
LARGE DISH WITH FEMALE HEAD

Deruta, c. 1520–30
Height 3⁵⁄₁₆" (8.6 cm); diameter 16¾" (42.6 cm)
Philadelphia Museum of Art. Purchased with the Elizabeth Wandell Smith Fund, 1951-107-2
PROVENANCE: [Dikran G. Kelekian, New York]
COMPARISONS: Rackham (1940) 1977, no. 435; Giacomotti 1974, cats. 582–87, 604, 619; Fiocco and Gherardi 1994, cat. 137
THERMOLUMINESCENCE ANALYSIS: Oxford Authentication Ltd., Wantage, England, report dated May 9, 2000, estimated the last firing was between 350 and 600 years ago.

Although it was more typical for Deruta dishes to have rims divided into sections with different patterns, this one bears a network of repeated quatrefoil motifs. The woman stands in an otherworldly space, behind her a stylized flower, and in front of her (as if she were gazing out a window), an abstract landscape with conelike hills and tiny buildings. This landscape convention was standard in these Deruta *piatti da pompa*, although its origin is unknown.

CAT. 58
ALBARELLO WITH FEMALE AND MALE HEADS

Venice, workshop of Maestro Domenego da Venezia, c. 1550–75
Height 9⁵⁄₁₆" (23.7 cm); width 5⅝" (14.2 cm)
Philadelphia Museum of Art. The Howard I. and Janet H. Stein Collection, in honor of the 125th Anniversary of the Museum, 1998-176-14
PROVENANCE: Sydney N. Blumberg, Newtown, Connecticut (died 1972) (his sale, Sotheby Parke-Bernet, New York, April 26, 1973, lot 58)
COMPARISONS: Morazzoni 1955, pl. 44b; Alverà Bortolotto 1987, cat. 13; Mazzucato 1990, pp. 66–67; Glaser 2000, cat. 228a, b; Salsi 2000, cat. 307

One reason for the consistency in the style of Venetian drug jars may stem from the protectionist

86. See, for example, Hausmann 1972, cats. 131–32; and Drey 1978, pl. 20b.

87. See Mallet 1991, pp. 62–73; and Musacchio 1999, figs. 79–80. The question of the plate's attribution will be treated in-depth in my forthcoming article.

88. See Fiocco and Gherardi 1988, pp. 57–69.

laws that banned the import of tin-glazed pottery made in other Italian centers, although the products of Majorca and Valencia were permitted.[89] And although drug jars of Venetian origin or style appear in Sicily, they seem not to have been exported to Germany, where quantities of Venetian tablewares are known to have been sent.

Cat. 58, reverse

odd for a pharmacy jar, there are equally strange subjects on some of the Orsini-Colonna pieces, like Cleopatra holding an asp, and a sexual allegory involving a woman displaying her bare breast.[92] This spouted container held a liquid compound made from the coltsfoot plant (*Tussilago farfara*), a traditional remedy for coughs and respiratory problems. Its use in herbal medicine ceased after it was discovered that it caused liver damage and cancer.

Cat. 59, reverse

CAT. 59
SPOUTED PHARMACY JAR WITH EMBRACING COUPLE

Castelli, 1548
Height 12⅜" (31.5 cm); width 9⅞" (25 cm)
Philadelphia Museum of Art. The Dr. Francis W. Lewis Collection, 1903–28
INSCRIPTIONS: (on front, on banderole above couple) *isoepiu / felice omo / dequesta / terra 1548.* (I am the happiest man in the world 1548); (on front, below couple) *AD.FARFARA* (acqua di farfara, liquified coltsfoot); (on reverse, under handle) *P. P. A. /.1.5.4.8.* (surmounted by a cross of Santo Spirito); (on underside, incised) cursive L-shaped *l* and 8½ 8½ (indicating the volume of the container)[90]
PROVENANCE: Dr. Francis W. Lewis, Philadelphia (died 1902)
REFERENCE: Fiocco and Gherardi 1992, p. 164 n. 34
COMPARISON: Fiocco and Gherardi 1992, pls. 27a–d, 29d, 31c.

A series of *porcellana colorata* albarelli and spouted jars was once thought to be Faentine, but has recently been attributed to Castelli. Dated 1548, the Philadelphia pitcher would be contemporary with some of the Orsini-Colonna ceramics, the most famous products of that center.[91] Stylistically, the amorous couple is consistent with the caricaturelike figures of the Orsini-Colonna group. Although this scene may seem

CATS. 60A, B
FOOTED BOWL AND LID OR TRAY FROM A CHILDBIRTH SET

The Marches, probably Urbino, Francesco Durantino, mid-1540s
Bowl (cat. 60a): height 3¾" (9.6 cm); width 6¹⁵⁄₁₆" (17.6 cm). Lid (cat. 60b): height ⅓" (1 cm); diameter 8¾" (22.3 cm)
Philadelphia Museum of Art. The Howard I. and Janet H. Stein Collection, in honor of the 125th Anniversary of the Museum, 2000-154-4, 2000-154-5
PROVENANCE: Eugène Piot, Paris (his sale, Pillet, Paris, April 23–24, 1864, lot 151); Baron Adolphe de Rothschild, Paris (died 1900); Baron Maurice de Rothschild, Paris; [Duveen Brothers, Paris, by 1914–15]; purchased, Norton Simon Foundation, Los Angeles, 1964 (Foundation sale, Parke-Bernet Galleries, New York, May 7–8, 1971, lot 85)
REFERENCE: Musacchio 1999, pp. 111–12, 128–29
COMPARISONS: Lessmann 1979, cats. 161–72 (for figure types); Musacchio 1999, figs. 88, 92 (for exterior landscape)

The distinctive style of Francesco Durantino reappears in this childbirth set, the only surviving example of this form from his hand. The scenes are remarkably well-painted, and Francesco skillfully compensates for the deeply curved interior surface of the

89. Alverà Bortolotto 1981, pp. 17–20.

90. See Mazzucato 1990, for illustrations of other examples.

91. See Fiocco and Gherardi 1992; and Baldisseri 1989, p. 186.

92. Watson 1986, cats. 17–18.

bowl. Also interesting is the lid, where the receding floorboards and borders of the room create an accurate sense of perspective. Francesco deftly applied shadows under the bed, at the edges of the framed mirror and, most remarkably, on the wall behind the maids making the bed. The grisaille frieze near the ceiling—painting that itself mimics relief sculpture—shows yet another dimension of the artist's imagination.[93] Although this set is uninscribed, it was probably painted by Francesco while he was still in Urbino, perhaps in 1545, when he executed the remarkable plate in the Herzog Anton Ulrich-Museum, with an elaborate triumphal arch.[94]

CAT. 61

SHORT ALBARELLO WITH PUTTO HOLDING A PINWHEEL

The Veneto, probably Venice, early seventeenth century
Height 6⅟₁₆" (15.4 cm); width 4½" (11.4 cm)
Philadelphia Museum of Art. The Howard I. and Janet H. Stein Collection, in honor of the 125th Anniversary of the Museum, 1998-176-6
PROVENANCE: (Sale, O. Rundle Gilbert & Son, Garrison-on-the-Hudson, New York, December 4, 1970, lot C217)
COMPARISONS: Alverà Bortolotto 1981, pls. CVI, CVIIa
THERMOLUMINESCENCE ANALYSIS: Oxford Authentication Ltd., Wantage, England, report dated June 19, 2001, estimated the last firing was between 200 and 400 years ago.

The influence of Maestro Domenego da Venezia was pervasive in Venice, as was his preference for an intense blue field with entwined foliage and flowers. This small albarello is a typical example of the persistence of that style with botanical elements that may have originated in reality, but was transformed into fanciful products of the imagination. Daisylike flowers and large trumpet-shaped blooms spring from the same leafy plants that also bear acorns. These fantasy plants are an amazing amalgamation of species indigenous to China, Turkey, Egypt, and Italy, perhaps known from actual specimens or reinterpreted from examples on Ming and Iznik ceramics or ancient Roman sculpture.

CAT. 62

LARGE DISH WITH SAINT JEROME

Deruta, first half of the sixteenth century
Height 3⅜" (8.6 cm); diameter 15⅞" (40.4 cm)
Philadelphia Museum of Art. Purchased with the Elizabeth Wandell Smith Fund, 1951-107-1
PROVENANCE: Hans von und zu Aufzeß, before 1862; Germanisches Nationalmuseum, Nuremberg, to 1922; purchased, H. Hoffmann, Munich, February 17, 1922; Kurt Glogowski, Berlin (his sale, London, Sotheby's, June 8, 1932, lot 38); Whitney Warren, New York (died 1943) (his sale, Parke-Bernet Galleries, New York, October 7–9, 1943, lot 498); [Dikran G. Kelekian, New York]
REFERENCES: Chompret 1949, vol. 2, fig. 227; Fiocco and Gherardi 1988, p. 317; Glaser 2000, p. x
COMPARISONS: Prentice von Erdberg and Ross 1952, cat. 19; Fiocco and Gherardi 1988, cat. 263
THERMOLUMINESCENCE ANALYSIS: Oxford Authentication Ltd., Wantage, England, report dated May 9, 2000, estimated the last firing was between 300 and 500 years ago.

Jerome is accompanied by a crucifix and his lion, whose head peeks up from the lower left of the composition. The saint is often shown on maiolica with his other main attribute, the cardinal's hat.[95] Jerome was normally depicted as a scholar ensconced in his study until around 1400, when Italian artists began to portray him as the penitent, beating his bare chest to tame his sinful heart. The establishment of Hieronymite congregations (hermetic orders associated with Saint Jerome) in Tuscany and Umbria certainly contributed to his popularity on Deruta wares. Given the association of Saints Jerome and Francis, it may be that display plates with their images were intended to be hung together, like those of the Turkish and western equestrian figures (see cat. 68).[96]

CAT. 63

PLAQUE WITH THE EMBLEM OF SAINT BERNARD OF SIENA

Emilia-Romagna, probably Faenza, mid- to late-sixteenth century
Height 8" (20.3 cm); width 7¾" (19.7 cm); depth ⅝" (1.6 cm)
Philadelphia Museum of Art. The Howard I. and Janet H. Stein Collection, in honor of the 125th Anniversary of the Museum, 1998-176-21
INSCRIPTION: (on front, in center) IHS

93. Compare a similar frieze in Ghirlandaio's *Birth of the Virgin* in Santa Maria Novella, Florence (Musacchio 1999, fig. 115).

94. Lessmann 1979, cat. 172.

95. See Bojani 1982, cat. 12.

96. See Fiocco and Gherardi 1994, cat. 113, for a plate showing both saints venerating the crucified Christ.

PROVENANCE: (Sale, Sotheby's, London, June 6, 1989, lot 12); [Cyril Humphris, London]; (Humphris sale, Sotheby's, New York, January 10, 1995, lot 41)

THERMOLUMINESCENCE ANALYSIS: Oxford Authentication Ltd., Wantage, England, report dated September 22, 2000, estimated the last firing was between 250 and 450 years ago.

This plaque has been variously ascribed to Faenza and Urbino, but its uniqueness makes it difficult to determine its place of manufacture. Another unique square tile has been described by Giuliana Gardelli as a *vassoio* (tray), but this use is not likely for the Philadelphia piece because of its relief decoration.[97] The Franciscan saint Bernard of Siena was, like Saint Francis, a beloved figure in popular belief. His distinctive symbol, the initials of Christ within a sunburst, appears in many places, including on the facades of buildings. It would not seem out of the ordinary for a plaque of this kind to be placed in a sacred or secular setting for either decoration or devotional inspiration.

CAT. 64
LARGE DISH WITH THE DEPOSITION OF CHRIST

Possibly Montelupo or Viterbo, seventeenth century
Height 3⁹⁄₁₆" (9 cm); diameter 20⅞" (53.1 cm)
Philadelphia Museum of Art. The Howard I. and Janet H. Stein Collection, in honor of the 125th Anniversary of the Museum, 1998-176-19
PROVENANCE: (Sale, Christie's, New York, June 13, 1981, lot 35)
THERMOLUMINESCENCE ANALYSIS: Oxford Authentication Ltd., Wantage, England, report dated May 30, 2001, estimated the last firing was between 350 and 600 years ago.

This puzzling work probably dates to the seventeenth century, but its source remains a mystery. The crude quality of the painting suggests a provincial workshop or simply a less accomplished painter. Although the Deposition of Christ is seldom found on maiolica, it was a very popular subject in painting. The maker of this dish appears to have based his own composition on a print after Federico Barocci's *Deposition* (1567–69) in the duomo of Perugia. Here the scene is reversed from the original, and the painter has added ornamental pilasters at the sides to compensate for the broader shape of the field on which he was working.

CAT. 65
HAND-WARMER IN THE SHAPE OF A SHOE

Emilia-Romagna, probably Faenza, eighteenth century
Height 4⅛" (10.2 cm); width 2⅝" (6.7 cm); length 8¼" (21 cm)
Philadelphia Museum of Art. Purchased with the Elizabeth Wandell Smith Fund from the Edmond Foulc Collection, 1930-1-72
PROVENANCE: Edmond Foulc, Paris (died 1916); by descent, Foulc family; [Wildenstein & Co., Paris and New York, by 1927]
COMPARISON: Ragona 1975, cat. 141 (for an early eighteenth-century example from Caltagirone)
EXHIBITION: Philadelphia 1930
THERMOLUMINESCENCE ANALYSIS: Oxford Authentication Ltd., Wantage, England, report dated May 30, 2001, estimated the last firing was between 150 and 250 years ago.

"Model" shoes like this one were often made in an archaic style, as some souvenirs are today. However, Edward Maeder has commented that the precise detailing of both shoe and stocking might suggest an early seventeenth-century date, although recent scientific testing has indicated that it might not have been made prior to c. 1750.[98] June Swann noted that other "Faenza footwear models" are shaped like ancient Roman boots and sandals.[99] In a recent lecture Timothy Wilson quoted a contract from 1543 in which Guido di Merlino and three other potters agreed to produce maiolica in various shapes, including the usual plates, wine coolers, and jugs, but also *"scarpe,"* which Wilson took to be vessels in the shape of shoes, perhaps pitchers, flasks, or hand-warmers.[100]

CAT. 66
MOLDED DISH ON A LOW FOOT

Faenza, c. 1550–70
Height 2⅝" (6.7 cm); width 10ⁱ⁄₁₆" (25.6 cm)
Philadelphia Museum of Art. The Howard I. and Janet H. Stein Collection, in honor of the 125th Anniversary of the Museum, 1999-99-9
PROVENANCE: Dr. Alfred Pringsheim, Munich, by 1923 (his sale, Sotheby's, London, June 7, 1939, lot 61); Robert Lehman, New York (died 1969), acquired through Goldschmidt Galleries, New York; his son, Robert Owen Lehman, New York (sale, Christie's, London, April 4, 1977, lot 44)
COMPARISONS: Baligand 1986, cat. 29; Fuchs 1993, cat. 71

97. Gardelli 1999, cat. 163.

98. Edward Maeder (Curator of Textiles, Historic Deerfield), conversation with the author, March 30, 2001.

99. Swann also noted in a letter in the Object files, Department of European Decorative Art and Sculpture, Philadelphia Museum of Art (July 24, 1991) that there are other related earthenware shoes in the collections of the Palazzo Davanzati, Florence, and the Northampton Museum, England.

100. Wilson 2001.

Pure landscapes rarely appear on Faentine maiolica of this type, or on maiolica in general. The most famous of them, probably made in the workshop of Guido Durantino, are the central feature of a large service with the Salviati family's coat of arms.[101] The landscape on the Philadelphia plate is embedded in the center of the *crespina* in the *a quartieri* style—a decorative mode illustrated in Piccolpasso's treatise.[102] The style was popular in Faenza between the 1530s and the late 1560s, and later enjoyed a revival in Sicily in the early seventeenth century. The *a quartieri* decoration on the front of the plate carefully echoes the contours of the mold, a practice that maiolica painters did not always follow. On its reverse (see appendix 9), rather cursorily painted blue and orange lines form an ornamental scheme that, by coincidence or not, resembles Deruta's earlier "petal-back wares" (see cat. 56).[103]

CAT. 67
VASE IN THE SHAPE OF A PINECONE

Deruta, c. 1500–1530
Height 7¾" (19.6 cm); width 6¾" (17.2 cm)
Philadelphia Museum of Art. Purchased with funds contributed by the Emerson Club from the Edmond Foulc Collection, 1930-1-68b
PROVENANCE: Edmond Foulc, Paris (died 1916); by descent, Foulc family; [Wildenstein & Co., Paris and New York, by 1927]
COMPARISONS: Rackham (1940) 1977, nos. 517–18; Giacomotti 1974, cats. 665–67, 669; Ladis 1989, cat. 9; Fiocco and Gherardi 1990, cat. 20; Salsi 2000, cat. 77
EXHIBITION: Philadelphia 1930
THERMOLUMINESCENCE ANALYSIS: Oxford Authentication Ltd., Wantage, England, report dated May 9, 2000, estimated the last firing was between 300 and 500 years ago.

The number of surviving jars in this shape—usually lustered in gold, but occasionally polychromed—suggests that they were produced in quantity and may have had multiple purposes. They were probably used to serve sweetmeats, but also may have functioned as pharmaceutical containers. Preparations made from pine nuts were prescribed for coughs and asthma and, according to Platina, helped to generate the proper humors, settle thirst, and even "excite latent passion."[104]

CAT. 68
LARGE DISH WITH AN EQUESTRIAN TURK

Deruta, first half of the sixteenth century
Height 3⅛" (7.9 cm); diameter 16¼" (41.3 cm)
The Howard I. and Janet H. Stein Collection
PROVENANCE: Private collector, San Francisco (sale, Sotheby Parke-Bernet, New York, November 10, 1972, lot 47)
COMPARISONS: Norman 1976, cat. C32; Join-Dieterle 1984, cat. 16; Poole 1995, cat. 273
THERMOLUMINESCENCE ANALYSIS: Oxford Authentication Ltd., Wantage, England, report dated May 10, 2000, estimated the last firing was between 300 and 500 years

Large-scale *piatti da pompa* with Turkish riders may have been intended to be seen alongside those with western lancers,[105] or even with allegorical dishes like one in this collection with the lion of Venice (see cat. 3). To judge from surviving works, it appears that the majority of Turkish-rider plates were painted in the polychrome scheme also favored by Deruta artisans, although some like this one were primarily blue with golden luster. In the fifteenth and sixteenth centuries, there was a steady escalation in the commissioning of images of horses in all media, which was part of the increasing display of wealth by European nobility.[106] Among the most prominent of these are the magnificent horses immortalized in fresco by Giulio Romano in Federico II Gonzaga's Palazzo del Te (1527–28).

CAT. 69
EWER BASIN WITH COAT OF ARMS

Deruta, c. 1520
Height 1⅜" (3.5 cm); diameter 13⁵⁄₁₆" (33.8 cm)
Philadelphia Museum of Art. The Howard I. and Janet H. Stein Collection, in honor of the 125th Anniversary of the Museum, 1999-99-14
INSCRIPTIONS: (on front) unidentified coat of arms; (on reverse, incised in center) *B*
PROVENANCE: Fernand Adda, Paris (his anonymous sale, Rheims & Laurent, Paris, December 1–3, 1965, lot 523); [Cyril Humphris, London]; Dr. Arthur M. Sackler, New York (died 1987) (his sale, part 1, Christie's, New York, October 6, 1993, lot 10)
REFERENCE: Rackham 1959, no. 374, pl. 162a
EXHIBITIONS: London, Cyril Humphris Ltd., *Sixty-nine Pieces of Islamic Pottery and Italian Maiolica from the Adda Collection*, 1967, cat. 41; San Francisco 1986–88, no. 35

101. At least fourteen pieces remain from that mid-century set; see Michael J. Brody, "'Terra d'Urbino tutta dipinta a paesi con l'armi de' Salviati': The *Paesi* Service in the 1583 Inventory of Jacopo di Alamanno Salviati (1537–1586)," *Faenza*, vol. 86 (2000), pp. 30–46.

102. Piccolpasso 1980, vol. 2, p. 119.

103. Wilson 1996a, cat. 123.

104. Platina 1998, p. 177.

105. See Poole 1995, cat. 274.

106. Jardine and Brotton 2000, pp. 150–51.

THERMOLUMINESCENCE ANALYSIS: The Research Laboratory for Archaeology and the History of Art, Oxford University, England, report dated January 1986, estimated the last firing was between 360 and 540 years ago.

Ewers and ewer basins were especially popular products of Deruta from the early sixteenth century. This spectacular and unusual polychromed example bears an unidentified coat of arms. On its white-glazed reverse, concentric blue bands encircle the letter *B*, scratched through the glaze. Ewers and basins were used not only in dining but also by women in bed after childbirth. Alessandro Allori shows this custom in his *Birth of the Virgin* (1595), where Saint Anne washes her hands using what appears to be a maiolica ewer and basin set.[107]

Cat. 69, reverse

CAT. 70
EWER

Deruta, first half of the sixteenth century
Height 7⅞" (20.1 cm); width (handle to spout) 6¾" (17.1 cm)
Philadelphia Museum of Art. Purchased with the Elizabeth Wandell Smith Fund from the Edmond Foulc Collection, 1930-1-69
PROVENANCE: Edmond Foulc, Paris (died 1916); by descent, Foulc family; [Wildenstein & Co., Paris and New York, by 1927]
COMPARISONS: Giacomotti 1974, cats. 626–28
EXHIBITION: Philadelphia 1930

Ewers like this one would have been paired with basins with a raised central emplacement (see cat. 69). Surviving examples of both suggest that these wares were produced in quantity. In the late-fourteenth century, the wife of Francesco Datini of Prato was asked to take "a bowl and an ewer, such as is customary to give to girls" to a birthday party for one of her daughter's friends. As Julia Poole notes, these probably would have been made of metal at the time, but if the custom persisted, maiolica would have been a suitable substitute.[108]

107. Santa Maria Nuova, Cortona; see Musacchio 1999, pp. 154–55.

108. Poole 1995, p. 168.

109. See Giacomotti 1974, cats. 651–53; see also Mancini della Chiara 1979, cat. 123, for a plate with a related border and different unidentified coat of arms.

110. For a good summary of Medici porcelain, see Wilson 1993, pp. 234–37; see also Spallanzani 1994.

CAT. 71
PLATE WITH COAT OF ARMS OF POPE CLEMENT VII MEDICI

Deruta, c. 1523–34
Height 1⅞" (4.8 cm); diameter 8⅞" (22.5 cm)
Philadelphia Museum of Art. The Howard I. and Janet H. Stein Collection, in honor of the 125th Anniversary of the Museum, 1999-99-8
INSCRIPTION: (on front, in center) .*CLEMENS*. (Clement); coat of arms of Pope Clement VII Medici
PROVENANCE: Robert Lehman, New York (died 1969); his son, Robert Owen Lehman, New York (sale, Christie's, London, April 4, 1977, lot 38)
REFERENCE: Morley-Fletcher and McIlroy 1984, cat. 8
COMPARISONS: Hausmann 1972, cat. 157; Giacomotti 1974, cat. 650; Join-Dieterle 1984, cat. 20; Gardelli 1999, cat. 191

This appealing lustered plate was one of a set made in Deruta during the pontificate of Clement VII (1523–34). The artist accurately depicted the Medici arms with its red and blue palle and fleur-de-lys, adding the name of their papal relation for additional prestige. Ruby luster was used for the Medici balls, since a true red pigment was not easily obtainable. At least four other plates remain from this set, as well as others with similar decoration but without the Medici heraldry.[109]

The Medici were major importers of Spanish lusterwares in the fifteenth century and also supported the establishment of a pottery at their villa in Cafaggiolo in the next century. In addition, they were avid collectors of Chinese wares and were instrumental in the experiments aimed at discovering the secrets of true porcelain. By 1575, Francesco de Medici had succeeded, at least in part, in producing exquisite soft-paste porcelain, mostly in imitation of blue and white Eastern wares. It was made in very restricted numbers because of the high failure rate of this complex technology, and only about seventy examples of the so-called Medici porcelain survive today.[110] Francesco's penchant for experimentation was directly in line with the *cortigiano* (courtier) way of thinking that gave rise to the term "Renaissance man."

CAT. 72
PLATE WITH THE LEGEND OF CIRCE

Urbino area, c. 1540–50
Height 1⅝" (4.2 cm); diameter 10⅜" (26.4 cm)
Philadelphia Museum of Art. The Howard I. and Janet H. Stein Collection, in honor of the 125th

Anniversary of the Museum, 1998-176-20
INSCRIPTIONS: (on reverse; see appendix 10) *Circera in / ca[n]t(?)atrice* (Circe the enchantress); coat of arms of the Lanciarini family
PROVENANCE: (Sale, Sotheby's, New York, December 3, 1982, lot 133)
COMPARISONS: Hausmann 1972, cats. 212–13; Giacomotti 1974, cats. 873–79; Wilson 1987b, cat. 212; Munarini and Banzato 1993, cat. 299; Crépin-Leblond and Ennès 1995, cats. 14–21

At least eighteen pieces (including a saltcellar) exist from the set made for the Lanciarini family of Rome. Perhaps more than three different artists shared the commission, since the handling of the coats of arms and inscriptions is divergent. The subjects on the plates are based on ancient history and mythology with only one showing a scene from the Old Testament.

CAT. 73
LOW-FOOTED DISH WITH SAMSON AND DELILAH

Urbino, workshop of Guido Durantino, 1535
Height 1¾" (4.4 cm); diameter 11" (28 cm)
The Howard I. and Janet H. Stein Collection
INSCRIPTION: (on reverse) *Sansone viene / ligato / p[er] Daliela / In vrbino / 1535* (Samson bound by Delilah, in Urbino, 1535)
PROVENANCE: Von K. estate, Dresden (sale, Paul Graupe, Berlin, October 20–21, 1936, lot 203); (sale, Sotheby Parke-Bernet, New York, 1972, lot 109)
COMPARISON: Rackham (1940) 1977, no. 627

This dish is almost certainly by the same artist who painted the unsigned and undated Montmorency candlestick in the Victoria & Albert Museum. The style of the faces, trees, drapery, and anatomy are extremely similar, and they were probably made in the same year. Although John Mallet wrote that the Victoria & Albert candlestick and an unmarked

Cat. 73, reverse with inscription

111. See Mallet 1987, p. 296.

112. See Poole 1995, cat. 431, for information on seven surviving examples from the Christell-Mair set.

113. Mallet 1998, pp. 39–51.

114. Quoted in ibid., p. 41.

Montmorency flask in Turin may have been made in different shops, the inscription on this piece (by the same person who inscribed cat. 18) ties them together and shows that all were made in the *bottega* of Guido Durantino.[111]

CAT. 74
PLATE WITH COATS OF ARMS OF THE BÖCKHLI AND CHRISTELL FAMILIES

Urbino, probably Patanazzi workshop, late-sixteenth century
Height 1⅜" (3.5 cm); diameter 9" (22.8 cm)
Philadelphia Museum of Art. The Howard I. and Janet H. Stein Collection, in honor of the 125th Anniversary of the Museum, 1999-99-11
INSCRIPTION: (on front, left and right, respectively) coats of arms of the Böckhli and Christell families
PROVENANCE: Umberto Melina (sale, Sotheby's, London, July 16, 1968, lot 81); private collector, Delaware (sale, Christie's, New York, June 13, 1981, lot 40)
COMPARISON: Rackham (1940) 1977, no. 884

The Christell family had a tradition of commissioning maiolica to commemorate marriages. To judge from the placement of the crests on this plate, it must have been made for the marriage of a Christell daughter to a Böckhli son. Other Urbino wares show the Christell arms linked with those of the Mair family; other families of Augsburg and Nuremberg continued the practice.[112] The Germans' original fondness for maiolica tablewares merged seamlessly with their collecting of them as antiques later, as John Mallet has noted.[113] In a 1614 letter, the gentleman-dealer Philipp Hainhofer mentioned some "beautiful, artistic, old maiolica dishes" that he had seen and actively acquired for some of his aristocratic clients. He wrote temptingly to one of them: "The painted Faenza dishes are a great rarity . . . the princesses [in Germany and Switzerland] use them when they want to welcome at their Court gentlefolk or company from foreign powers with sweetmeats and refreshments."[114]

CATS. 75A, B
PAIR OF PHARMACY BOTTLES WITH COAT OF ARMS OF THE GONZAGA FAMILY

Faenza, c. 1530–40
Cat. 75a: height 9⅟₁₆" (23 cm); width 6¾" (17.2 cm)
Cat. 75b: height 9⁷⁄₁₆" (24 cm); width 6⅞" (17.4 cm)
Philadelphia Museum of Art. Purchased with the Elizabeth Wandell Smith Fund from the Edmond

Foulc Collection, 1930-1-67a, 1930-1-67b
INSCRIPTIONS: (on body of cat. 75a) *A. cucurbite:* (liquified pumpkin seeds); (on body of cat. 75b) *A. mente:* (liquified mint); (on body of both, above) coat of arms of the Gonzaga family
PROVENANCE: [Delange, unconfirmed]; Edmond Foulc, Paris (died 1916); by descent, Foulc family; [Wildenstein & Co., Paris and New York, by 1927]
REFERENCES: Carmen Ravanelli Guidotti, *La farmacia dei Gesuiti di Novellara* (Faenza: Edit Faenza, 1994), pp. 43–45, 67 n. 3, figs. 16a, b
COMPARISONS: Rackham 1959, no. 315; Legge 1986, pp. 23–24, no. 14
EXHIBITION: Philadelphia 1930
THERMOLUMINESCENCE ANALYSIS: Oxford Authentication Ltd., Wantage, England, report dated May 30, 2001, estimated the last firing was between 300 and 500 years ago.

Berettino glaze—a blue-tinged form of the usual tin glaze—was popular with potters in both Faenza and Venice, as we see in this pair of albarelli (see cats. 77a,b). Such bottles or flasks contained liquid preparations, the narrow necks helping to prevent evaporation of the compounds. They reflect a shape common in both glass tablewares and containers used for alchemical experiments. The compounds contained in these two particular flasks were liquids derived from gourd or pumpkin seeds and from mint leaves.

Cats. 75a, b, reverses

CAT. 76
ALBARELLO WITH COAT OF ARMS

Castel Durante, first half of the sixteenth century
Height 9⅛" (23.1 cm); width 5⅜" (13.6 cm)
Philadelphia Museum of Art. The Howard I. and Janet H. Stein Collection, in honor of the 125th Anniversary of the Museum, 1999-99-13
INSCRIPTIONS: (on body, in central band) *Myrrhe*; (on body, above) heart-shaped mark with a star-cross and

letters *RD/G*; (on body, below) unidentified coat of arms
PROVENANCE: [Martin Shopland, New York, March 7, 1991]
COMPARISONS: Lessmann 1979, cat. 24; Bojani et al. 1985, cat. 300 (as Salviati family); Mariaux 1995, cat. 105

Castel Durante was a center of production for these white-ground albarelli, which often bear a pharmacy emblem above and a family's coat of arms below. The arms and insignias on other related examples are as inscrutable as these, leading to speculation that they were commissioned by less-prominent families. Past publications describe these arms as those of the Salviati family, despite the fact that their crenellated bands were normally red and white, not blue and white.[115] Although the true red required for Salviati heraldry was not easily obtainable, painters normally substituted dark orange in such situations. Various heraldic treatises illustrate blue and white coats of arms like this one, associating them with various families (such as the Avogadro and the Benci), but no evidence has surfaced to link this jar and its mates definitively to any of them. Myrrh, the contents of the albarello, is a gum resin usually employed in the making of perfumes and incense.

CATS. 77A, B
PAIR OF ALBARELLI WITH ANGELS AND COATS OF ARMS

Venice, second half of the sixteenth century
Cat. 77a: height 7⅜" (18.7 cm); width 4½" (11.4 cm)
Cat. 77b: height 7½" (19.1 cm); width 4½" (11.4 cm)
Philadelphia Museum of Art. The Howard I. and Janet H. Stein Collection, in honor of the 125th Anniversary of the Museum, 1999-99-4, 1999-99-5
INSCRIPTIONS: (on body of cat. 77a) *.ell. de gemmi[l?].* (electuary of poplar buds); (on body of cat. 77b) *.zuc. borag.* (sweet borage compound); (on body of both, below) unidentified coat of arms with the letters *.M.* and *.C.* on the left and right of the crest, and a rampant dog facing left
PROVENANCE: Maurice Chabrières-Arlès, Paris (died 1897); Chabrières-Arlès collection, Paris; [purchased, Duveen Brothers, New York, 1916]; Carl W. Hamilton, New York; George R. Hann, Treetops, Sewickley Heights, Pennsylvania (his sale, part 2, Christie's, Treetops, Sewickley Heights, May 19, 1980, lot 93)
REFERENCE: Rasmussen 1984, p. 245 (as Hann collection)

115. See Bojani and Vossilla 1998, cat. 34, for a pitcher with the red and white arms of the Salviati family impaled with those of the Capponi family, and an inscription identifying them.

COMPARISONS: Rackham 1959, nos. 463–64; Rasmussen 1984, cats. 161–63; Wilson 1996a, cats. 185–86

EXHIBITIONS: Montclair 1925–26, cats. 59–60; Buffalo 1926–28, cat. 35; Newark 1929

In addition to displaying a coat of arms, all nine extant jars from this set have a medallion with an angel bearing the palm of martyrdom, perhaps another symbol of the particular hospital or monastic apothecary to which they belonged. If the coat of arms does indeed belong to the Dominican order (see page 159), these jars may have been made for one of its monastic apothecaries or hospitals. The Dominicans operated the famous and still-active pharmacy of Santa Maria Novella in Florence. In Venice, a hospital at the Dominican church of Santi Giovanni e Paolo dates back to the 1520s, founded during what was probably a typhus epidemic.[116] Further research is necessary to solidify the link between these *berettino* drug jars and a particular Venetian pharmacy.

Cats. 77a, b, reverses

CATS. 78A, B
PAIR OF ALBARELLI WITH SEATED QUEENS

Urbino, probably workshop of Orazio Fontana, c. 1565–71
Cat. 78a: height 8¹³⁄₁₆" (22.5 cm); width 5³⁄₁₆" (13.2 cm)
Cat. 78b: height 9¹⁄₁₆" (23 cm); width 5³⁄₁₆" (13.2 cm)
Philadelphia Museum of Art. The Howard I. and Janet H. Stein Collection, in honor of the 125th Anniversary of the Museum, 2000-154-2, 2000-154-3
INSCRIPTIONS: (on body of cat. 78a) *.E.D.SVCO.D. ROSE.* (a sweet-tasting elixir made from rose petals); (on body of cat. 78b) *DIAPENTA* (made from penta-phyllum, also known as cinquefoil or *Potentilla reptans*)
PROVENANCE: [Alexander Barker, London]; Sir Francis W. Cook, Baronet, Doughty House, Richmond Hill, Surrey, England, c. 1870 (died 1901);

his son Wyndham F. Cook, London (died 1905); his son, Humphrey W. Cook (his sale, Christie's, London, July 7–10, 1925, lot 36); [purchased, Rosenbach Company, New York and Philadelphia]; The Philip H. & A.S.W. Rosenbach Foundation, Philadelphia, 1954 (sale, Sotheby Parke-Bernet, New York, March 2, 1974, lot 48)
REFERENCE: Poole 1995, p. 377 (as New York private collection with erroneous inscriptions)
COMPARISON: Poole 1995, cat. 411

There is a link between the Queen and Fortune services (see cats. 80a,b) despite their having been produced in different centers. Two pill jars, one in the Bayer Collection (its lid dated 1575) and another in the Victoria & Albert Museum closely resemble the Fortune series in terms of style, palette, and the use of trophies.[117] But their main decorative feature is a seated queen drawn from the same unknown print source as these albarelli. Perhaps this connection is pure coincidence, but further research remains to be done to determine between these two very important services. According to Giuseppe Donzelli, rose syrup was sold by spice-sellers to cleanse bile, phlegm, and the humors; and to satisfy thirst, strengthen the stomach, and quell high fevers.[118]

CAT. 79
SPOUTED DRUG JAR WITH SEATED QUEEN

Urbino, probably workshop of Orazio Fontana, c. 1565–71
Height 8⁵⁄₁₆" (22.6 cm); width (handle to spout) 8⁵⁄₁₆" (21.1 cm)
Philadelphia Museum of Art. The Howard I. and Janet H. Stein Collection, in honor of the 125th Anniversary of the Museum, 2000-154-1
INSCRIPTIONS: (on body) *.S.D. INCRI.S.A.* (syrup made with an unidentified substance)
PROVENANCE: Hermann Emden, Hamburg, Germany (his sale, Lepke, I, Berlin, November 3–7, 1908, lot 71); [Jacques Seligman & Co., New York]; purchased, George G. Booth, Bloomfield Hills, Michigan, June 14, 1929; Cranbrook Museum of Art, Cranbrook Academy of Art, Bloomfield Hills, Michigan, 1929 (sale, Sotheby Parke-Bernet, New York, March 25, 1972, lot 110)
REFERENCES: Poole 1995, p. 377 (as formerly in Hermann Emden collection)
COMPARISON: Poole 1995, cat. 411

This set was probably made in Orazio Fontana's

116. Michelle Laughran (Professor of History, St. Joseph's College of Maine), conversation with the author, May 18, 2001.

117. See Biscontini Ugolini 1997, cat. 2; and Rackham (1940) 1977, no. 1010.

118. Donzelli 1686, p. 155; cited in Biscontini Ugolini 1997, p. 78.

Urbino workshop after 1565, when he left the service of the duke of Savoy in Turin, and before his death in 1571.[119] A pair of related jars with similar seated figures is inscribed *fatto in Urbino* (made in Urbino), corroborating the attribution to that city.[120] Stylistic differences confirm that several painters worked on the service. At least forty pieces remain from what was probably a single set, since no drug names are repeated. The surviving shapes include albarelli and two sizes of spouted jars, of which this is the smaller version. The figure—perhaps meant to invoke the goddess Hera or another mythological character—may derive from a woodcut that was used in its original orientation on some pieces and in reverse on others. A stylistically related set of jars commissioned by Duke Guidobaldo II, was later given by his successor, Duke Francesco Maria II, to the Santa Casa at Loreto.[121]

CATS. 80A, B

PAIR OF ALBARELLI WITH TROPHIES AND FEMALE FIGURES REPRESENTING FORTUNE

Pesaro or Castel Durante, c. 1580
Cat. 80a: height 7¼" (18.4 cm); width 4¾" (12.1 cm)
Cat. 80b: height 7⁵⁄₁₆" (18.6 cm); width 4¾" (12.1 cm)
Philadelphia Museum of Art. The Howard I. and Janet H. Stein Collection, in honor of the 125th Anniversary of the Museum, 2000-154-8, 2000-154-9
INSCRIPTIONS: (on body of cat. 80a) .*CONFEZI*[O]. *AME.* (or *confectio Hamech*, purgative syrup); (on body of cat. 80b) .*DIA.DRAGAN.F.* (gum tragacanth)
PROVENANCE: [Martin Shopland, New York, May 18, 1991]
COMPARISONS: Giacomotti 1974, cats. 979–92; Wilson 1996a, cats. 146–48; Bojani 2000, cats. 38–39

Although painted by several hands, the figures on this suite must have been based on a print circulating in the workshop.[122] The service includes covered pill-boxes, albarelli, spouted jars, pitchers, bottles, and large vases with covers. In the past, the set was assigned to Castel Durante, but similar fragments have surfaced in excavations at Pesaro. Documents from the second half of the sixteenth century have noted the existence in Pesaro of a pharmacy known as *Ad signum fortune* (At the sign of fortune), following the tradition of naming such establishments by the symbols they used.[123] One of the compounds held in these albarelli was a purgative syrup believed to be named after the Arab physician Hamech. The other contained a medicine made from a fine, dried gummy

exudate obtained from a plant of the *Astragalus* genus.[124]

Cats. 80a, b, reverses

CAT. 81

DRUG JAR WITH COAT OF ARMS

Sicily, Trapani, first half of the seventeenth century
Height 13½" (34.3 cm); width 12" (30.5 cm)
Philadelphia Museum of Art. The John D. McIlhenny Collection, 1943-40-92
INSCRIPTION: (on body) unidentified coat of arms
PROVENANCE: [Sangiorgi Gallery, Rome]; purchased, John D. McIlhenny, Parkgate, Philadelphia, February 27, 1917 (died 1925)
COMPARISONS: Ragona 1975, no. 85; Governale 1986, no. 429; Donatone 1998, cats. 87, 107; Glaser 2000, cat. 159
EXHIBITION: Philadelphia 1944

The folded ribbon motif on the reverse of this jar appears in Neapolitan wares, as well as those of Sicily—evidence of the continued relationship, both artistic and political, between these two cities.[125] The coat of arms repeated on three related pieces was identified on the original 1917 bill of sale as those of Marchese Favara di Mozzara of Trapani, although this has not been confirmed.

Cat. 81, reverse

119. See the recent article by Paola Casati Migliorini, "Tra ipotesi storiche e suggestioni simbolishe: Un corredo farmaceutico ancora in cera della sua spezieria," *CeramicAntica*, vol. 11 (May 2001), pp. 12–27.

120. Poole 1995, p. 376.

121. The church at Loreto was built around the "sacred house" of the Virgin, which was said to have been brought there by angels from Nazareth; see Floriano Grimaldi, *Le ceramiche da farmacia della Santa Casa di Loreto* (Rome: Autostrade), 1979.

122. Pierre-Alain Mariaux offers a possible source by Nicoletta da Modena, although the comparison is not entirely convincing; see his catalogue, *La Majolique: La Faïence italienne et son décor dans les collections suisses, XVe–XVIIIe siècles* (Geneva: Skira, 1995), p. 78.

123. See Bojani 2000, p. 94.

124. See Drey 1978, pp. 205, 235.

125. Compare an albarello with ribbon decoration in Donatone 2000 (cat. 4) and a globular vase of related shape and decoration marked *fatta in Napule* (made in Naples) in Ragona 1975 (fig. 27).

CAT. 82
BOWL FROM A CHILDBIRTH SET

Urbino, c. 1560–70[126]
Height 2 1/16" (5.3 cm); diameter 8 11/16" (22 cm)
Philadelphia Museum of Art. The Howard I. and Janet H. Stein Collection, in honor of the 125th Anniversary of the Museum, 1999-99-7
PROVENANCE: [Alexander Barker, London]; Sir Francis W. Cook, Baronet, Doughty House, Richmond Hill, Surrey, England, c. 1870 (died 1901); his son Wyndham F. Cook, London (died 1905); his son, Humphrey W. Cook (his sale, Christie's, London, July 7–10, 1925, lot 2); [purchased, Tancred Borenius, London, 1925]; private collector, New York (sale, Sotheby Parke-Bernet, New York, February 17, 1976, lot 48)
COMPARISONS: Giacomotti 1974, cat. 1070; Kube 1976, cat. 86; Musacchio 1999, fig. 116
EXHIBITION: Leeds, England, *National Exhibition of Works of Art,* 1868, cat. 1035

Urbino was an important production center for childbirth sets that reflected the *istoriato* style of the time. Beautiful grotesques ornament the rims of childbirth bowls like this one, echoing the borders of contemporaneous Urbino plates and platters. These wares—and their increasingly specific applications and uses—were clearly part of the expansion of the "empire of things," since every household would have had perfectly serviceable bowls and plates that could have been used by new mothers. Two *scodelle da parto* (birth bowls) from Urbino are listed in the Medici inventory of 1588, one of only a few such documents that records personal possessions, especially in the case of important families.[127]

CATS. 83A, B
BOWL AND RELATED LID OR TRAY FROM A CHILDBIRTH SET

Urbino, c. 1560–80
Bowl (cat. 83a): height 1 7/8" (4.9 cm); diameter 8 1/8" (20.8 cm). Lid (cat. 83b): height 3/4" (2 cm); diameter 7 7/16" (18.9 cm)
Philadelphia Museum of Art. The Howard I. and Janet H. Stein Collection, in honor of the 125th Anniversary of the Museum, 2000-154-6, 2000-154-7
PROVENANCE: Maurice Chabrières-Arlès, Paris (died 1897); Chabrières-Arlès collection, Paris; [purchased, Duveen Brothers, New York, 1916]; purchased, Norton Simon Foundation, Los Angeles, 1964 (Foundation sale, Parke-Bernet Galleries, New York, May 7–8, 1971, lot 86)
COMPARISON: Giacomotti 1974, cats. 1071–73
NOTE: Repaint from an old restoration campaign obscures the original decoration of these pieces, notably in the borders with grotesques.

A woodcut by Bernard Salomon of the birth of Joseph served as a model for this and several other paintings on childbirth sets, although here the painter decided to include only a few figures.[128] The two babies appear much older than newborns, which leads one to wonder whether the painter intended to evoke the young Christ and Saint John the Baptist, a common pairing in Renaissance art and an ostensible link to the older Saint John on the lid.[129]

CATS. 84A, B, C, D, E
SPINDLE WHORLS OR BEADS

Possibly Faenza, sixteenth century
Cat. 84a: height 5/8" (1.6 cm); diameter 15/16" (2.3 cm)
Cat. 84b: height 5/8" (1.6 cm); diameter 7/8" (2.2 cm)
Cat. 84c: height 9/16" (1.4 cm); diameter 5/8" (1.6 cm)
Cat. 84d: height 7/16" (1.2 cm); diameter 1/2" (1.3 cm)
Cat. 84e: height 9/16" (1.4 cm); diameter 5/8" (1.6 cm)
Philadelphia Museum of Art. The Howard I. and Janet H. Stein Collection, in honor of the 125th Anniversary of the Museum, 1999-99-15, 1999-99-16, 1999-99-17, 1999-99-18, 1999-99-19
INSCRIPTIONS: (cat. 84a) *[C]HIARA.B[ELLA]* (Beautiful Chiara); (cat. 84b) *IODE[?].CA.B[ELLA]* (sic. Lode [?]; praise to the beautiful Catherine [?]); (cat. 84c) a design of leaves or feathers; (cat. 84d) *.POLISENA.B.* (Beautiful Polisena); (cat. 84e) *SOBASTIANA.[?]B[E]LLA* (Beautiful Sebastiana)
PROVENANCE: [Martin Shopland, New York, 1994]
COMPARISONS: Rasmussen 1984, cat. 69; Wilson 1987b, cat. 233; Musacchio 1999, fig. 77

Spindle whorls of this type have traditionally been attributed to Faenza, although their style of ornament could also link them to Deruta, where some have also been found.[130] The examples shown here were destined for young women named Chiara, Polisena, Sebastiana, and one other, whose name is no longer legible, may have been Catherine. It has been suggested that the smaller pieces may have been worn as beads, although no proof of that practice exists. One of the examples in the British Museum was also made for a nun, as the inscription, *Sor Eustochia* (Sister Eustochia), shows.[131]

126. In the past, this bowl and cats. 83a,b were among the works ascribed generally to the Fontana workshop. Recently, John Mallet, Timothy Wilson, and others have made important progress in distinguishing between the output of Guido Durantino (later called Fontana), his son Orazio Fontana, and grandson Flaminio Fontana, as well as other painters working in their shops. Cats. 82 and 83a,b have yet to be attributed to specific hands, but were almost certainly produced in Urbino during the years in which the Fontana flourished.

127. Spallanzani 1994, p. 192.

128. See Salomon's woodcut from Damiano Maraffi, *Figure del Vecchio Testamento* (Lyon: Jean de Tournes, 1554); illustrated in Musacchio 1999, fig. 83. For comparisons, see Rasmussen 1984, cat. 136; and Giacomotti 1974, cat. 1071.

129. Musacchio (1999, fig. 150) ponders the same anomaly in a piece from the Kunstgewerbemuseum, Berlin, which may have some deeper significance; see also Hausmann 1972, cat. 209.

130. Timothy Wilson, in a conversation with the author (February 1994), noted that there is a private collection in Deruta that contains several examples in addition to the unpublished pieces in the Ashmolean Museum, Oxford (inv. nos. C 487–490 and C 509).

CATS. 85A, B
INKSTAND IN THE FORM OF A BOAT WITH FISHERMEN

Urbino, Patanazzi workshop, c. 1580–90
Top (cat. 85a): height 7¹¹⁄₁₆" (19.5 cm); width 13"
(32.9 cm); depth 6⁷⁄₁₆" (16.2 cm). Base (cat. 85b):
height 4¾" (12.1 cm); width 17³⁄₁₆" (43.7 cm); depth
10⅜" (26.3 cm)
Philadelphia Museum of Art. The Howard I. and
Janet H. Stein Collection, in honor of the 125th
Anniversary of the Museum, 1999-99-2a, 1999-99-2b
PROVENANCE: [Stefano Bardini, Florence]; (Bardini
sale, Christie's, London, May 26–31, 1902, lot 235);
[purchased, Durlacher Brothers, London, 1902]; purchased, J. Pierpont Morgan, London and New York,
1902 (died 1913); [possibly Duveen Brothers, New
York]; (sale, Christie's, London, March 12, 1990,
lot 325)
COMPARISONS: Giacomotti 1974, cats. 1113–14;
Norman 1976, cat. C112; Wilson 1996a, cat. 153
EXHIBITION: New York 1914–16
THERMOLUMINESCENCE ANALYSIS: Oxford Authentication Ltd., Wantage, England, report dated May 10,
2000, estimated the last firing was between 250 and
450 years ago. A sample was taken from the top and
the bottom of the inkstand.

The Patanazzi *bottega* in Urbino was responsible for a
number of these delightful inkstands, two of which
are dated 1584.[132] Some examples include the coat of
arms of the owner, adding further prestige to the
object. This piece once held a third figure in the center
of the boat, of which only the feet remain. What at
present is a pure genre scene—a rather rustic story to
grace the desktop of a member of the elite—would
be significantly transformed if the missing figure were
one of Christ. In that case, a simple boat with fishermen would become the apostle Luke's story of the
miraculous draught of fishes, immortalized by Raphael
in his great tapestry cartoon of 1519–20.[133] This example is the only known instance in the shape of a boat,
although Renaissance cradles, saltcellars, and dining-
table ornaments often made use of the form.

CAT. 86
VIRGIN AND CHRIST CHILD

Emilia-Romagna or the Marches, c. 1487–1500
Height 16½" (42 cm); width 9½" (24 cm); depth 7⅛"
(18.1 cm)
Philadelphia Museum of Art. Gift of Henry P.
McIlhenny, 1956-107-8

PROVENANCE: Elia Volpi, Palazzo Davanzati, Florence
(his sale, American Art Galleries, New York,
November 21–27, 1916, lot 151); purchased, John D.
McIlhenny, Parkgate, Philadelphia, 1916 (died 1925);
his son, Henry P. McIlhenny, Philadelphia
COMPARISONS: Ballardini 1930, vol. 1, cats. 7, 17;
Berardi 1984, fig. 93

Sculptural ceramics were first made in Florence by the
della Robbia. Works like this one have traditionally
been attributed to Faenza, although Pesaro is now
thought to be the site of such manufacture as well.[134]
Less sophisticated and classical than della Robbia
products, such figures are often decorated with patterns found on other Pesaro wares. Here the Christ
child cradles a bird in his hand, a traditional symbol
of the soul carried over from antiquity and frequently
seen in medieval stone sculpture and Renaissance
painting. The goldfinch, often kept as a child's pet,
had special christological symbolism based on the
legend that it had acquired the red spot on its breast
from being pierced by Christ's crown of thorns.[135]

CAT. 87
TABERNACLE WITH THE GATHERING OF MANNA

Possibly Viterbo, probably late-nineteenth century in
the style of the seventeenth century
Height (at knob) 13¹³⁄₁₆" (35.1 cm); diameter (at base)
9⅞" (25.1 cm)
The Howard I. and Janet H. Stein Collection
PROVENANCE: J. Pierpont Morgan, London and New
York (died 1913); [Duveen Brothers, New York]; Carl
W. Hamilton, New York; George R. Hann, Treetops,
Sewickley Heights, Pennsylvania (his sale, part 2,
Christie's, Treetops, Sewickley Heights, May 19, 1980,
lot 89)
COMPARISONS: Bojani et al. 1985, cat. 253; Rosea 1995,
cat. 17
EXHIBITIONS: New York 1914–16; Montclair 1925–26,
cat. 101; Buffalo 1926–28, cat. 80; Newark 1929
THERMOLUMINESCENCE AND OTHER TECHNICAL
ANALYSES: Oxford Authentication Ltd., Wantage,
England, report dated September 22, 2000, estimated
the last firing was less than 100 years ago. Other exam-
inations at the Philadelphia Museum of Art indicate
that the tabernacle's base and body were thrown as
one piece, that repairs have been made to the frame
of the doorway, and that the object has not been
reglazed.

131. Wilson 1987b, cat. 233.

132. Rackham (1940) 1977, no. 897; the
Metropolitan Museum of Art, New York
(inv. 32.100.383a–c).

133. British Royal Collection, on loan to the
Victoria & Albert Museum.

134. See Berardi 1984, pp. 212–15.

135. Hall 1999, p. 331.

This tabernacle was originally thought to have been made in the sixteenth century, although scientific tests now suggest that it may belong to the late-nineteenth century. Further research—on both the clay tabernacle and its bronze door—is needed to confirm the attribution and date and to determine whether or not this work was made as an intentional forgery. The few related works from the seventeenth century are also religious in nature, as would befit the products of Viterbo in the Papal States. Statutes governing the manufacture of ceramics are noted there as early as the mid-thirteenth century. Obviously, there was interchange between the workshops of this city and those of nearby Orvieto and more distant Deruta, as can be seen by the similarities of some wares.[136]

Cat. 87, detail of right side

CAT. 88

PUZZLE JUG WITH PHILYRA AND SATURN

Urbino, late-sixteenth or early seventeenth century
Height 7⅞" (20.1 cm); width (handle to spout) 6" (15.2 cm)
Philadelphia Museum of Art. The Howard I. and Janet H. Stein Collection, in honor of the 125th Anniversary of the Museum, 1998-176-8
PROVENANCE: (Sale, Sotheby Parke-Bernet, New York, November 10, 1972, lot 51)
COMPARISONS: Giacomotti 1974, cats. 1036–37

The subject of this piece is recounted by Hyginus in his *Fabularum liber* (1535) and regularly appears on other works of maiolica.[137]

CAT. 89

SPOUTED JAR WITH COAT OF ARMS AND BUST OF A MOOR

Possibly Umbria, c. 1500–1510, or nineteenth century in the style of the sixteenth century
Height 10⁵⁄₁₆" (26.1 cm); width (handle to spout) 9⅜" (23.9 cm)

The Howard I. and Janet H. Stein Collection
INSCRIPTION: (on body) *SYᵒ DEPITTA*ᴹ (probably a syrup of *pitimo* or *epitimo*, a form of thyme)
PROVENANCE: Edward Hutton, Casa di Boccacio, Corbignano, Italy (died 1969); [Kate Foster Ltd., London, 1978]
COMPARISON: Poole 1995, cat. 212

To date, no comparisons have been found for this jar except a similarly problematic one at the Fitzwilliam Museum.[138] It could date to the early part of the sixteenth century and resembles the spouted jars of Deruta. The unusual arms are identical in form, if not in color, to those depicted on a fourteenth-century Orvieto *boccale* in the Museo Internazionale delle Ceramiche.[139] The Moor emblem on this pitcher is very similar to the one on the important 1501 Deruta albarello in this collection (see cat. 10), perhaps disturbingly so. The shiny glaze and running pigments, also seen in the Fitzwilliam jug, add to

Cat. 89

suspicions about its authenticity. The compound described on the label might represent a syrup made from thyme, the sweet herb that had multiple medicinal applications in the Renaissance, including the treatment of eye and menstrual problems.

CAT. 90

HEXAGONAL WRITING BOX

Urbino, Fontana or Patanazzi workshop, late-sixteenth century (with later additions)
Height 4⅝" (11.8 cm); width 11⅜" (29 cm); depth 9¾" (24.9 cm)
Philadelphia Museum of Art. Purchased with the Bloomfield Moore Fund and with other Museum funds, 1944-15-16b
PROVENANCE: (see cat. 19)
REFERENCES: Olivar 1953, pp. 119–22, pl. 35
EXHIBITION: Philadelphia 1992

As Melissa Meighan and Dean Walker have demonstrated, this writing box was given a lid and base in the nineteenth century, perhaps for the collector, Baron Adolphe de Rothschild, to turn it into a

136. See Ragona 1975, p. 36; see also Gardelli 1999, p. 435.

137. The *Fabularum liber* was first published in Basel, Switzerland. For examples from the text in other works of maiolica, see Watson 1986, cat. 67; and Rackham (1940) 1977, no. 855.

138. Poole 1995, cat. 212.

139. Fiocco and Gherardi 1988, cat. 33.

pedestal for the large *Amadis de Gaula* vase (see cat. 19).[140] The lion's paw feet were part of the original box, but were cut off and reattached to the new bottom plate in order to support the new structure. The decorations have much in common with the Jacques Androuet I Ducerceau prints that were used as design sources by the painters of white-ground grotesque maiolica.[141] Further research may produce direct links to those prints.

Cat. 90

CAT. 91

PLATE WITH JACOB OBTAINING A BLESSING INTENDED FOR ESAU

France, probably Lyon or Nevers, last quarter of the sixteenth century
Height 1³⁄₁₆" (3 cm); diameter 9" (22.8 cm)
Philadelphia Museum of Art. Purchased with the John D. McIlhenny Fund, 1965-116-1
INSCRIPTION: (on reverse) *GENESIS III./.XXV*
PROVENANCE: (Sale, Sotheby's, London, November 20, 1962, lot 110); [purchased, Peel and Humphris, London, 1962]; [Cyril Humphris, London]
REFERENCE: Norman 1976, p. 320
COMPARISONS: Giacomotti 1974, cat. 1160; Norman 1976, cat. C164
EXHIBITION: Philadelphia 1987

Cat. 91

Like the plate depicting the story of Joseph and Potiphar's wife (see cat. 25), this scene is taken from the Book of Genesis and is also based on one of Bernard Salomon's woodcut illustrations. The painter has taken some liberties with the original composition, changing the background at the left and altering some of the details of clothing and setting. Both plates appear to have been executed by the same unnamed painter.

CAT. 92

FOOTED DISH WITH HERCULES AND CACUS

Pesaro, possibly workshop of Girolamo di Lanfranco dalle Gabicce, c. 1540–50
Height 2⁵⁄₁₆" (5.9 cm); diameter 11⁹⁄₁₆" (29.3 cm)
Philadelphia Museum of Art. The Dr. Francis W. Lewis Collection, 1893–43
INSCRIPTION: (on reverse) *Erchole et caco* (Hercules and Cacus)
PROVENANCE: [Possibly Sangiorgi Gallery, Rome]; Dr. Francis W. Lewis, Philadelphia
COMPARISON: Wilson 1987b, cat. 213

The story of Hercules and Cacus, or the tenth labor of Hercules, is told in several classical sources, including Ovid's *Fasti*, Livy's *History of Rome*, and Virgil's *Aeneid*. In the tale Cacus steals the cattle of the three-headed monster Geryon. Later Hercules discovers the herd inside a cave, and kills Cacus. The hero appears at right in his signature lion skin and club.

Cat. 92

140. Illustrated in Olivar 1953, pl. 35.

141. See Poke 2001.

SELECTED BIBLIOGRAPHY

Adams 2001
Adams, Laurie Schneider. *Italian Renaissance Art.* Boulder, Colo.: Westview Press, 2001.

Agnellini 1992
Agnellini, Maurizio, ed. *Maioliche: Storia e produzione italiana dalla metà del Quattrocento ai primi decenni del Novecento.* Milan: Giorgio Mondadori & Associati, 1992.

Ajmar and Thornton 1998
Ajmar, Marta, and Dora Thornton. "When Is a Portrait Not a Portrait? *Belle Donne* on Maiolica and the Renaissance Praise of Local Beauties." In Mann and Syson 1998, pp. 138–53.

Alverà Bortolotto 1981
Alverà Bortolotto, Angelica. *Storia della ceramica a Venezia: Dagli albori alla fine della repubblica.* Florence: Sansoni, 1981.

Alverà Bortolotto 1987
Alverà Bortolotto, Angelica. *Maioliche veneziane.* Florence: Museo Nazionale del Bargello, 1987.

Alverà Bortolotto 1988
Alverà Bortolotto, Angelica. *Maiolica a Venezia nel Rinascimento.* Bergamo: Bolis, 1988.

Baldisseri 1989
Baldisseri, Giorgio, et al. *Le maioliche cinquecentesche di Castelli: Una grande stagione artistica ritrovata.* Pescara: Carsa, 1989.

Baligand 1986
Baligand, Françoise. *La Majolique italienne dans les musées du Nord-Pas-de-Calais.* Lille, France: Association des conservateurs de la région Nord-Pas-de-Calais, 1986.

Ballardini 1930
Ballardini, Gaetano, ed. *Corpus della maiolica italiana.* 2 vols. Rome: Libreria dello Stato, 1930 and 1938.

Bartsch
Bartsch, Adam. *The Illustrated Bartsch.* Edited by Walter L. Strauss; subsequent editor, John T. Spike. New York: Abaris, 1978–.

Beckerath 1913
Von Falke, Otto. *Die Majolikasammlung Adolf von Beckerath.* Berlin: Rudolph Lepke's Kunst-Auctions-Haus, 1913.

Berardi 1984
Berardi, Paride. *L'antica maiolica di Pesaro dal XIV al XVII secolo.* Florence: Sansoni, 1984.

Bernardi 1980
Bernardi, Carla, ed. *Immagini architettoniche nella maiolica italiana del Cinquecento.* Milan: Electa, 1980.

Berti 1984
Berti, Fausto. *Antiche maioliche di Montelupo, secoli XIV–XVII.* Pontedera: Bandecchi & Vivaldi, 1984.

Berti 1986
Berti, Fausto. *La maiolica di Montelupo, secoli XIV–XVIII.* Milan: Electa, 1986.

Biavati 1987
Biavati, Eros. "Oro metallico: Decorazione a terzo fuoco sulla maiolica italiana da Quattrocento al secolo XVIII." In *7. Convegno della ceramica: 3. rassegna nazionale,* pp. 11–26. Pennabili: Comitato Mostra Mercato Nazionale d'Antiquariato, 1987.

Biringuccio 1959
Biringuccio, Vannoccio. *The Pirotechnia of Vannoccio Biringuccio.* Edited by Derek J. Price. New York: Basic Books, 1959.

Biscontini Ugolini 1979
Biscontini Ugolini, Grazia. "Sforza di Marcantonio: Figulo pesarese cinquecentesco." *Faenza,* vol. 65 (1979), pp. 7–10.

Biscontini Ugolini and Petruzzellis Scherer 1992
Biscontini Ugolini, Grazia, and Jacqueline Petruzzellis Scherer. *Maiolica e incisione: Tre secoli di rapporti iconografici.* Vicenza: Neri Pozza, 1992.

Biscontini Ugolini 1997
Biscontini Ugolini, Grazia, ed. *I vasi da farmacia nella collezione Bayer: Pharmacy Jars in the Bayer Collection.* Ospedaletto (Pisa): Pacini, 1997.

Bode 1899
Bode, Wilhelm, ed. *Ausstellung von Kunstwerken des Mittelalters und der Renaissance aus Berliner privatbesitz veranstaltet von der Kunstgeschichtlichen Gesellschaft, 20. Mai bis 3. Juli 1898.* Berlin: G. Grote, 1899.

Bode 1911
Bode, Wilhelm. *Die Anfänge der Majolikakunst in Toskana.* Berlin: J. Bard, 1911.

Bojani 1982
Bojani, Gian Carlo, et al. *Maioliche umbre decorate a lustro, il rinascimento e la ripresa ottocentesca: Deruta, Gualdo Tadino, Gubbio.* Florence: Nuova Guaraldi, 1982.

Bojani 1988
Bojani, Gian Carlo. *Ceramica nelle Marche.* Bergamo: Bolis, 1988

Bojani 2000
Bojani, Gian Carlo, ed. *Gaetano Ballardini e la ceramica a Roma: Le maioliche del Museo Artistico Industriale.* Florence: Centro Di, 2000.

Bojani and Vossilla 1998
Bojani, Gian Carlo, and Francesco Vossilla, eds. *Capolavori di maiolica della collezione Strozzi sacrati.* Florence: Centro Di, 1998.

Bojani et al. 1985
Bojani, Gian Carlo, Carmen Ravanelli Guidotti, and Angiolo Fanfani, eds. *La Donazione Galeazzo Cora: Ceramiche dal medioevo al XIX secolo.* Vol. 1. Milan: Fabbri 1985.

Breck and Rogers 1925
Breck, Joseph, and Meyric R. Rogers. *The Pierpont Morgan Wing.* New York: The Gillis Press, 1925.

Brody 1997
Brody, Michael. "Un piatto di Nicola da Urbino proveniente dalla credenza di Isabella d'Este-Gonzaga nel Philadelphia Museum of Art." *CeramicAntica*, vol. 7 (July–August 1997), pp. 36–62.

Burke 1986
Burke, Peter. *The Italian Renaissance: Culture and Society in Italy.* Rev. ed. Cambridge: Polity Press, 1986.

Caiger-Smith 1973
Caiger-Smith, Alan. *Tin-Glaze Pottery in Europe and the Islamic World: The Tradition of 1000 Years in Maiolica, Faience & Delftware.* London: Faber & Faber, 1973.

Caiger-Smith 1985
Caiger-Smith, Alan. *Lustre Pottery: Technique, Tradition and Innovation in Islam and the Western World.* London: The Herbert Press, 1985.

Castellani Collection 1877
Catalogue of the Castellani Collection in the Loan Exhibition of the Metropolitan Museum of Art. Vol. 2, *Maiolica, & c.* New York: Francis & Loutrel, 1877.

Chambers and Martineau 1981
Chambers, David, and Jane Martineau, eds. *Splendours of the Gonzaga.* London: Victoria & Albert Museum, 1981.

Chompret 1949
Chompret, J. *Répertoire de la majolique italienne.* 2 vols. Paris: Les Editions Nomis, 1949.

Cioci 1987
Cioci, Francesco. *Xanto e il duca di Urbino.* Milan: Fabbri, 1987.

Clifford 1991
Clifford, Timothy. "Some Unpublished Drawings for Maiolica and Federigo Zuccaro's Role in the 'Spanish Service.'" In Wilson 1991a, pp. 166–76.

Cole 1995
Cole, Alison. *Virtue and Magnificence: Art of the Italian Renaissance Courts.* New York: Harry N. Abrams, 1995.

Collins 1987
Collins, Patricia. "Prints and the Development of *Istoriato* Painting on Italian Renaissance Maiolica." *Print Quarterly*, vol. 4 (September 1987), pp. 222–35.

Concina 1975
Concina, Ennio. "Un contributo alla definizione della cronologia ed all'ambiente di Maestro Domenico da Venezia." *Faenza*, vol. 61 (1975), pp. 136–39.

Conforti 1995
Conforti, Michael. "European Decorative Arts at the Taft Museum." In Taft Museum 1995, pp. 323–26.

Conti 1971
Conti, Giovanni, ed. *Catalogo delle maioliche: Museo Nazionale di Firenze, Palazzo del Bargello.* Florence: Centro Di, 1971.

Conti 1980
Conti, Giovanni. *L'arte della maiolica in Italia.* 2nd. ed., rev. Busto Arsizio: Bramante, 1980.

Cora 1973
Cora, Galeazzo. *Storia della maiolica di Firenze e del contado secoli XIV e XV.* 2 vols. Florence: Sansoni, 1973.

Crépin-Leblond and Ennès 1995
Crépin-Leblond, Thierry, and Pierre Ennès. *Le Dressoir du Prince: Services d'apparat à la Renaissance.* Ecouen: Musée National de la Renaissance, 1995.

Crollalanza 1886–90
Crollalanza, Giovanni Battista di. *Dizionario storico-blasonica delle famiglie nobili e notabili italiane, estinte e fiorenti.* 3 vols. Pisa: Giornale Araldico, 1886–90.

Curnow 1992
Curnow, Celia. *Italian Maiolica in the National Museums of Scotland.* Edinburgh: National Museums of Scotland, 1992.

Dacos 1969
Dacos, Nicole. *La Découverte de la Domus Aurea et la formation des grotesques à la Renaissance.* London: The Warburg Institute, University of London; Leiden: E. J. Brill, 1969.

Dean and Lowe 1998
Dean, Trevor, and K.J.P. Lowe, eds. *Marriage in Italy, 1300–1650.* Cambridge and New York: Cambridge University Press, 1998.

De Pompeis 1990
De Pompeis, Claudio, et al. *Castelli e la maiolica cinque-centesca italiana: Atti del convegno in Pescara, 22–25 Aprile, 1989.* Pescara: Sala, 1990.

Distelberger 1993
Distelberger, Rudolf, et al. *The National Gallery of Art, Systematic Catalogue: Western Decorative Arts.* Part 1, *Medieval, Renaissance, and Historicizing Styles Including Metalwork, Enamels, and Ceramics.* Washington, D.C.: National Gallery of Art; Cambridge and London: Cambridge University Press, 1993.

Donatone 1970
Donatone, Guido. *Maioliche napoletane della spezieria aragonese di Castelnuovo.* Naples: Luigi Regina, 1970.

Donatone 1998
Donatone, Guido, ed. *Maioliche delle due Sicilie.* Naples: Edizioni Scientifiche Italiane, 1998.

Donzelli 1686
Donzelli, Giuseppe T. *Teatro farmaceutico dogmatico, e spargico. . . .* Venice: Paolo Baglioni, 1686.

Drey 1978
Drey, Rudolf E. A. *Apothecary Jars: Pharmaceutical Pottery and Porcelain in Europe and the East, 1150–1850.* London: Faber and Faber, 1978.

Drey 1991
Drey, Rudolf E. A. "*Istoriato* Maiolica with Scenes from the Second Punic War: Livy's History of Rome as Source Material." In Wilson 1991a, pp. 51–61.

Fiocco and Gherardi 1988
Fiocco, Carola, and Gabriella Gherardi. *Ceramiche umbre dal Medioevo allo storicismo.* Part 1. Faenza: Museo Internazionale delle Ceramiche, 1988.

Fiocco and Gherardi 1990
Fiocco, Carola, and Gabriella Gherardi. *Ceramiche di Deruta, secoli XV–XVI.* Florence: Museo Nazionale del Bargello, 1990.

Fiocco and Gherardi 1992
Fiocco, Carola, and Gabriella Gherardi. "Alcune considerazioni sull'Orsini-Colonna: Il servizio B°, il servizio T e la 'porcellana colorata.'" *Faenza,* vol. 78 (1992), pp. 157–65.

Fiocco and Gherardi 1994
Fiocco, Carola, and Gabriella Gherardi. *La ceramica di Deruta dal XIII al XVIII secolo: Deruta Pottery from the 13th to the 18th Century.* Perugia: Volumnia, 1994.

Fowles 1976
Fowles, Edward. *Memories of Duveen Brothers.* London: Time Books, 1976.

Fuchs 1993
Fuchs, Charles Dominique. *Maioliche istoriate rinascimentali del Museo statale d'arte medioevale e moderna di Arezzo.* Arezzo: Centro Affari e Promozioni, 1993.

Gardelli 1987
Gardelli, Giuliana. *"A Gran Fuoco": Mostra di maioliche rinascimentali dello stato di Urbino da collezioni private.* Urbino: Accademia Raffaello, 1987.

Gardelli 1991
Gardelli, Giuliana. "Urbino nella storia della ceramica: Note sulla grottesca." In Wilson 1991a, pp. 126–35.

Gardelli 1999
Gardelli, Giuliana. *Italika: Maiolica italiana del Rinascimento, saggi e studi.* Faenza: Edit Faenza, 1999.

Gentilini 1993
Gentilini, Anna Rosa. "Circolazione libraria e committenza artistica nel Cinquecento: Ricerche su tradizione libraria e tradizione ceramica di Livio e di Ovidio." In Ravanelli Guidotti 1993, pp. 11–29.

Gentilini 1992
Gentilini, Giancarlo. *I Della Robbia: La scultura invetriata nel Rinascimento.* 2 vols. Florence: Cantini, 1992.

Gentilini 1998
Gentilini, Giancarlo, ed. *I Della Robbia e l'arte nuova della scultura invetriata.* Florence: Giunti Gruppo, 1998.

Gere 1963
Gere, John A. "Taddeo Zuccaro as a Designer for Maiolica." *Burlington Magazine,* vol. 105 (July 1963), pp. 306–15.

Giacomotti 1974
Giacomotti, Jeanne. *Catalogue des majoliques des Musées nationaux: Musées du Louvre et de Cluny, Musée national de céramique à Sèvres, Musée Adrien-Dubouché à Limoges.* Paris: Editions des Musées Nationaux, 1974.

Glaser 2000
Glaser, Silvia. *Majolika: Die italienischen Fayencen im Germanischen Nationalmuseum Nürnberg, Bestandskatalog.* Nuremberg: Germanischen Nationalmuseums, 2000.

Goldthwaite 1987a
Goldthwaite, Richard A. "The Economy of Renaissance Italy: The Preconditions for Luxury Consumption." *I Tatti Studies: Essays in the Renaissance,* vol. 2 (1987), pp. 15–39.

Goldthwaite 1987b
Goldthwaite, Richard A. "The Empire of Things: Consumer Demand in Renaissance Italy." In *Patronage, Art, and Society in Renaissance Italy,* edited by F. W. Kent and Patricia Simons with J. C. Eade, pp. 153–75. Oxford: Clarendon, 1987.

Goldthwaite 1989
Goldthwaite, Richard A. "The Economic and Social World of Italian Renaissance Maiolica." *Renaissance Quarterly,* vol. 42 (Spring 1989), pp. 1–32.

Goldthwaite 1993
Goldthwaite, Richard A. *Wealth and the Demand for Art in Italy, 1300–1600.* Baltimore: Johns Hopkins University Press, 1993.

Governale 1986
Governale, Antonello. *Rectoverso: La maiolica siciliana, secoli XVI e XVII; Maestri, botteghe, influenze.* Palermo: Altamura Editrice, 1986.

Gruber 1994
Gruber, Alain, ed. *The History of Decorative Arts: The Renaissance and Mannerism in Europe.* Translated by John Goodman. New York: Abbeville, 1994.

Hall 1979
Hall, James. *Dictionary of Subjects and Symbols in Art.* New York: Harper & Row, 1979.

Hall 1999
Hall, Marcia B. *After Raphael: Painting in Central Italy in the Sixteenth Century.* Cambridge and New York: Cambridge University Press, 1999.

Hausmann 1972
Hausmann, Tjark. *Majolika: Spanische und italienische Keramik vom 14. bis zum 18. Jahrhundert.* Berlin: Mann, 1972.

Hiesinger 1987
Hiesinger, Kathryn B. "Fiske Kimball and the Collection of Edmond Foulc." In *Hommage à Hubert Landais: Art, Objets d'art, collections; Etudes sur l'art du Moyen Age et de la Renaissance sur l'histoire du goût et des collections,* pp. 238–42. Paris: Blanchard, 1987.

Hess 1988
Hess, Catherine. *Italian Maiolica: Catalogue of the Collections.* Los Angeles: The J. Paul Getty Museum, 1988.

Holman 1997
Holman, Beth L., ed. *Disegno: Italian Renaissance Designs for the Decorative Arts.* New York: Cooper-Hewitt, National Design Museum, Smithsonian Institution, 1997.

Horvitz Roth 1987
Horvitz Roth, Linda, ed. *J. Pierpont Morgan, Collector: European Decorative Arts from the Wadsworth Atheneum.* Hartford, Conn.: Wadsworth Atheneum, 1987.

Italian Maiolica 1876
Italian Centennial Commission. *Special Catalogue of the Collection of Antiquities Exhibited by Signor Alessandro Castellani of Rome in Rooms U.V.W, Memorial Hall.* Section 2, *Italian Maiolica.* Philadelphia: Edward Stern, 1876.

Jardine 1998
Jardine, Lisa. *Worldly Goods: A New History of the Renaissance.* New York: W. W. Norton & Co., 1998.

Jardine and Brotton 2000
Jardine, Lisa, and Jerry Brotton. *Global Interests: Renaissance Art between East and West.* Ithaca, N.Y.: Cornell University Press, 2000.

Johnston 1999
Johnston, William R. *William and Henry Walters: The Reticent Collectors.* Baltimore: Johns Hopkins University Press in association with The Walters Art Gallery, 1999.

Join-Dieterle 1984
Join-Dieterle, Catherine. *Catalogue de ceramiques: Musée du Petit Palais.* Paris: Musée du Petit Palais, 1984.

Kidwell 1991
Kidwell, Carol. *Pontano: Poet and Prime Minister.* London: Gerald Duckworth & Co., 1991.

Kingery and Aronson 1990
Kingery, W. David, and Meredith Aronson. "The Glazes of Luca della Robbia." *Faenza,* vol. 76 (1990), pp. 221–35.

Klapisch-Zuber 1985
Klapisch-Zuber, Christiane. *Women, Family, and Ritual in Renaissance Italy.* Translated by Lydia Cochrane. Chicago and London: University of Chicago Press, 1985.

Klesse 1966
Klesse, Brigitte, ed. *Majolika.* Vol. 2, *Kataloge des Kunstgewerbemuseums der Stadt Köln.* Cologne: Kunstgewerbemuseum der Stadt Köln, 1966.

Krahn and Lessmann 1987
Krahn, Volker, and Johanna Lessmann. *Italienische Renaissancekunst im Kaiser Wilhelm Museum Krefeld.* Krefeld: Kaiser Wilhelm Museum Krefeld, 1987.

Kremers and Urdang 1986
Kremers, Edward, and George Urdang. *History of Pharmacy.* 4th ed., rev. by Glenn Sonnedecker. Madison, Wis.: American Institute of the History of Pharmacy, 1986.

Kube 1976
Kube, A. N. *Italian Majolica, XV–XVIII Centuries.* Moscow: State Hermitage Collection, 1976.

Ladis 1989
Ladis, Andrew. *Italian Renaissance Maiolica from Southern Collections.* Athens: Georgia Museum of Art, University of Georgia, 1989.

Landau and Parshall 1994
Landau, David, and Peter Parshall. *The Renaissance Print, 1470–1550.* New Haven and London: Yale University Press, 1994.

Lawner 1987
Lawner, Lynne. *Lives of the Courtesans: Portraits of the Renaissance.* New York: Rizzoli, 1987.

Lawner 1988
Lawner, Lynne, ed. and trans. *I Modi, the Sixteen Pleasures, an Erotic Album of the Italian Renaissance: Giulio Romano, Marcantonio Raimondi, Pietro Arentino, and Count Jean-Frederic-Maximilien de Waldeck.* Evanston, Ill.: Northwestern University Press, 1988.

Legge 1986
Legge, Margaret. *The Apothecary's Shelf: Drug Jars and Mortars, 15th to 18th Century.* Melbourne: National Gallery of Victoria, 1986.

Leman 1927
Leman, Henri, ed. *La Collection Foulc: Objets d'art du Moyen Age et de la Renaissance.* 2 vols. Paris: Les Beaux-arts, édition d'études et de documents, 1927.

Leonardi 1982
Leonardi, Corrado, ed. *La ceramica rinascimentale metaurense.* Rome: Paleani Editrice, 1982.

Lessmann 1979
Lessmann, Johanna. *Italienische Majolika: Katalog der Sammlung.* Braunschweig, Germany: Herzog Anton Ulrich-Museum, 1979.

Lincoln 2000
Lincoln, Evelyn. *The Invention of the Renaissance Printmaker.* New Haven and London: Yale University Press, 2000.

Liverani 1958
Liverani, Giuseppe. *La maiolica italiana sino alla comparsa della porcellana europea.* 2nd ed. Milan: Electa, 1958.

Livy 1982
Livy. *Livy in Fourteen Volumes.* Translated by B. O. Foster. Cambridge: Harvard University Press; London: William Heinemann, 1982–88.

Lutteman 1981
Lutteman, Helena Dahlbäck. *Majolika från Urbino och andra orter i Italien i Nationalmuseum Stockholm.* Stockholm: LiberFörlag, 1981.

McNab 1995
McNab, Jessie. "Sixteenth-Century Italian Maiolica." In Taft Museum 1995, pp. 517–41.

Mallet 1970
Mallet, J.V.G. "Maiolica at Polesden Lacey I." *Apollo,* n.s., vol. 92 (October 1970), pp. 260–65.

Mallet 1980
Mallet, John V. G. "I suoi compagni e seguaci." In Xanto 1988, pp. 67–108.

Mallet 1981a
Mallet, John V. G. *The John Philip Kassebaum Collection.* Vol. 1. Kansas City, Kans.: Lowell Press, 1981.

Mallet 1981b
Mallet, J.V.G. "The Este-Gonzaga Service, Made for Isabella d'Este c. 1525 by Nicolò da Urbino (active c. 1520–40)." In Chambers and Martineau 1981, pp. 175–78.

Mallet 1987
Mallet, J.V.G. "'In Botega di Maestro Guido Durantino in Urbino.'" *Burlington Magazine,* vol. 129 (May 1987), pp. 284–98.

Mallet 1991
Mallet, J.V.G. "The Painter of the Coal-Mine Dish." In Wilson 1991a, pp. 62–73.

Mallet 1996
Mallet, J.V.G. "Au Musée de Céramique à Sèvres: Majoliques historiées provenant de deux ateliers de la Renaissance." *Revue du Louvre,* vol. 1 (1996), pp. 45–61.

Mallet 1998
Mallet, J.V.G. "Introduction to Italian Maiolica." In Mallet and Dreier 1998, pp. 12–53.

Mallet and Dreier 1998
Mallet, J.V.G., and Franz Adrian Dreier. *The Hockemeyer Collection: Maiolica and Glass.* Bremen, Germany: H. M. Hauschild, 1998.

Mancini della Chiara 1979
Mancini della Chiara, Maria, ed. *Maioliche del Museo civico di Pesaro.* Pesaro: Regione Marche, Comune di Pesaro, 1979.

Mann and Syson 1998
Nicholas, Mann, and Luke Syson, eds. *The Image of the Individual: Portraits in the Renaissance.* London: British Museum Press, 1998.

Mariaux 1995
Mariaux, Pierre-Alain. *La Majolique: La faience italienne et son décor dans les collections suisses, XVe–XVIII siècles.* Geneva: Skira, 1995.

Marquand 1912
Marquand, Allan. *Della Robbias in America.* Princeton, N.J.: Princeton University Press, 1912.

Mazzucato 1990
Mazzucato, Otto, ed. *Le ceramiche da farmacia a Roma tra '400 e '600.* Viterbo: FAUL Edizioni Artistiche, 1990.

Miller 1994
Miller, Paul F. "The Gothic Room in Marble House, Newport, Rhode Island." *Antiques: The Magazine,* vol. 146 (August 1994), pp. 176–85.

Molinier 1889
Molinier, Emile. *Collection Emile Gavet: Catalogue raisonné.* Paris: D. Jouaust, 1889.

Moore 1988
Moore, Andrew. "The Fountaine Collection of Maiolica." *Burlington Magazine,* vol. 130 (June 1988), pp. 435–47.

Morazzoni 1955
Morazzoni, Giuseppe. *La maiolica antica veneta.* Milan: Luigi Alfieri, 1955.

Morley-Fletcher and McIlroy 1984
Morley-Fletcher, Hugo, and Roger McIlroy. *Christie's Pictorial History of European Pottery.* Oxford: Phaidon—Christie's, 1984.

Munarini and Banzato 1993
Munarini, Michelangelo, and Davide Banzato. *Ceramiche rinascimentali dei Musei Civici di Padova.* Milan: Electa, 1993.

Musacchio 1997
Musacchio, Jacqueline Marie. "Imaginative Conceptions in Renaissance Italy." In *Picturing Women in Renaissance and Baroque Italy*, edited by Geraldine A. Johnson and Sara F. Matthews Grieco, pp. 42–60. Cambridge and New York: Cambridge University Press, 1997.

Musacchio 1999
Musacchio, Jacqueline Marie. *The Art and Ritual of Childbirth in Renaissance Italy*. New Haven and London: Yale University Press, 1999.

Negroni 1985
Negroni, F. "Nicolò Pellipario: Ceramista fantasma." *Notizie da Palazzo Albani*, vol. 14, no. 1 (1985), pp. 13–20.

Negroni 1998
Negroni, F. "Una famiglia di ceramisti Urbinati: I Patanazzi." *Faenza*, vol. 84 (1998), pp. 104–15.

Norman 1976
Norman, A.V.B. *Wallace Collection: Catalogue of Ceramics.* Vol. 1, *Pottery, Maiolica, Faience, Stoneware*. London: Trustees of the Wallace Collection, 1976.

Olivar 1953
Olivar, Marçal. "Su alcuni esemplari urbinati con iscrizioni spagnole, della bottega di Orazio Fontana." *Faenza*, vol. 39 (1953), pp. 119–22.

Ovid 1980
Ovid. *Metamorphoses.* Translated by Mary M. Innes. Harmondsworth and New York: Penguin Books, 1980.

Palvarini Gobio Casali 1987
Palvarini Gobio Casali, Mariarosa. *La ceramica a Mantova.* Ferrara: Belriguardo arte, 1987.

Passeri 1980
Passeri, Giovanni Battista. *Istoria delle pitture in majolica fatte in Pesaro e ne'luoghi circonvicini.* Venice, 1752. Reprint (in 2 vols.), Bologna: Arnaldo Forni, 1980.

Pataky-Brestyánszky 1967
Pataky-Brestyánszky, Ilona. *Italienische Majolikakunst: Italienische Majolika in ungarischen Sammlungen.* Budapest: Corvina, 1967.

Philadelphia 1995
Philadelphia Museum of Art. *Handbook of the Collections.* Philadelphia: Philadelphia Museum of Art, 1995.

Piccolpasso 1980
Piccolpasso, Cipriano. *The Three Books of the Potter's Art: I tre libri dell'arte del vasaio.* 2 vols. Translation and introduction by Ronald Lightbown and Alan Caiger-Smith. London: Scolar Press, 1980.

Pier 1911
Pier, Garrett Chatfield. *Catalogue of the Collection of Pottery, Porcelain, and Faience.* New York: The Gilliss Press, 1911.

Platina 1998
Platina. *On Right Pleasure and Good Health.* Critical edition and translation by Mary Ella Milham. Tempe, Ariz.: Medieval and Renaissance Texts and Studies, 1998.

Poke 2001
Poke, Christopher. "Jacques Androuet I Ducerceau's 'Petites Grotesques' as a Source for Urbino Maiolica Decoration." *Burlington Magazine*, vol. 143 (June 2001), pp. 332–44.

Pontano 1965
Pontano, Giovanni. *I trattati delle virtù sociali.* Edited by Francesco Tateo. Rome: Edizioni dell'Ateneo, 1965.

Poole 1995
Poole, Julia. *Italian Maiolica and Incised Slipware in the Fitzwilliam Museum, Cambridge.* Cambridge and New York: Cambridge Unviersity Press, 1995.

Prentice von Erdberg and Ross 1952
Prentice von Erdberg, Joan, and Marvin C. Ross. *Catalogue of the Italian Majolica in the Walters Art Gallery.* Baltimore: The Walters Art Gallery, 1952.

Pringsheim 1994
Von Falke, Otto. *Die Majolikasammlung Alfred Pringsheim: Le maioliche italiane della collezione Pringsheim: Italian Maiolica of the Pringsheim Collection.* 3 vols. Ferrara: Belriguardo arte, 1994.

Rackham (1940) 1977
Rackham, Bernard. *Victoria & Albert Museum: Catalogue of Italian Maiolica.* 2 vols. 1940. Reprint, with emendations and additional bibliography by J. V. G. Mallet, London: Her Majesty's Stationery Office, 1977.

Rackham 1959
Rackham, Bernard. *Islamic Pottery and Italian Maiolica: Illustrated Catalogue of a Private Collection.* [Fernand Adda Collection, London]. London: Faber, 1959.

Raffaelli 1846
Rafaelli, Giuseppe, comp. *Memorie istoriche delle maioliche lavorate in Castel Durante o sia Urbania.* Fermo: Tipografia Paccasassi, 1846.

Ragona 1975
Ragona, Antonino. *La maiolica siciliana dalle origini all'Ottocento.* Palermo: Sellerio, 1975.

Rasmussen 1984
Rasmussen, Jörg. *Italienische Majolika.* Hamburg, Germany: Museum für Kunst und Gewerbe Hamburg, 1984.

Rasmussen 1989
Rasmussen, Jörg. *The Robert Lehman Collection: X, Italian Majolica.* New York: The Metropolitan Museum of Art in association with Princeton University Press, 1989.

Ravanelli Guidotti 1985
Ravanelli Guidotti, Carmen. *Ceramiche occidentali del Museo civico medievale di Bologna*. Bologna: Grafis, 1985.

Ravanelli Guidotti 1987
Ravanelli Guidotti, Carmen. *Donazione Paolo Mereghi: Ceramiche europee ed orientali*. Casalecchio di Reno (Bologna): Grafis, 1987.

Ravanelli Guidotti 1990
Ravanelli Guidotti, Carmen, ed. *La donazione Angiolo Fanfani: Ceramiche dal Medioevo al XX secolo*. Faenza: Edit Faenza, 1990.

Ravanelli Guidotti 1991
Ravanelli Guidotti, Carmen. "Un singolare ritrovamento: Un piatto del servizio di Isabella d'Este Gonzaga." In Wilson 1991a, pp. 13–23.

Ravanelli Guidotti 1992
Ravanelli Guidotti, Carmen. *Mediterraneum, ceramica spagnola in Italia tra Medioevo e Rinascimento: Ceramica espanola en Halia entre el medioevo y el Rinascimiento*. Viterbo: FAUL Edizioni, 1992.

Ravanelli Guidotti 1993
Ravanelli Guidotti, Carmen, ed. *L'istoriato: Libri a stampa e maioliche italiane del Cinquecento*. Faenza: Gruppo Editoriale Faenza, 1993.

Reitlinger 1963
Reitlinger, Gerald. *The Economics of Taste*. Vol. 2, *The Rise and Fall of Objets d'art Prices since 1750*. London: William Clowes and Sons, 1963.

Ray 2000
Ray, Anthony. *Spanish Pottery, 1248–1898: With a Catalogue of the Collection in the Victoria & Albert Museum*. London: V&A Publications, 2000.

Rietstap 1887
Rietstap, Johannes Baptista. *Armorial général*. 2nd ed. Vol. 2. Gouda, Netherlands: G. B. Van Goor Zonen, 1887.

Roberts and Roberts 1959
Roberts, George, and Mary Roberts. *Triumph on Fairmount: Fiske Kimball and the Philadelphia Museum of Art*. Philadelphia and New York: J. B. Lippincott, 1959.

Robinson 1914
Robinson, Edward, et al. *The Metropolitan Museum of Art: Guide to the Loan Exhibition of the J. Pierpont Morgan Collection*. New York: The Gilliss Press, 1914.

Rosea 1995
Rosea, Paola. *Le maioliche: Le arti decorative nelle collezioni Doria Pamphilj*. Genoa: Tormena, 1995.

Salsi 2000
Salsi, Claudio, ed. *Museo d'arti applicate: Le ceramiche*. Milan: Electa, 2000.

Shearman 1979
Shearman, John. *Mannerism*. Harmondsworth, England, and Baltimore: Penguin Books, 1979.

Shinn 1982
Shinn, Deborah. *Sixteenth-Century Italian Maiolica: Selections from the Arthur M. Sackler Collection and the National Gallery of Art's Widener Collection*. Washington, D.C.: The National Gallery of Art, 1982.

Shoemaker 1981
Shoemaker, Innis H., and Elizabeth Broun. *The Engravings of Marcantonio Raimondi*. Lawrence: The Spencer Museum of Art, University of Kansas, 1981.

Spallanzani 1994
Spallanzani, Marco. *Ceramiche alla corte dei Medici nel Cinquecento: Collezionismo e storia dell'arte, studi e fonti*. Vol. 3. Modena: Franco Cosimo Panini, 1994.

Spreti 1928–35
Spreti, Vittorio. *Enciclopedia storico-nobiliare italiana. . . .* 8 vols. Milan: Enciclopedia Storico-Nobiliare Italiana, 1928–35.

Strouse 2000
Strouse, Jean. "J. Pierpont Morgan, Financier and Collector." *The Metropolitan Museum of Art Bulletin*, vol. 57 (Winter 2000), pp. 1–64.

Summers 1981
Summers, David. *Michelangelo and the Language of Art*. Princeton, N.J.: Princeton University Press, 1981.

Syson and Thornton 2001
Syson, Luke, and Dora Thornton. *Objects of Virtue: Art in Renaissance Italy*. London: British Museum Publications, 2001. Forthcoming.

Taft Museum 1995
The Taft Museum: European Decorative Arts. New York: Hudson Hills Press, 1995.

Tait 1991
Tait, Hugh. "Ormolu-mounted Maiolica of the Renaissance: An Aspect of the History of Taste." In Wilson 1991a, pp. 267–78.

Talvacchia 1994
Talvacchia, Bette. "Professional Advancement and the Use of the Erotic in the Art of Francesco Xanto." *Sixteenth Century Journal*, vol. 25 (Spring 1994), pp. 121–53.

Talvacchia 1999
Talvacchia, Bette. *Taking Positions: On the Erotic in Renaissance Culture*. Princeton, N.J.: Princeton University Press, 1999.

Thornton 1997
Thornton, Dora. *The Scholar in His Study: Ownership and Experience in Renaissance Italy*. New Haven and London: Yale University Press, 1997.

Thornton 1991
Thornton, Peter. *The Italian Renaissance Interior, 1400–1600*. New York: Harry N. Abrams, 1991.

Triolo 1996
Triolo, Julia Catherine. "The Armorial Maiolica of Francesco Xanto Avelli." Ph.D. diss., The Pennsylvania State University, 1996.

Vanzolini 1879
Vanzolini, Giuliano, ed. *Istorie delle fabbriche di majoliche metaurensi*. 2 vols. Pesaro: Annesio Nobili, 1879.

Vasari-Milanesi 1878–85
Vasari, Giorgio. *Le vite de 'piu eccellenti pittori, scultori ed architettori, scritte da Giorgio Vasari pittore aretino, con nuove annotazione e commenti di Gaetano Milanesi*. 9 vols. Florence: G. C. Sansoni, 1878–85.

Virgil 1962
Virgil. *Aeneid*. Translation and introduction by W. F. Jackson Knight. Baltimore: Penguin Books, 1962.

Walker 1974
Walker, John. *Self-Portrait with Donors: Confessions of an Art Collector*. Boston: Little, Brown, 1974.

Wallis 1905
Wallis, Henry. *XVII Plates by Nicola Fontana da Urbino at the Correr Museum Venice: A Study in Early XVIth Century Maiolica*. London: s.n., 1905.

Watson 1986
Watson, Wendy M. *Italian Renaissance Maiolica from the William A. Clark Collection*. London: Scala, 1986.

Wilson 1987a
Wilson, Timothy. "Maiolica in Renaissance Venice." *Apollo*, vol. 125 (March 1987), pp. 184–89.

Wilson 1987b
Wilson, Timothy. *Ceramic Art of the Italian Renaissance*. London: British Museum Publications, 1987.

Wilson 1989a
Wilson, Timothy. "Maioliche rinascimentali armoriate con stemmi fiorentini." In *L'Araldica: Fonti e metodi: Atti del Convegno internazionale di Campiglia Marittima, Marzo 6–8, 1987*, pp. 128–38. Florence: Giunta Regionale Toscana, 1989.

Wilson 1989b
Wilson, Timothy. *Maiolica: Italian Renaissance Ceramics in the Ashmolean Museum*. Oxford: Ashmolean Museum, 1989.

Wilson 1991a
Wilson, Timothy, ed. *Italian Renaissance Pottery: Papers Written in Association with a Colloquium at the British Museum*. London: British Museum, 1991.

Wilson 1991b
Wilson, Timothy. "Girolamo Genga: Designer for Maiolica?" In Wilson 1991a, pp. 157–65.

Wilson 1993
Wilson, Timothy. "Renaissance Ceramics." In Distelberger 1993, pp. 120–241.

Wilson 1994
Wilson, Timothy. "Alfred Pringsheim and His Collection of Italian Maiolica." In Pringsheim 1994, vol. 3, pp. 79–99.

Wilson 1996a
Wilson, Timothy. "Italian Maiolica of the Renaissance." Milan, 1996.

Wilson 1996b
Wilson, Timothy. "The Beginnings of Lustreware in Renaissance Italy." In *The International Ceramics Fair and Seminar*, June 1996, pp. 35–43.

Wilson 2001
Wilson, Timothy. "Francesco Durantino: Mobility and Collaboration in Urbino *Istoriato* of the 1540s." Paper presented at the Germanisches National Museum, Nuremberg, Germany, February 12–14, 2001.

Xanto 1988
Francesco Xanto Avelli da Rovigo: Atti del Convegno Internazionale di Studi, Accademia dei Concordi, Rovigo, 3–4 Maggio 1980. Rovigo: s.n., 1988.

LIST OF EXHIBITIONS

Buffalo 1926–28
Buffalo, New York, Buffalo Fine Arts Gallery/Albright Art Gallery; The Art Gallery of Toronto; San Francisco, California Palace of the Legion of Honor; Saint Louis City Art Museum, *A Group of Italian Renaissance Paintings, Sculpture, Furniture, Maiolica Vases and Other Objects from the Collection of Carl W. Hamilton, New York*, 1926–28

London 1862
London, South Kensington Museum, *Special Exhibition of Works of Art of the Mediaeval, Renaissance, and More Recent Periods, on Loan at the South Kensington Museum*, 1862

London 1921–22
London, Burlington Fine Arts Club, *Catalogue of Pictures and Other Objects of Art Selected from the Collections of Mr. Holford (1808–1892), Mainly from Westonbirt in Gloucestershire, Lent by Lt. Col. Sir George Holford, Chosen from Collections of His Father Mr. Holford*, 1921–22

Montclair 1925–26
Montclair, New Jersey, Montclair Art Museum, *Loan Exhibition of Paintings, Furniture & Art Objects from the Collection of Carl W. Hamilton*, 1925–26

Newark 1929
Newark, New Jersey, The Newark Museum, *The Carl W. Hamilton Collection*, 1929

New York 1914
New York, The Metropolitan Museum of Art, *Loan Exhibition of the J. Pierpont Morgan Collection*, 1914–16

New York 1917–19
New York, The Metropolitan Museum of Art, Exhibition of Objects on Extended Loan from the Collection of Mortimer L. Schiff, 1917–19

New York 1923
New York, The Metropolitan Museum of Art, *The Arts of the Italian Renaissance*, 1923

New York 1923–38
New York, The Metropolitan Museum of Art, Exhibition of Objects on Extended Loan from the Collection of William Randolph Hearst, 1923–38

New York 1937–41
New York, The Metropolitan Museum of Art, Exhibition of Objects on Extended Loan from the Collection of Mortimer L. Schiff, 1937–41

Philadelphia 1930
Philadelphia Museum of Art, *The Edmond Foulc Collection*, 1930

Philadelphia 1944
Philadelphia Museum of Art, *The McIlhenny Collection Inaugural Exhibition*, 1944

Philadelphia 1987
Philadelphia Museum of Art, *European Sculpture and Decorative Art: Acquisitions by David DuBon (1958–1985)*, 1987

Philadelphia 1992
Philadelphia Museum of Art, *An Examination of Renaissance Maiolica*, 1992

San Francisco 1986–88
The Fine Arts Museums of San Francisco, California Palace of the Legion of Honor, *Italian Maiolica from the Arthur M. Sackler Collection*, 1986–88

Washington, D.C. 1982–83
Washington, D.C., *National Gallery of Art, Sixteenth-Century Italian Maiolica: Selections from the Arthur M. Sackler Collection and the National Gallery of Art's Widener Collection*, 1982–83

INDEX

OF COLLECTORS, LOCATIONS, AND MAKERS

The index references catalogue numbers (rather than page numbers), since both the main text and the checklist are arranged by these numbers.

PHOTOGRAPHIC CREDITS   All photography is by Graydon Wood unless otherwise indicated.

DEAN WALKER'S ESSAY
The Corcoran Gallery and School of Art Archives, Washington, D.C.: fig. 3
The Metropolitan Museum of Art, New York: figs. 5–6, 8
Philadelphia Museum of Art: fig. 7
Photograph courtesy of The Preservation Society of Newport County, Rhode Island: fig. 2
Mattie Edwards Hewitt Collection, Courtesy of The Rhode Island Historical Society Library, Providence, RHi (x3) 6774: fig. 1
Rosenbach Museum & Library, Philadelphia: fig. 9
Archival photograph courtesy of The Walters Art Museum, Walters Art Museum Archives, Baltimore: fig. 4

MAIN TEXT
Scala / Art Resource, New York: figs. 1–2, 7
Victoria & Albert Picture Library, London: figs. 3–6

CHECKLIST
Eric Mitchell: cat. 92
Lynn Rosenthal: cat. 87